Morgan Horses

By the same author

THE BACK-YARD HORSE
THE BACK-YARD FOAL
RESCHOOLING THE THOROUGHBRED
THE WONDERFUL WORLD OF PONIES

Morgan Horses

By Peggy Jett Pittenger

arco

New York

Published 1974 by ARCO PUBLISHING COMPANY, Inc.
219 Park Avenue South, New York, N.Y. 10003

Library of Congress Catalog Card Number 73-89232
ISBN 0-668-03392-4

Printed in the United States of America

For Nancy Jett Boardman

Acknowledgments

I am indebted to the following persons and organizations for locating facts, figures and photographs:

Margaret Gardiner, Wiscasset, Maine
Chicago Historical Society
Dr. Imogene P. Earle, U.S. Department of Agriculture
W. T. Carter, Fresno, California
Roy Brunk, Rochester, Illinois
J. Cecil Ferguson, Green, Rhode Island
Mary Turgeon, Brownsville, Vermont
Mosher Brothers, Salt Lake City, Utah
The Summit County Historical Society, Akron, Ohio
Joseph E. Olsen, St. George, Utah
Charles Hamilton, Triangle A Ranch, Parkman, Wyoming
Seth Holcombe, Hartford, Connecticut
Cooper Square Publishers
Vermont Historical Society, Montpelier, Vermont
Barbara Cole, Leesburg, Virginia
Marilyn Childs, Tunbridge, Vermont
Maurine Holloway, Barrington, Illinois
Western Reserve Historical Association, Cleveland, Ohio
The United States Department of Agriculture Library
Olin S. Nye, Elizabethtown, New York
The Essex County Historical Society, Elizabethtown, New York
The Penfield Museum, Ironville, N. Y.
Merle D. Evans, Massilon, Ohio
Green Mountain Horse Association, South Woodstock, Vermont

The Historical Society of Pennsylvania, Philadelphia
The Library of Congress
Robert Hayes, Missoula, Montana
American Horse Shows Association, Inc.

Contents

PART I

Introduction

Woodcut that appeared in the *Ohio Farmer* on Thursday, May 12, 1853. "From Life." The article by James D. Ladd says: "All unprejudiced minds speak well of the sprightly Morgan. The only difference is in the degree of praise." (Courtesy Western Reserve Society, Cleveland, Ohio.)

1

Morgan Characteristics

THE MORGAN IS THE OLDEST BREED OF HORSE DEVELOPED IN THE UNITED States. He grew up with the emerging nation and was influential in shaping its growth. The breed is unique in that all its members trace in direct male line to a single foundation sire, Justin Morgan. His descendants ten and eleven generations removed exhibit to a surprisingly uniform degree the qualities that made their progenitor famous almost two hundred years ago.

The ideal Morgan stands between 14:1 and 15:1 hands high. There are occasional individuals as little as 13 hands or as tall as 16, while Eucre (Monterey–Bronita), foaled at the United States Range Experiment Station in Montana, stood a remarkable 17 hands.

Although the usual standards of good conformation apply to the Morgan, he appears to be more compact than the ordinary horse. The compactness in no way suggests coarseness. One of the most outstanding characteristics of the breed is the long, sloping shoulder with withers and mane hair extending well into the back, which is short and broad with just enough room for a saddle. Morgans are well ribbed up, short in their coupling, with little space between the last rib and the point of the hip. The extreme shoulder angle accounts for the upright head carriage. The neck is full in both mares and stallions, with a heavy deposit of nuchal fat giving the typical crested contour in both sexes which is so characteristic of the breed. The head is wide between the eyes, wide at the jaw and tapers to a fine muzzle. Ideally it should be breedy looking with a chisled appearance, free from any fleshiness. The set of the eye is quite characteristic; it is prominent, large and round, and often shows part of the sclera. The ears are small, taper to a point, are set rather wide apart and incline slightly toward each other. They are often described as foxy.

THE MORGAN LOOK: Little Hawk (Devan Hawk–Double H. Cindy): Note powerful hind quarters, short back, well-sprung ribs, short clean cannons, heavily crested neck, luxuriant mane and tail hair and the kind, alert expression. (Courtesy of Norman and Phyllis Dock, Sunset Farm, Bethel, Maine.)

THE MORGAN LOOK: Parade (Cornwallis–Mansphyllis): Note short back, good shoulder, crested neck, substance combined with refinement. (Courtesy J. Cecil Ferguson, Green, Rhode Island)

THE MORGAN LOOK: Tally Ho (Lippit Moro Ash–Ruthven's Beatrice Ann), a Morgan gelding. Note the crested neck, distinct throttle, head wide between the eyes tapering to a fine
muzzle and alert, kind expression. (Courtesy Robert Nierman, Cumberland, Md.)

Viewed from the front, the chest is wide and the ribs well-sprung, making
room for extraordinary heart and lung capacity. The development of the
forearm and gaskin suggest great power, while short, flat cannons and clean,
distinct tendons standing well away from the bone indicate enduring soundness. The hooves are neat, the horn flinty and dense, not likely to split or
chip. The frog is large, the heel open. The original Morgan seldom was shod
although he did hard work all of his life. Similarly, many modern Morgans
have such excellent feet that they never require shoes.

Due to his short cannons and the tremendous slope of his shoulder, the
Morgan seems to be longer than he is tall, in spite of his short back. All in
all, he gives the impression of being big for his size and exudes the appear-

ance of tremendous muscular power and nervous energy. His eye is bright, his ears alert, his step quick and elastic. In temperament he is cheerful, endlessly willing, definitely playful and spirited, but so gentle that many stallions —including the founder of the breed—can be ridden by women and children. Courageous, but docile, according to Lady Wentworth, the Morgan is second only to the pure Arab in endurance and soundness. At the trot his gait should be perfection—balanced, square and airy.

Although the original Morgan was a dark bay or brown, most modern Morgans are chestnut (69 per cent in Volume VIII of the *Register*) of which 11 per cent have flaxen manes and tails. Bay accounts for only 21 per cent, while black and brown together make up another 8 per cent. There are a few palomino Morgans; 63 were listed in Volume VII. The occasional grays add up to less than 1 per cent of the total. There are even a few pintos, although they are now barred from registration. At the present the most fashionable coat color is liver chestnut with lighter mane and tail. All coat colors tend toward saturation. Light or golden chestnuts are rare, while pale bay and dun are seldom seen. Extreme white markings are not characteristic of the breed, the greatest majority having a star, strip, and, perhaps, a modest pastern

THE MORGAN LOOK: Performance and Western Champion Chico's Flame (L. U. Colonel-Tippy Dee), owned by Dot Chapman, Spencer, Ohio. (Courtesy Dot Chapman)

THE MORGAN LOOK, relaxed and unposed: Blackacre Mandamus (Devan Marsh Hawk–Replevin), yearling colt. Note sloping shoulder, short cannons, finely chiseled head, distinct throttle, good top line, and full body.

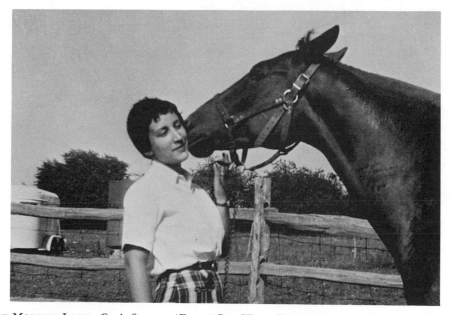

THE MORGAN LOOK: Cap's Stormy (Devan Cap–Tippy Dee), Morgan gelding with Carolyn Baker. Note crested neck, distinct throttle, tapering head, and affectionate nature. (Courtesy Mrs. Jess Baker, Solon, Ohio)

THE MORGAN LOOK: Four month old colt Blackacre Wildfire (Devan Marsh Hawk–Tippy Dee) owned by Mrs. Robert Tempest. (Boyajian photo)

THE MORGAN LOOK: Ten-year-old stallion UVM Cantor (Tutor–Sugar) owned by the University of Vermont. (Courtesy the *Morgan Horse Magazine*)

THE MORGAN LOOK: Note width between eyes, rounded contour of body. Tippy Dee (Hawk Jim–Tippy Tin) at twenty.

Morgans can live outdoors the year around. Replevin (O C R–Tippy Dee) as a three-year-old-filly. Note the strong Morgan type: width through chest and fine head, alert expression.

Morgan mares and suckling foals at Triangle A Ranch, Parkman, Wyoming. (Courtesy, Charley Hamilton)

or two. Horses with natural marks above the knees or hocks, except on the face, and those with glass, wall or watch eyes are denied registration.

Morgans running out of doors in winter grow dense body hair; while not particularly long, it is extremely thick and has the look and feel of high-quality plush. In the spring when it is shed, it is replaced by a very fine, slick coat. The mane and tail hair is usually heavy with a tendency to wave, or even to curl in some strains. Because the long hairs have great vitality, they grow to extreme length before breaking off.

Due to their compact build Morgans are very easy keepers. They stay in good flesh on a small portion of the hay and grain required by other light horse breeds. In fact, is it possible to maintain a whole family of Morgans on the oats that one growing Thoroughbred will consume! Morgans are hardy

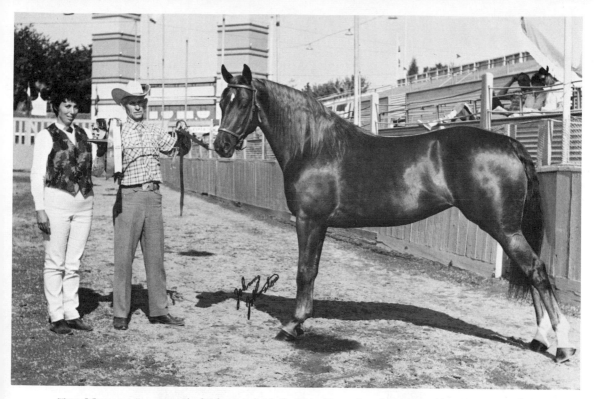

THE MORGAN LOOK: Albafield (Sonfield–Proba) Champion four-year-old mare. Note balance and refinement, finely chiseled head, crested neck, and kind expression. (Courtesy of Arthur and Gloria Jones, Diablo, Calif.)

THE MORGAN LOOK: Cap's Stormy (Devan Cap–Tippy Dee) combines substance in neck, quarters and barrel with refined head. (Courtesy, Mrs. Jess Baker, Solon, Ohio)

and can live out of doors the year round, provided they have adequate forage. Windbreak provided by the lee of a hill or by a dense stand of trees is all the shelter they require, even in severe weather. With hardiness goes longevity. Morgans retain their good looks and vigor well into their twenties. Flyhawk 7526(Go Hawk–Florette), foaled in 1926, was still siring foals at the age of

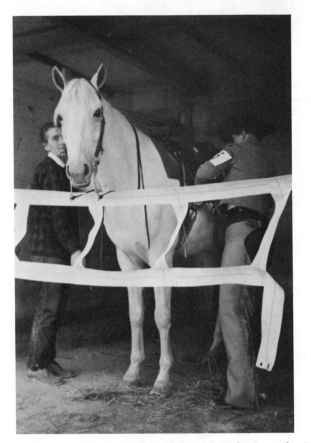

Rare gray Morgan: Captain Paleface (Easter Twilight–Lavender Lassie)

twenty-eight. His sons Linsley de Jarnette and Illiniwek were foaled in 1955. Similarly, mares of the breed are famous for being life-long producers.

Although Morgans have been adversely criticized for their small stature, and it is true that many of them fall into the pony category, they are quite capable of carrying weight while being less likely to break down doing so than taller, leggier horses. Morgans have also been criticized for being too short in the neck, too short in the pastern and too short from the point of the hip to the point of the buttocks. Undeniably these shortcomings exist in cer-

Morgans enjoy being outdoors the year around. Tippy Dee and her weanling daughter Debt by Devan Marsh Hawk.

THE MORGAN LOOK: Windsor's Mr. Chaplin (Trilbrook Joel–Fire's Chigger), owned and bred by Theodore Niboli, Windsor, Vermont. (Courtesy *Morgan Horse Magazine*)

THE MORGAN LOOK: Astronaut (Ulendon–Silkolene) now senior sire at the University of New Hampshire. (Courtesy *Morgan Horse Magazine*)

THE MORGAN LOOK: Morgans retain their good looks even with advancing years. Patricia Gates (Roubidoux–Quaker Maid) at the age of twenty. (Courtesy, Mr. and Mrs. Harold Jenkins, Medina, Ohio)

THE MORGAN LOOK: Debt (Devan Marsh Hawk–Tippy Dee) month-old filly. Note round, bold eye, alert expression. (Photo by John Boardman)

Morgan mares are lifelong producers. Tippy Dee at twenty-one, with her tenth foal, Black-acre Wildfire by Devan Marsh Hawk. (Photo by George Shepard)

Tippy Dee (Hawk Jim–Tippy Tin) enoying a romp: age, twenty-one.

Longevity is a Morgan characteristic. Stresa (Powhattan–Daisy Dean) was foaled August 30, 1928. She is shown here at age thirty-three with her owner, Gardner N. Cobb, M. D., of Strafford, Vermont. He said of her that "Her prime lasted over 20 years." She was humanely destroyed at age thirty-five because Dr. Cobb, who was in failing health, feared that she might be neglected should something happen to him.

tain individuals but are no more typical of the breed than cowhocks in the Arab or lack of substance in the Thoroughbred. There is variation in type between East and West. In the East, due to outcrossing with Saddle Horses prior to 1947, Morgans average somewhat taller than in the West where they have been bred primarily as stock horses and are, therefore, smaller, more compact and closer to the old type.

Considering his good characteristics, the Morgan is the ideal family and all-purpose horse. Although his basic needs are simple, he blooms with loving care. Because of his kindness and small size he can be easily handled by children, yet can carry a heavy rider all day, if necessary. His great versatility and willingness to try anything make him suitable for almost any light horse purpose. What he does, he does well, cheerfully, jauntily and with his own inimitable style.

He is rightfully known as "The Pride and Product of America."

PART II

Beginnings

2

Probable Origins of the Morgan Horse

THE HORSE JUSTIN MORGAN BECAME A LEGEND DURING HIS OWN LIFETIME. The tales of his prowess were repeated by word of mouth, changing and growing with each telling, until he emerged as a super-horse, a veritable Paul Bunyan of the equine world.

There is disagreement as to his actual foaling date which is generally accepted as being 1789, although some authorities believe it was several years later, while others place it a year or two earlier.

There is no irrefutable proof of his pedigree which has been variously described as Dutch, French, Spanish, Canadian, Arab and Thoroughbred. Opinion as to his antecedents has been strongly influenced by the personal bias of various researchers. Admirers of the Thoroughbred present him as being pure bred while those to whom Thoroughbred is a term of opprobrium deny the presence of any hot blood whatsoever in his veins.

It was not until long after the horse's death that an attempt was made to trace his origin. By then, of course, the trail was cold. Memories of people who had known the horse varied; dates and descriptions were often incompatible, or even contradictory. Mixed with the fascination and romance that have always surrounded the horse, according to John Hervey, "have been also much controversy, dispute and collar-and-elbow rough-and-tumble literary and other hard scrabbling. At every step we are confronted by flat contradictions, vague or discrepant statements, conflicting testamonies and (most to be deplored) that acrimony, truculence and disposition to calumniate and abuse that was so often a conspicuous factor of those old time pedigree wars.

For wars they were, fought with a grim persistance and animosity that sometimes stopped little short of bloodshed."

The picture was further confused by the unfortunate manner in which horses of that era changed names almost as often as they changed hands, the same horse being known by many different designations during his lifetime. Sometimes an outstanding physical characteristic suggested a name, such as Bloody Buttocks for a gray with a remnant of chestnut foal hair on the quarters, Old Bald Peg for a mare with a splashy blaze, One Eye, or the Straddling Turk. A horse might simply be known by his owner's name, as the Morgan Horse was, or compounding the confusion, by his sire's name, as Young Traveller. He might be known by the locality in which he stood, or by his supposed place of origin as the Dutch Horse or the Spanish Horse. The famous Alcock Arabian (1704–23), the ancestor of all gray Thoroughbreds, at one time or another was also called the Akaster Turk, Ancaster Arabian, Holderness Turk, Sutton Arabian, Honeywood Arabian and Brownlow Turk. Mares were usually known simply by their sires, as Mare by Cygnet, Daughter of Childers, Cub Mare, Byerly Turk Mare, Sister to Stripling or even less specifically Mare by Gascoigne's Foreign Horse!

From the welter of information, misinformation, opinion, hearsay and recollections, a more or less definite pattern began to emerge concerning Justin Morgan's background. From old tax records, newspaper accounts of the day, stallion advertisements and broadsides, death lists, probate records, contemporary letters and family traditions certain definite facts and dates were ascertained which tend to corroborate certain theories while discrediting others.

Justin Morgan was often referred to as a "Dutch Horse" both in advertisements and in a letter by Justin Morgan, Jr. printed in the Albany *Cultivator* in 1842. This caused endless confusion and misunderstanding.

The horses which the Dutch had imported to New Netherland were heavy draft type animals, plain headed, slow, logy and not suited to saddle purposes. It is stretching the credulity to believe that the lively little horse of song and story descended from such lethargic stock. After the colony became British in 1664, however, New Englanders continued to call "Dutch" anything that was brought into their area from New York, although the equine importations during British rule were principally Arab or Thoroughbred.

In a later letter, Justin Morgan, Jr. said that his father always spoke of the horse as being "of the best blood," which, at that time, meant English racing stock. While living in West Springfield, Massachusetts, Justin Morgan had supplemented his income by leasing various Thoroughbred stallions which he offered at public service. One of these was True Briton, beyond a reasonable doubt the sire of Mr. Morgan's remarkable horse.

True Briton belonged to, and was believed by some authorities to have been bred by James De Lancey (1733–1800). There is also strong evidence that he was bred in England and imported by De Lancey. The De Lancey family, of French Hugenot descent, dominated Manhattan socially, economically and politically. They were related by birth or marriage to most of the prominent families of New York. James De Lancey is known as the father of the American Turf because he was the first to import English horses to America on a large scale for racing and breeding. He had inherited the estate, Bouwerie, located in what is now the Bowery, from his father Steven. Educated in England, as were many wealthy young men of the day, he remolded his farm in the manner of a British stud and laid out a half-mile training course. He was a fine horseman and an excellent judge of foundation stock.

Although De Lancey's sentiments were Tory, he was reluctant to bear arms against his fellow countrymen in the Revolution. Instead, in 1775 he dispersed his horses and land holdings and returned to England. He remained in voluntary exile for the rest of his life.

Before his horses were offered for sale he gave his favorite riding horse, True Briton, to his uncle, General Oliver De Lancey, who kept him for several years before giving him to another nephew, also named James.

Colonel James De Lancey commanded the Westchester County Light Horse Troop which served with the British. The group was also called "the cowboys," whence the term originated. They raided and ravaged the countryside, confiscating livestock and supplies. The handsome colonel cut a fine figure on his beautiful bay charger and, one of the troopers in his old age recalled that he had seen De Lancey repeatedly clear a five-barred gate with True Briton for the delight of onlookers. The speed and beauty of the elegant stallion were soon well-known throughout both armies.

According to an account which appeared in the Connecticut *Gazette* on October 31, 1780, Lieutenant Weight Carpenter, whose property had been pillaged by the raiders, vowed revenge. He and two companions lay in wait for Colonel De Lancey outside his mother's house. De Lancey was in the habit of visiting his widowed mother rather frequently. She lived at the family home, Rosehill, on high ground overlooking the Bronx River, on the present site of the Bronx Zoological Gardens. De Lancey rode from his camp at Kingsbridge and tied his horse to a tree near the house, for, since it was war time, he wanted him close at hand whenever he was absent from his post. While De Lancey was in the house, Carpenter and his friends stole the horse. They galloped off with him, down the long, tree-lined driveway and clattered across a wooden bridge that spanned the river. The Colonel and his servants gave pursuit, but were unable to catch the horse-thieves. They spirited True

Briton to White Plains which was outside the circle of British control. He was later taken to Connecticut where he was sold to Joseph Ward of Hartford who kept him for several years for driving and riding. He was later sold to Selah Norton of East Hartford who kept him at stud at his own stable or leased him to others, including Justin Morgan of West Springfield in 1785; and to his distant cousin, John Morgan of Springfield, in 1788 and 1789.

True Briton(Traveller, Hero, Beautiful Bay) was not advertised at stud during the years immediately following his capture for fear that the Tories would try to recover him. In November of 1783 the British troops were evacuated and Tory property was confiscated by the patriots. The following spring Selah Norton first advertised True Briton at stud. In 1785 he was leased by Morgan who advertised him as follows in the May 3rd Hampshire *Herald*:

"The elegant full-blooded horse called Beautiful Bay will cover this season at Justin Morgan's stables in West Springfield, at twenty shillings the season, ten shillings the leap in cash or produce by the first day of January next, and allowance for cash in hand. Said horse is fifteen hands, takes his name from his shape and color, which is beautiful perhaps as any horse in the thirteen states. Trots and canters exceedingly light; is famous for getting fine colts and is very sure."

He was indeed sure with his mares and was reported to have gotten 16 foals in a single day!

According to De Lancey tradition, True Briton was an imported Thoroughbred. But there is no record of his importation. It is possible that he was of James De Lancey's own breeding. Selah Norton was a knowledgeable horseman but was not above stretching a point in order to make his horse attractive to potential customers. He advertised True Briton as "said to be by the imported horse, Traveller and out of Colonel De Lancey's imported racer." A later ad said: "by the famous old Traveller imported from Ireland." The only one of De Lancey's imported mares that raced in this country was Betty Leedes by Babraham by the Godolphin Arabian. Joseph Battell, who compiled the first there volumes of the *Morgan Horse and Register,* assumed her to be the dam of True Briton. Since contemporary records do not substantiate this theory, it cannot be accepted as fact. Writing in the *Chronicle,* Alexander Mackay-Smith says, "Joseph Battell, who spent a lifetime and a fortune gathering, cataloguing, and publishing source materials for the history of the horse in America, threw out the window his knowledge and integrity as an historian . . . and entered into a series of assumptions." Mr. Mackay-Smith concluded that True Briton was foaled in 1768, or earlier, of unknown pedi-

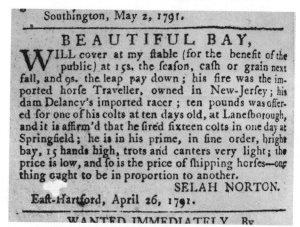

Southington, May 2, 1791.

BEAUTIFUL BAY,

WILL cover at my ftable (for the benefit of the public) at 15s. the feafon, cafh or grain next fall, and 9s. the leap pay down; his fire was the imported horfe Traveller, owned in New-Jerfey; his dam Delancy's imported racer; ten pounds was offered for one of his colts at ten days old, at Lanefborough, and it is affirm'd that he fired fixteen colts in one day at Springfield; he is in his prime, in fine order, bright bay, 15 hands high, trots and canters very light; the price is low, and fo is the price of fhipping horfes—one thing ought to be in proportion to another.

SELAH NORTON.

Eaft-Hartford, April 26, 1791.

WANTED IMMEDIATELY. By

Advertisement in the *Connecticut Courant,* Hartford, Connecticut. Courtesy *Hartford Courant* (founded 1764) and the *Chronicle of the Horse.*

gree, and was imported along with several hunters and fox hounds, by James De Lancey of the Bouwerie Farm, Manhattan.

The dam of Justin Morgan was described as being of medium height with a light bay coat and heavy mane and tail of mixed black and brown. She was foaled in 1784 at West Springfield and was probably sired by Diamond by Mister Church's Wildair, a son of Mr. De Lancey's imported Wildair. Cade, the sire of Wildair, was by the Godolphin Arabian and was both bred and owned by Lord Godolphin. The dam of Church's Wildair was also of the Wildair strain.

Wildair had been imported to America by De Lancey in 1764. He got such elegant foals that he was returned to England in 1773 where he stood for the then astounding price of 40 guineas. Wildair breeding became very popular in the colonies and was considered to be a family in its own right; it was also known as the Wild Deer Breed.

The dam of Justin Morgan was said to be a smooth traveller. She was owned by Mr. Morgan who was her breeder also, in all probability, for her sire was Diamond, one of the stallions which he had leased. It is likely that the second dam, too, was bred by Mr. Morgan from the stallion he stood in 1778, Sportsman by Ranger, also known as Lindsey's Arabian.

Repeatedly in the outer reaches of the possible pedigree of Justin Morgan, as drawn up by Daniel Chapman Linsley, author of the first history of the breed, there appear the names of the foundation sires and dams of the English racing horse that later was to develop into the modern Thoroughbred.

Desert-bred animals imported from Arabia, Persia, Turkey and Morocco increased greatly in size due to the superior forage of their adopted land.

The Darley Arabian, ancestor of the modern Thoroughbred, was also a distant ancestor of Justin Morgan. (Courtesy Keeneland Library)

England is ideally suited to raising horses. Its limestone subsoil, and damp, mild climate in a comparatively short time produced radical changes in the original Arab stock, especially those selected for their racing speed. From an average height in 1700 of 13.3 hands, the English horse gained approximately an inch every twenty-five years. The average at present is about 16 hands. Conversely, adverse conditions result in stunting. Australian hunter stock was introduced to the Dutch Indies with the expectation of up-grading the local stock; the second generation, however, grew no larger than the native Javanese and Sandlewood ponies which they had been imported to improve.

There had been much discussion and speculation about "native English mares" and their influence on the Thoroughbred. But the mares in England before the Arab importation were either of draft or pony type. The vast majority of the foundation mares were also imported Arabs, the best of which were *Kehilan,* or pure bred. Better living conditions rather than introduction of common blood resulted in the dramatic increase in size.

At the end of his exile, Charles II set about rebuilding his stud. He repossessed the holdings that had been confiscated by Cromwell. According to tradition, he sent his agents to the East to import the finest mares. His Master-of-Horse was said to have spent fabulous sums securing the best Arab racing stock of the *Naseri* strain. The horses were taken by sea—with favorable winds a journey of three months. Both the imported mares and their daughters were designated as Royal Mares.

According to Lady Wentworth, "Remembering that true Arabian blood has the power of transmitting quality and vitality unimpaired over centuries there can be . . . no doubt that the Royal Mares were not only Oriental and not only Arabian, but Arabian blood of the very highest class just as the Darley Arabian and the other three sires whose influence has been indelible and overwhelming in its prepotency."

In the pedigree of Justin Morgan, as worked out by Linsley, in addition to the Royal Mares appear many other illustrious names: D'Arcy's Yellow Turk (seven crosses); D'Arcy's White Turk; Old Bald Peg, progenitor of Bruce Lowe's Family No. 6; The Brownlow Turk or Alcock Arabian, (four crosses); The Leedes Arabian (eight crosses); Flying Childers; The Byerly Turk (four); the Godolphin Arabian (three); and the Darley Arabian (two).

Many times the theory has been advanced that the Morgan Horse was a mutant, a genetic sport, a wonder horse that sprang, as it were, full blown from Zeus's skull. This belief is only another of the quaint legends that make up the aura of fantasy surrounding the horse. Mutation is rare, almost always recessive and is usually undesirable. "Taking everything into consideration, it is very probable that animal breeders are almost never concerned with mutation."[1] Rather, it is the homozygous blood of the Arab, bred for centuries for purity, which accounts for the prepotency of the original Morgan horse and his decendants.

The short back of the Morgan also indicates a high percentage of oriental blood. Not only are the Arab's individual vertebrae shorter in length than the common horse, they are also fewer in number. Similarly many Morgans have one less than the usual six lumbar vertebrae and one fewer pair of ribs than the usual 18 or 19. According to H. H. Reese of the Bureau of Animal Industry, at post-mortem exhamination General Gates 666, Donald 5224,

[1] A. L. Hagendoorn, Ph.D., *Animal Breeding*, Crosby Lockwood & Son, Ltd., London, 1939. p. 33.

The Godolphin Arabian, one of the three imported Oriental sires to which Thoroughbreds trace in direct male line, was also an ancestor of Justin Morgan. Note the heavily crested neck, extremely short back, and powerful loins. These characteristics are typical of the Morgan. (Courtesy Keeneland Library)

Dude 4673 and a weanling colt by Troubadour of Willowmoor 6459 were found to have only five lumbar vertebrae. The round eye socket, short frontal bones and, occasionally the dished face of modern Morgans indicate their Arab heritage.

These two descriptions make an interesting comparison. The first is by the veterinary surgeon Omer, who saw the Godolphin Arabian in his prime: ". . . his shoulders were deeper and lay further into his back than any horse as yet seen. Behind the shoulders there was but very small space before the muscles of his loins rose excessively high, broad and expanded, which were inserted into his quarters with greater strength and power than in any horse I believe ever seen of his dimensions." The second is by Daniel Chapman Linsley, of the original Morgan horse: "His back and legs were perhaps his most noticeable points. The former was very short; the shoulder blades and hip bones being very long and oblique, and the loins exceedingly broad and muscular."

3

Justin Morgan, the Man

JUSTIN MORGAN WAS BORN IN 1747 IN WEST SPRINGFIELD, MASSACHUSETTS, which is just across the Connecticut River from Springfield. He suffered from tuberculosis, or consumption as it was then called, and was not able to do hard labor after the age of twenty. Fortunately he had other skills and was called upon to fill many jobs requiring more than the average degree of literacy. In spite of his delicate health he was industrious, and tried his hand at many tasks at one time or another. He taught school, he served as town clerk, he conducted singing classes. He wrote a beautiful hand and gave lessons in penmanship when that art was considered one of the hallmarks of gentility. He was a composer of some note and several of his compositions have come down to us. He owned a small plot of land with a house and barn. The land, amounting to less than an acre, sloped gently down to the river's edge where Mr. Morgan kept a small inn and tavern for the boatmen.

Mr. Morgan was very much liked because of his gentility, fine manners and sterling character. He was described as being "upright, industrious and poor." He was also a lover of fine horses and supplemented his meagre income from tavern and teaching by acting as stallioneer. Throughout his lifetime he owned, bred and trained blooded horses. While living in West Springfield he leased and offered at public service several Thoroughbred stallions which he advertised in the local newspapers: Sportsman in 1778, Diamond in 1783, and in 1785, True Briton or Beautiful Bay. All were at least part Thoroughbred. True Briton was possibly clean-bred. All came from Hartford, Connecticut, 25 miles south of West Springfield on the Connecticut River and, in that day, the center for buying, selling and breeding fine horses.

Statue erected by descendants of Miles Morgan, great-grandfather of Justin Morgan. The Morgans were leading citizens of the Springfield area. Financier J. P. Morgan was a great-grandson of a first cousin of Justin Morgan. (Courtesy Margaret Gardiner, Wiscasset, Maine)

Also, in addition to the stallions that he leased, Mr. Morgan kept from time to time one or two mares from which he raised a few foals.

In 1788 when he was forty-one years old, Mr. Morgan moved his family to Randolph, Vermont. He and his wife Martha had two children, a daughter Emily, and a son Justin, Jr.; three other children, born in Springfield, had not survived. Another child Nancy was born in Randolph in September of the following year.

It is difficult to understand why Mr. Morgan, who was already in delicate health, would choose to undergo the hardships of a frontier life. The living was still meager in the new state and many of the Vermont pioneers were near starvation before the bitter winters passed. Sometimes they eked out an existence by subsisting on wild onions. The actual threat of famine was always at hand. The houses were little more than log cabins.

In the isolated pioneer communities, long before the days of elaborate entertainment and mass media, the simple pleasures were very important. The singing-school movement took New England by storm and everywhere

To all People to whom these Presents shall come,

Greeting.

KNOW YE, That *Isaac Morgan of Springfield in the County of Hampshire & Province of the Massachusetts Bay in New England yeoman*

For and in consideration of the Sum of *Thirty pounds* Current Money of the Commonwealth aforesaid, to *me* in Hand paid before the Ensealing hereof by

my son Justin Morgan of Springfield & County aforesaid husbandman

the Receipt whereof *I* do hereby acknowledge and *am* fully satisfied, contented and paid, HAVE given, granted, bargained, sold, aliened, released, conveyed and confirmed, and by these Presents, do freely, clearly and absolutely give, grant, bargain, sell, aliene, release, convey and confirm unto *him* the said *Justin Morgan his* Heirs and assigns forever,

A certain tract or piece of land situate lying & being in the township of Springfield aforesaid & on the west side of the great River being part of my home lot on which I now dwell being the east side of my said home lot containing twenty two acres bounded northerly on Israel Brooks land easterly partly on Israel Brooks land & partly on Thomas Baggs land southerly on Thomas Baggs land westerly on my own land together with one third part of my barn with the privilege of the yard as he has need of going in & out of my barn.

TO HAVE AND TO HOLD the before-granted Premises, with the Appurtenances and Privileges thereto belonging, to *him* the said *Justin Morgan his* Heirs and Assigns : To *his* and *their* own proper Use, Benefit and Behoof forever more. And *I,* the said *Isaac Morgan for me and my* Heirs, Executors, and Administrators, do Covenant, Promise and Grant unto and with the said *Justin Morgan his* Heirs and Assigns forever. That before and until the Ensealing hereof, *I am* the true, sole, proper and lawful Owner and Possessor of the before-granted Premises, with the Appurtenances. And have in *myself* good Right, full Power and lawful Authority to give, grant, bargain, sell, aliene, release, convey and confirm the same as aforesaid ; and that free and clear, and freely and clearly executed, acquitted and discharged of and from all former and other Gifts, Grants, Bargains, Sales, Leases, Mortgages, Wills, Intails, Joyntures, Dowries, Thirds, Executions and Incumbrances whatsoever.

AND FURTHERMORE, *I* the said *Isaac Morgan for me my* Heirs, Executors and Administrators, do hereby Covenant, Promise and engage the before-granted Premises, with the Appurtenances, unto the said *Justin Morgan his* Heirs and Assigns forever, to Warrant, Secure and Defend against the lawful Claims or Demands of any Person or Persons whatever. *In witness whereof I the said Isaac Morgan have hereunto set my hand & seal this 26 day of May, Anno Domini 1771 & in the 11 year of his Majesty's Reign George the third King &*

Signed Sealed & delivered in presence of

Nath'l Atchinson Gideon Morgan   *Isaac Morgan & Seal*

Rec'd Jan'y 31 1786 & Recorded from the Original
Pr Wm Pynchon Reg'r

Deed transferring piece of property from Isaac Morgan to his son Justin in 1771. (Courtesy Margaret Gardiner)

people were eager for singing lessons to brighten the austerity and monotony of their days.

As was typical of other New England singing masters, Justin Morgan went from village to village organizing singing schools from which the best voices were chosen to make up choirs. Where cash was short—as was usually the case—lessons were paid for in grain or other produce. The classes which were held at a school or tavern were open to all the young people of the parish, and to their elders in the evening after the day's work was done. The choirs drawn from the singing classes participated at various church holidays, often singing hymns especially written for the occasion by their singing master. The simple harmonies are reminiscent of the counterpoint of Bach and his contemporaries and are our first truly American folk music. These primitive yet strong and expressive melodies also enriched the daily religious services held by many individual families.

The Morgans' life in Vermont followed very much the same pattern that it had in West Springfield. Mr. Morgan continued to give singing lessons and to stand a stallion. In 1789 he was chosen lister and in 1790 he was elected town clerk. As before he kept a small tavern.

Martha died on the 20th of March, 1791, ten days after giving birth to their seventh child, a daughter named Polly. For two years Justin Morgan struggled to keep his family together, but finally the children were divided among neighbors to be brought up. The family was never together again after 1793, nor did Mr. Morgan have a permanent home after that time. He continued to ride from town to town, boarding with various families, much as the village school master was accustomed to board in turn with several citizens of the community. While riding from one village to another he would often drop the reins while he composed a new song for his pupils.

Justin Morgan's health continued to decline and in 1798 he died at the age of fifty-two. In Spooner's *Vermont Journal,* April 15, 1799, there appeared an advertisement for the settlement of his estate. A bridle and saddle were appraised at $7.00, a whip at 25¢, his clothes and personal effects at $23.06. His books were a Bible, Scott's *Lessons* and Pope's *Essay on Man* valued at a total of 65¢. The entire estate was appraised at $160.13. The meagre list of articles enumerated in the probate records include no horse or other kind of livestock. Probably his horse had been disposed of to settle a debt some time before his death. He left his children nothing but debts and in 1800 his creditors were paid 18 cents on the dollar for what was owed them.

Although Morgan's personal life was marred by tragedy, his spirit rose above the hardships which he always endured with fortitude. All recollections of him mention his gentle, urbane ways and his integrity of character.

Justin Morgan lived and died in obscurity where he would have remained had it not been for the stallion he brought to Vermont which later bore his name and founded the first American breed of horse.

4

The Life and Times of the Original Morgan Horse

DANIEL CHAPMAN LINSLEY (1827–1889) WHILE ENGAGED IN A GOVERN-MENT construction project in the West in 1852 was impressed with the hardiness, speed and endurance of Morgan horses, as well as their ability to withstand the hardship of severe daily use. He therefore decided to discover the origin of this remarkable breed of horse and to preserve what records were available under one cover. The task proved to be a tremendous one extending over several years and ending in 1856 with the publication of the classic *Morgan Horses* which earned him First Premium from the Vermont State Agricultural Society.

Thirty years had passed since the death of the horse when Linsley began his research into the stallion's background, ownership, life history and descendants. In Linsley's own words:

It is exceedingly difficult to obtain accurate information respecting the changes in owners that occurred to the horse at different times. To account for this uncertainty we must consider that his fame has been almost entirely posthumous, that although the champion of the neighborhood, he was little valued, on account of his small size; and it was not until after his death, and his descendants were exhibiting the powers of their sire in speed, strength and endurance, in almost every village of Eastern Vermont, that people began to realize that they had not properly appreciated him. For this reason, little notice was taken, at that time, of any changes of owners, and many persons who very well recollect the horse, recollect nothing of these changes; and those who claim to recollect them disagree much as to the dates at which his several owners purchased him.

It is certain, however, that the horse changed hands frequently and never for a sum of more than one or two hundred dollars. From time to time the horse disappears from sight entirely; there are periods of more than a year which are unaccounted for before he reappears in the form of a tax record, advertisement or definite recollection. The confusion is further compounded by the fact that during his lifetime the original Morgan horse, as was the custom of the times, was known by several names. During his youth when he was owned by the singing teacher he was called Figure. Later he was known as the Morgan Horse, but only after he had already passed from Morgan's ownership. He also was called the Goss Horse because he was owned at various times by several members of the Goss family. Later still — and probably not until after his death — he was known as Justin Morgan.

Vermont is rocky and mountainous, the soil ungenerous, the climate harsh. Difficult tasks become doubly so, and in the post-Revolutionary days tillable fields had to be hewn from the virgin forest. The people were poor, life was a constant struggle for survival and the Morgan Horse was worked hard all the days of his life. In the evenings after an arduous day's labor he was matched in races and pulling contests at neighborhood taverns for wagers of coin or rum. He was ridden on holidays in military reviews and because of his gay and jaunty air was much in demand for parades. Yet he was gentle enough to be ridden and driven by children. He stood at stud in Montpelier, Randolph, Lydon, Williston and Hinesburg; there is a likelihood that he crossed the border into Canada during one of the unaccounted-for periods in his history. He stood at crossroads, taverns and livery stables often covering ten or twelve mares in a single day.

The horse lived to a remarkable thirty-two years, during all of which time he did the roughest of farm labor. He had a succession of owners all of whom used him hard and he finally died of neglect, ill-usage and exposure. Despite the disparity and generally indifferent and nondescript quality of the mares sent to him, his get was amazingly uniform and even during his lifetime began to be known as Morgan horses.

Among his many owners were Justin Morgan, Samuel Whitman, Jonathan Shepard, William Rice, James Hawkins, Robert Evans, John Goss, David Goss, Joel Goss, Joseph Rogers, Jacob Sanderson, William Langsmaid, Levi Bean, plus several others now unknown.

Even the exact date of the horse's birth is a matter of dispute. Linsley sets it at 1793 while Battell places it in 1789, basing his belief upon the fact that the horse was advertised at stud by Justin Morgan in Spooner's *Vermont Journal,* published at Windsor in April of 1793, as follows: "Will cover this

WILL Cover this feason at Captain
Elias Biffell's ftable in Randolph,
and at Captain Josiah Cleveland's ftable
in Lebanon, the famous FIGURE
HORSE, from Hartford, in Connecticut, at fifteen fhillings for the feafon
if paid down, or eighteen fhillings if
paid in the fall, in Cafh or Grain at cafh
price. Said Horfe's beauty, ftrength,
and activity, the fubfcriber flatters himfelf the curious will be beft fatisfied to
come and fee.
₊ Said Horfe will be in Lebanon
the fecond Monday in May next, there to
continue two weeks, and then return to
Randolph; fo to continue at faid Cleveland's and Biffell's, two weeks at each
place, through the feafon.
              JUSTIN MORGAN.
Randolph, April 8th, 1793.   7t9

A 1793-stallion ad for Figure, two years before (according to legend) Justin Morgan had accepted a worthless two-year-old castoff in lieu of payment of a debt. Ad originally appeared in Spooner's *Vermont Journal,* and is reproduced by courtesy of Vermont Historical Society and Margaret Gardiner.

season at Captain Elias Land's stable in Lebanon, the famous Figure horse from Hartford, Connecticut at fifteen shillings the season, if paid down, or eighteen shillings if paid in the fall, in cash or grain at cash prices. Said horse's beauty, strength and activity the subscriber flatters himself the curious will be satisfied to come and see . . . JUSTIN MORGAN." And in 1794, he advertised the horse: "The beautiful horse, Figure, will cover this season at the moderate price of one dollar the single leap, two dollars the season, if paid down by the first of September next . . . the horse's strength, beauty and activity will bear examination by the curious." In another ad in 1795 he stated that, "Figure sprang from a curious horse owned by Col. De Lancey of New York, but the greatest reccommend I can give him is, he is exceedingly sure and gets curious colts." "Curious" was used to mean of exceedingly fine quality.

It is evident from the above dates that Figure could not have been the unbroken two-year-old runt said to have tagged along behind a gelding that Justin Morgan brought back with him in 1795 from West Springfield in lieu of settlement of a debt, for by that time Figure had already stood two seasons

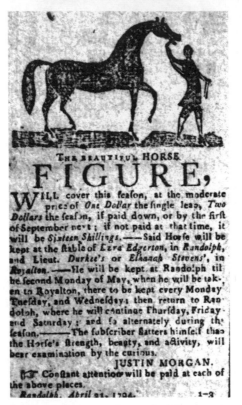

A 1794 stallion ad from Spooner's *Vermont Journal*. (Courtesy Vermont Historical Society and Margaret Gardiner)

in and around Randolph. The story of the worthless colt that was thrown in for good measure, scorned and ill-thought-of by all, which made liars of his detractors and founded a dynasty, is a pretty tale and for that reason has persisted. Sometimes fiction seems to have a greater validity than truth, especially if it points a moral. American folklore is full of the rags-to-riches tradition, but the account of Figure as a worthless castoff must be dismissed as but another of the myths, legends, half-truths and pure fantasies that grow up around any famous personality. It belongs in the same apocryphal catagory as Eugène Sue's tale of the Godolphin Arabian pulling a water cart through the streets of Paris or Parson Weems' parable of George Washington and the cherry tree, both of which are spurious in origin, but have such great appeal and have been repeated so often that they are widely accepted as gospel.

By 1795 the horse was already well-known in Randolph and had previously served a season in West Hartford, as attested by an advertisement of one Samuel Whitman in 1792 who described him as "a beautiful bay horse."

FIGURE,
WILL COVER

THIS feafon at the ftable of Samuel Allen, in Williston, and at a ftable in Hinfburgh formerly owned by Mr. Munfon. He will ftand at Williston till the 18th of May, then to Hinfburgh, where he will ftand one week, then back to Williston ; to continue through the feafon one week in each place. With regard to faid horfe's beauty, ftrength, and activity, the fubfcriber flatters himfelf the curious will be beft fatisfied to come and fee.

FIGURE fprang from a curious horfe owned by Col. Delanfey, of New-York, but the greateft recommend that I can give him is, he is exceeding fure and, gets curious Colts.

JUSTIN MORGAN.

Williston, April 30, 1795.   345

Stallion ad, May 11, 1795, *Rutland Herald,* Rutland, Vermont. (Courtesy Vermont Historical Society and Margaret Gardiner.

Justin Morgan, from Linsley's *Morgan Horses.* ("A very faithful representation of him as he appeared while I owned him."—DAVID GOSS.)

Nothing further appeared in Connecticut in regard to Figure after 1792, but the following spring Justin Morgan's ad was published offering the services of "the famous Figure horse from Hartford." No further published record of Figure can be found after 1795 because subsequent to that time he was known as the Morgan Horse or the Goss Horse.

Daniel Lindsley's description of Figure is a classic and bears repeating:

The original, or Justin Morgan, was about fourteen hands high, and weighed about nine hundred and fifty pounds. His color was dark bay with black legs, mane and tail. He had no white hairs on him. His mane and tail were coarse and heavy, but not so massive as has been sometimes described; the hair of both was straight, and not inclined to curl. His head was good, not extremely small, but lean and bony, the face straight, forehead broad, ears small and very fine, but set rather wide apart. His eyes were medium size, very dark and prominent, with a spirited but pleasant expression, and showed no white around the edge of the lid. His nostrils were very large, the muzzle small, and the lips close and firm. His back and legs were perhaps his most noticeable points. The former was very short; the shoulder blades and hip being very long and oblique, and the loins exceedingly broad and muscular. His body was rather long, round and deep, close ribbed up; chest deep and wide, and breast-bone projecting a good deal in front. His legs were short, close jointed, thin, but very wide, hard and free from meat, with muscles that were remarkably large for a horse of his size, and this superabundance of muscle exhibited itself at every step. His hair was short, and at almost all seasons soft and glossy. . . . His feet were small but well shaped, and he was in every respect perfectly sound and free from any sort of blemish. He was a very fast walker. In trotting his gait was low and smooth, and his step short and nervous. . . . Although he raised his feet but little he never stumbled. His proud, bold and fearless style of movement and his vigorous, untiring action, have, perhaps, never been surpassed. When a rider was on him he was obedient to the slightest motion of the rein, would walk backward as willingly as he moved foreward; in short, was perfectly trained to all the paces and evolutions of a parade horse; and when ridden at military reviews (as was frequently the case) his bold, imposing style, and spirited, nervous action attracted universal attention and admiration.

In general, Battell agreed with Lindsley's description, except that he believed the horse's height to be nearer 15 than 14 hands. To substantiate this assertion he quoted Solomon Yurann of West Randolph as saying that the horse was ". . . bay with mane and tail black and very long; of fair height, fifteen hands or a little less; eyes very prominent; flat legs, big cords, good feet; a horse that was right every way under the heavens and would go very fast; an awful good horse." Whitman's ad also describes Figure as standing 15 hands.

There was, as far as is known, no contemporary portrayal of the horse. The woodcut, however, which appears as the frontispiece of Lindsley's *Mor-*

gan Horses was thought to be an excellent likeness of Figure by those who had known him, including David Goss who owned him for about seven years. He called the drawing "a very faithful representation of him as he appeared while I owned him." Solomon Steele who knew the horse well, having seen him almost every day during the height of his popularity, said that the print "is remarkably correct and gives a *very* accurate delineation of the horse . . ." Daniel Baldwin who once kept the horse while he was owned by Joel Goss, and described him as the best horse he ever had anything to do with, said that the woodcut "is a very excellent likeness of him."

As we have seen, there is a strong likelihood that Justin Morgan not only owned Figure's dam but was also her breeder since her sire, Diamond, was one of the Thoroughbred stallions he had leased while operating the boatmen's tavern in West Springfield. It is probable that he bred her to True Briton before moving his family to Randolph in 1788. After a season at stud in West Hartford as a three-year-old, Figure appeared in Randolph where the now seriously ailing singing master again attempted to eke out his humble livelihood by acting as stallioneer in 1793 and 1794. Great credit should be given to the frail, gentle man who trained the spirited young stallion to go so kindly that ladies and children could ride him.

His wife dead, his children divided among neighbors and his own health rapidly failing, Justin Morgan's struggle to make ends meet became increasingly hopeless. In the fall of 1795 he attempted to apply his horse against the payment of a note. He was not able to get what he thought Figure was worth, nor did he have the means to keep him through the severe Vermont winter. Therefore he leased the horse to a farmer named Robert Evans for $15 a year.

Robert Evans was a poor man with a large family. In addition to doing the work around his own place, he hired out to do chores for his neighbors — clearing land, hauling logs and building fences. Evans' only team was the little horse, Figure, which he used no less severely than he did himself. Shortly after leasing the horse from Morgan, he contracted to clear 15 acres of heavily timbered land, and before the first of June of the following year had completed the job — truly a herculean task for one man and one horse working together.

It was during the year of Evans' lease that the stallion's remarkable capabilities were first realized. After a day of the most severe labor, he would be matched in all sorts of contests and earned the reputation of being able to out-walk, out-trot, out-run and out-pull any horse that was put against him. Impromptu pulling matches were held at sawmills or at the inns and taverns where the tired farmers and loggers gathered for a glass of cheer after the

"Whatever he was hitched to generally had to come the first time trying." — ROBERT EVANS. Drawing by Peggy Pittenger

long day's work. A stirring though exaggerated account by Nathan Nye of one such contest, of which he had been an eyewitness, was quoted by Solomon Steele in a letter to Linsley.

At the time Evans had the horse, a small tavern, a grist mill, and a saw-mill were in operation on the branch of White River, in Randolph, and at this place the strength of men and horses in that settlement, were generally tested. On one occasion I went to these mills, where I spent most of a day, and during the time, many trials were had, for a small wager, to draw a certain pine log, which lay some ten rods from the saw mill.

Some horses were hitched to it that would weigh twelve hundred pounds, but not one of them could move it its length. About dusk, Evans came down from his logging field, which was near by, and I told him the particulars of the drawing match. Evans requested me to show him the log, which I did; he then ran back to the tavern and challenged the company to bet a gallon of rum, that he could not draw the log fairly on to the logway, at three pulls with his colt. The challenge was promptly accepted, and each having "taken a glass" the whole company went down to the spot.

Arrived on the ground, Evans says, "I am ashamed to hitch my horse to a little log like that, but if three of you will get on and ride, if I don't draw it, I will forfeit the rum." Accordingly, three of those least able to stand were placed upon the log. I was present with a lantern, and cautioned those on the log to look out for their legs, as I had seen the horse draw before, and knew something had got to come. At the word of command the horse started, log and men, and went more than half the distance before stopping. At the next pull, he landed his load at the spot agreed upon to the astonishment of all present.

Not many days after this, the beaten party proposed to Evans to run a certain horse against his, eighty rods for another gallon. Evans accepted, went from his work, and matched his horse against four different horses the same evening, and beat them all with ease.

In Vermont in those days there were no race courses as such. Usually a tavern, inn, mill, cross-road general store or other gathering place was the starting point for these impromptu match races. According to Phil Stong, "We can assume from the fact that the pulling contest was held by lantern light that most of the notable races were held under the same conditions; that is, in dusk or dark, with tired horses ridden by owners at no particular weight, and with well moistened whistles."

The course extended an agreed upon distance down the public road; 80 rods, the equivalent of two furlongs, or one-quarter mile was the usual length. Because of the narrowness of the road, which was often a mere wagon track through the brush, only two horses at a time raced against each other. Like the Quarter Horse, which also developed from English racing stock in Colonial Virginia and the Carolinas, Figure had a great burst of early speed and was able to get the jump on his larger rivals. Tremendous muscular development is the distinguishing feature of the sprinter — a characteristic which Figure had in great abundance.

The horses paired against each other stood behind a mark, or "scratch" drawn with a stick across the roadway and went off at the word "go," the drop of a hat, or other such signal. "When brought up to the line, his eyes flash and his ears quiver with great excitement, he grinds the bit with his teeth, his hind legs are drawn under him, every muscle of his frame trembles, and swells almost to bursting, and at the given signal he goes off like the spring of a steel trap," Linsley wrote of Figure.

There were many accounts of races the little horse won, but because the details were in disagreement with each other, Linsley described only two, which were run in 1796 at Brookfield, Vermont, when the horse was seven.

Apparently renown of Figure's prowess as a sprinter had spread, for two runners from New York, one from Long Island and the other from St. Lawrence County were brought in to race against him. Figure easily defeated

"At the given signal he goes off like the spring of a steel trap." — DANIEL LINSLEY. Drawing
by Peggy Pittenger

both Sweepstakes and Silver Tail. His owner — whom Linsley says was
Justin Morgan, but according to Battell's calculations would have been Jonathan Shepard — offered the owner of Silver Tail two more chances to win
the $50-stake by matching his horse with Figure in both a walking and trotting
race; but the offer was declined.

It is probable that Figure had passed out of Justin Morgan's possession
by the fall of 1795; his last known advertisement of the horse is at Williston
and Hinesborough during the 1795 season. Formerly it was believed that
Morgan willed his horse to William Rice in payment for debts he had incurred,
but the tax records show that at the time of his death in 1798, Justin Morgan
no longer owned a horse of any sort. Therefore, the horse must have gone
to Rice at an earlier date.

In 1796, Rice took Figure to Woodstock where he kept him only long enough to find a buyer for him. Jonathan Shepard bought the horse and took him to Montpelier where he made the 1796 season. Shepard thought highly of the horse's racing ability and often matched him against other horses for wagers of money or spirits.

In the *History of Montpelier*, Shepard is quoted as saying that he had purchased the horse from a man in Woodstock for about $200 — a large sum for the times, when cash was short — and that he had been told that the horse had been raised by Justin Morgan who had also owned his dam. It was during this time that Figure began to be known as the Morgan Horse.

Shepard had built the village's first blacksmith shop which he later traded, along with the horse, to James Hawkins, for the latter's farm. The transfer took place on February 14, 1797, when the horse was rising eight years of age.

It is not certain how long Hawkins kept the Morgan Horse for it is at this point that we lose track of him for several years. It is probable that he had several different owners during the period and that he was kept at several different places. Often, due to the pioneer conditions in the new state, records were sketchy or nonexistant and it is therefore impossible to pinpoint his location each year.

Apparently, Robert Evans, who had found the little horse to be such a willing worker when he had leased him from Justin Morgan, awaited an opportunity to purchase him, for the Morgan Horse next appeared in 1801 under Evans' ownership. Things continued much as before with the horse cheerfully and kindly doing all the rough work that was asked of him by a poor but ambitious man with a large family to feed and clothe. The horse was never known to refuse a draw nor to pull as often as was needed to get the job done, but, as his owner remarked, "I didn't very often have to ask him but once, for whatever he was hitched to generally had to come the first time trying."

Despite his industry, Robert Evans had trouble making ends meet. In 1804 he was sued by his creditors. Colonel John Goss of Randolph went bail for Evans, taking the horse as security. Later, the Colonel paid off the note and kept the horse but since he was not much of a horseman, he sent the horse to be kept at his brother David's farm near St. Johnsbury. David Goss was an excellent and knowledgeable horseman and immediately recognized the stallion's unusual merit. So greatly pleased was he with the horse's quality, manners and all-round usefulness that he traded his brother a fine mare in addition to cash and goods for the horse. Although he was worked hard during the seven years that David Goss owned him, the Morgan Horse was never overworked or abused, but was always well-treated, well-fed and well-cared-for.

The most successful and best recorded portion of his stud career was served in and around St. Johnsbury. It was here that his sons Sherman, Fox (Corbin's), Rover, Highlander, The Fenton Horse (Weasel) and the Hawkins Horse were gotten. In the spring, in breeding condition, he was described as being a very dark bay, almost brown, with an overlay of dapples.

At the age of fifteen the Morgan Horse — or Goss Horse — was still being used in drawing matches, and was entered in a pulling bee at General Butler's Tavern in St. Johnsbury in 1804. Although many of the horses competing were draft type, outweighing him by several hundred pounds, the gallant little horse was equal to the occasion and out-pulled them all.

Forty-odd years later, an elderly lady who had grown up in St. Johnsbury said she could recall the horse's jaunty appearance perfectly and that she had delighted in riding him, while she was still a young girl, to balls and other parties. She spoke with great enthusiasm of the little stallion's noble looks, high spirits and perfect docility.

By this time, many of his sons and daughters around the Randolph area had grown into useful, handsome animals. They were all remarkably like, having inherited their sire's good looks, hardiness and seemingly endless willingness to get the job done. Even at this early date his progeny were beginning to be known as Morgan Horses. Consequently, because of the great demand for his services, the old horse was returned to Randolph for the 1807 season during which time he was stabled at John Goss's. He also stood part of the season at Claremont, New Hampshire.

In 1811, when the horse was twenty-two, David Goss sold him to his son Philip who returned him to Randolph since, again, there were many people who wished to breed their mares to him. Robert Evans again cared for him, and it was during this period that his famous son, Bulrush, was sired.

From this time on during his declining years the old horse changed hands frequently, according to Linsley, "for those who owned him . . . seemed eager to get rid of him, for fear he should die on their hands." Philip Goss sold him to Jacob Sanderson after the 1811 breeding season. Sanderson in turn sold him to Jacob Langsmade, who put the stallion to very severe use, considering his age. He was worked in a six-horse hitch hauling freight between Windsor and Chelsea. Not only was the work hard in the extreme, it required intelligence, endurance and courage — qualities that the Morgan Horse had in abundance and of which he was willing to give generously, even while his reserves of strength were running out.

In the spring, the wagon would often become mired axle-deep and the horses would have to strain mightily to free it. In winter on the icy mountain roads, through blinding sleet and heavy drifts — often traveling at a gallop, with the heavily loaded vehicle sliding and careening along the precipitous track — the nimble horse had to scrabble and scramble, using his waning powers to the utmost to prevent an accident. Sometimes a double trip had to be made because one of the other team was laid up due to lameness; and it was always the Morgan that was equal to the task.

Under such treatment, the old horse for the first time in his life became thin and poor. Hollows appeared over his eyes, his ribs showed and his hip bones protruded. But his eye was still bright, his step lively and his spirit willing. When pitifully worn down by hard work, he was sold for a trifle to Joel Goss, another member of the family who had owned him for much of his life. He kept the horse in partnership with Joseph Rogers who lived near the ferry in Claremont, New Hampshire, where the horse was at stud in 1814, 1815 and 1817. It was here that his son Revenge was sired. Joel Goss then sold the horse to Samuel Stone of Randolph who had handled the horse at various times while he had been at stud in that village, but while owned by others. After a couple of years, Stone sold him to Levi Bean, his last owner.

During the winter of 1821 the horse was kept at the farm of Clifford Bean, about three miles south of Chelsea. The horse was not stabled, but was running loose in an open lot with other horses — without shelter from the severe weather. He was kicked in the flank; the untreated wound became infected and the horse died of the combined effects of neglect and old age. Before receiving the injury that led to his death he had been perfectly sound and free from any sort of blemish. Those who remember having seen him during his last years always remarked upon his youthful appearance, the cleanness and suppleness of his limbs. He bore his age lightly. His eyes was undimmed, his air still jaunty and gay, his step light, quick and elastic.

It is a sad commentary on human nature that this gallant little horse which had done so much to improve the lot of Vermonters was not treated with kindness and consideration during his last years. But as Battell said, Vermont is a place where nature has done little to smooth the path of man or beast and luxury was something neither could expect in the pioneer days when scratching a bare existence out of rocky soil occupied everyone's energies to the fullest. The people fared little better than their animals and it is only in terms of the times that one can understand their apparent callousness in allowing the old horse to die from lack of proper care. Maintaining a no-longer-productive animal was an indulgence better suited to a more affluent age.

PART III

The Begats

5

The Less Well Known Sons of
Justin Morgan

ALTHOUGH THE ORIGINAL MORGAN HORSE DIED IN 1821, HE WAS ALREADY assured of a measure of immortality. Not only did his sons and daughters closely resemble him in temperament, size and conformation, they also passed on to their progeny the same qualities which they had inherited from their sire. These characteristics are still readily evident in his present-day descendants which are removed from Justin Morgan by ten, twelve, or more generations. This similarity is all the more remarkable when it is considered that in twelve generations a horse has a total of 8,190 possible ancestors — a figure that doubles with each generation — and that outside blood was continually being introduced into the breed until the book was officially closed in 1947.

According to Hervey, "In his capacity to propagate a family of horses that was in effect a 'new thing' and to stamp it with his own image so strongly that eight or ten generations subsequent to himself and despite all admixtures of foreign blood, its members showed a family likeness, a uniformity of type so striking that they could be spotted upon sight, he ranks most assuredly in a class by himself so far as America is concerned." Further, the Morgan Horse's descendants were able to withstand the test of inbreeding, a practice which while fixing type, runs the risk of bringing to light recessive defects, if present. Also, Morgans have been and are still a great source of improvement when crossed upon other breeds.

Positive statements of fact concerning the Morgan Horse have always resulted in disagreement, first as to the stallion's origin, and, later, to the number of entire sons that he left. F. A. Weir of Walpole, New Hampshire, an early student of the breed, stated that only four sons were kept for breeding — Sherman, Bulrush, Woodbury and Revenge. Linsley states that it is certain that there were six sons kept as stallions, the four listed by Weir plus the Hawkins Horse and the Fenton Horse. John Hervey, authority on the American trotting horse, believes that there were twelve, while Joseph Battell claims information, more or less reliable, on twelve, possibly fourteen, entire sons. Doubtless there were others, quite likely in Canada, recalling that there is a strong indication that the Morgan Horse crossed over the border and served one or more seasons in Quebec between 1797 when owned by James Hawkins and 1801 when purchased by Robert Evans, for during that period there are no definite records of his ownership in either Vermont or New Hampshire. The fact that the Canadian Pacer greatly resembled the Morgan in looks and temperament tends to substantiate this theory.

Certainly the three most famous and prolific sons were Sherman (1808), Bulrush (1812) and Woodbury (1816) each of which established a line of his own, though the greatest number of modern Morgans trace to Sherman. Of the other three sons that Linsley lists for certain as entire sons, he states that it is extremely doubtful if any stock could be traced to the Fenton Horse and that very little was descended from either Revenge or the Hawkins Horse. This was well over a century ago (1856) and their influence must be considered to be negligible today.

The earliest of the Morgan Horse's sons to be kept as a stallion was Brutus, foaled in 1794 in Lebanon. He was from the first crop Figure had sired after coming from Hartford in 1793, the year in which he had alternated at stud between Randolph and Captain Josiah Cleveland's stables in Lebanon, New Hampshire. Brutus was a bay, 15:3, weighing about 1,100. He had a beautiful front, long, elegant neck and breedy head. He had good action at the trot and great endurance. Like his sire, he was a good sprinter and could run away and hide from all competition at 80 rods. Those who knew the horse described him as "the best horse of all and got the best stock."

The Fenton Horse (Weasel) was foaled in St. Johnsbury in 1806. He was named for his first owner, Richard W. Fenton, who bred his mare to Justin Morgan while owned by David Goss. Weasel greatly resembled his sire and was a beautiful blood bay, 15 hands, stoutly built with an airy way of going. Linsley believed him to be the best of all the old horse's sons. He stood a couple of seasons at St. Johnsbury Plains, but there is no record of any of his sons being kept as stallions. At the age of six, Weasel bit his owner severely; as a consequence he had the horse castrated, putting an abrupt end to his career at stud.

The Hawkins Horse was foaled during the same period at St. Johnsbury, in 1806 or 1807. He was bred by a Mr. Melvin from his good bay mare said to be Thoroughbred. The colt was sold as a three-year-old to a near neighbor, Olney Hawkins, whose name he bore. He was a flashy black with no marks, standing 15 hands and not as compact as the others. The high headed horse was a smart trotter, and exceedingly fast runner and in general more inclined toward the Thoroughbred type. His expression was described as "fierce," nor was he as tractable as the other sons, but Linsley described him as "one of the best acting and finest looking horses ever seen under saddle in the state."

Captain Hawkins commanded a troop and he used the colt in the parades, musters and military reviews which were so very popular in that day. The officer and his dashing black charger cut a fine figure. Later Captain Hawkins sold his horse to a brother, who kept him a couple of years before taking him into Canada where in 1817, he was advertised as being "descended from the old Dutch Goss Horse." In Canada he gained renown both as a runner and as a sire of runners. After a few years, he was taken into the northern provinces and trace of him was lost.

Revenge was of Joel Goss's breeding, but was foaled at the farm of Cyrus Moore, also from Claremont, New Hampshire. He was a very compact horse with a smooth, swift gait and less action than either Woodbury or Sherman. Like all Morgans, he had great endurance and was an excellent road horse. Revenge was a dark bay or brown, standing about 14:2 and weighing about 1,000 pounds. The breeding of his dam, a light bay, is uncertain, but she had a tendency to mix gaits, not a surprising trait, considering that her dam was said to have been a pacer of Narraganset stock. As a two-year-old, Revenge was sold to Neamiah Rice, and two or three years later to a Mr. Tyler who kept him in and around Claremont until he was nine.

The sons of Revenge were, for the most part, bay or brown. They all showed great trotting speed although some of them had a tendency to pace. Only one of his sons was known to have been kept entire and he was taken into Canada from Windsor by John Clark.

Battell advances the theory that the dam of the celebrated trotting stallion Henry Clay (founder of the Clay family of trotters), a mare named Lady Surry, was a daughter of Revenge. She had come to Kentucky from Surry, New Hampshire, where presumably she had also been bred. Lady Surry was foaled in 1824, the year following the season Revenge stood at Walpole, a village adjoining Surry.

Blazing Star, a 15:1 hand black horse was foaled about 1814 at Woodstock and is believed to have been by the Morgan Horse. He was compact and muscular, much used as a parade horse. His get was said to resemble the old horse very closely.

Fox (Corbin's, Young Traveller, Paddy) was a brown, 14:3 horse, a good roadster, wide between the eyes, a very pleasant animal and most easy to handle. He was said to be by the Morgan Horse but possibly was a son of the Hawkins Horse who was also known as Traveller, a popular name at the time. Elsewhere he is referred to as "brother to Sherman" which would, of course, make him by Justin Morgan.

Rover, a very dark bay, was also said to be by Justin Morgan. He stood in and around St. Johnsbury where the original Morgan had had his longest and most rewarding years at stud.

Highlander (Kellog's Morgan, Morgan Highlander, Billy Morgan) was a 14:1 bob tail bay foaled in Vermont in 1810 and taken to Boston, where he was used as a dray horse. He was a smooth, high-headed, sound horse with excellent legs and feet. His stock were also described as sound and hardy. Thomas Kellog saw the horse and recognized his fine qualities, bought him and took his to East Bloomfield, New York, where he had a long and successful career at stud.

The Gordon Horse (Gordon Morgan) was a dark bay, 1,400 pound stallion bred by Joseph Gordon of Danville, Vermont. His dam was a chestnut mare from Canada, said to be of French descent.

The Nicholas Horse (Weasel) was also bay, 900 pounds foaled in 1817 or 1818. He was bred by Robert Nicholas of Caledonia County, Vermont. His dam was said to be English. It is doubtful that he left many offspring, since he was gelded as a four-year-old.

Brandywine was a dark bay with a very heavy mane and tail and a forelock that hung nearly to his nose. His dam was of unknown background. When already a mature stallion he was brought to Mercer, Maine by a Mr. Bean in 1829. His get were mostly bay. A horse of the same name and said to be Morgan was brought to Trois Rivières, Province of Quebec. He was the progenitor of the famous Brandywine Family in Canada, but whether or not he was the same horse is uncertain.

Defiance, a 15 hand gray was foaled in Claremont, New Hampshire, and was said to be by Justin Morgan — though he may have been a grandson — sired by Revenge, who also stood in Claremont. He was a good trotter and sire of horses with trotting speed.

Dutch Morgan Trotter was another horse said to be by the old Morgan Horse, as was the Randolph Horse. The latter was a 1,200 pound bay, owned by David Carpenter of Randolph who sold him to a Mr. Buckminster. The horse was described as being low and well built.

Battell rather arbitrarily assigned Copperbottom 66 a fraction of ½ in Vol. II of *The Morgan Horse and Register* indicating that he believed him to be a son of Justin Morgan although he offers little evidence other than similarity of type to substantiate his theory.

Of all of the horses alleged to have been sired by Justin Morgan, much is made of their good looks, compactness, willingness and ability to stand up under hard work. Although the quality of the stock they got was highly praised, there is no record of any of it that has come down to us. Undoubtedly many of the hardy, useful New England mares which were "said to be Morgan" or "of Morgan Type" descended from these little known sons of the old Morgan Horse.

6

Sherman and His Descendants

THE SHERMAN HORSE (LORD NORTH) WAS BRED BY JAMES SHERMAN OF Lyndon, Vermont, and was gotten while the Morgan Horse was the property of David Goss of St. Johnsbury.

The breeding of Sherman's dam is uncertain. She was a high spirited, elegant chestnut which Mr. Sherman had brought with him from Cranston, Rhode Island when he first moved to St. Johnsbury. She was said to have been of Spanish blood, which meant Barb or Arab type. She has also been called an imported English horse. There is a possibility that she may have come to Rhode Island by way of Virginia where high-quality English stock had been bred since earliest Colonial times. All sources are in agreement, however, in praising her beauty, refinement, speed and ease under saddle. Her golden coat was marked with a stripe and three stockings. She had a fine head at the end of an elegant, swan-like neck. Her disposition was the best and she was a willing worker.

Sherman inherited his dam's color and, in part, her markings. He is described as a bright chestnut with a small stripe and a half-stocking on the off hind. He was just under 14 hands, but weighed 925 pounds; for he had his sire's blocky build. His head was breedy, chiseled and fine, with eyes prominent and kind, but not as large as the other sons'. He had the full chest, sloping shoulder, generous heart girth and ample quarters characteristic of Justin Morgan's get. In fact, his conformation was hard to fault except for the fact that he was a trifle low in the back. This was in no way a sign of weakness, for had it been, he surely would have broken down under the hard work and rough treatment he received during his early years.

When the colt was a three-year-old, James Sherman let his recently mar-

64

Sherman Morgan. (Courtesy *Morgan Horse Magazine*)

ried son, George, take the horse to keep and use at his place. Even at this young age, the horse was put to hard work, for George's farm was a new one. Much of the work consisted of clearing the land — timbering and removing stumps and boulders from the rocky fields. New England's picturesque stone walls are not the direct result of any lack of wood for fencing; rather they were constructed of rocks which had to be removed from the soil before the land could be tilled. The rocks were prized up, loaded on a stone boat and dragged to the edge of the clearing where they were piled into a wall.

Mr. Sherman was industrious and there was little rest for his horses. Sherman was worked in double harness with a gelding also sired by the Morgan Horse and not a great deal bigger. In the winter they were used to haul a sledge of freight between Lyndon, Vermont, and Portland, Maine. The "Little Team" soon became locally famous, because Mr. Sherman was always ready and willing to match them against all comers, either pulling or running.

The cross-roads tavern was still the gathering place, the center of social activities and the site of pulling bees, wrestling matches and other contests of strength held between men and their teams. At Lyndon, the winter contests consisted of hitching a horse to a sled filled with men and pulling the load up a steep hill just north of the tavern. When each of the other horses had pulled to the limit of his strength, Mr. Sherman would add a small boy to the load, attach his horse to the sled and pull a bit farther than the best. Nothing daunted the little horse and it was difficult to load him in such a way that he could not move the sledge a little.

Sherman Morgan's kind, generous disposition, his tractability in spite of high spirits and his remarkable powers of endurance were commented upon by all who knew him. In spite of the backbreaking work to which he was subjected, his spirit did not flag. He needed neither whip nor spur to urge him to greater effort.

Mr. Sherman kept the horse for seven years before selling him. After that time the horse changed hands rather frequently. He stood in Littleton, New Hampshire; Dover, Durham, Danville, Vermont; and Lancaster and Charlestown, Massachusetts. He died in John Bellow's Stable in Lancaster on January 9, 1835 of unknown causes. At ten in the morning he had seemed perfectly well, but by one in the afternoon he was found dead in his stall. Apparently he had been dead for a couple of hours, for he was already turning cold. He seemed to have died without a struggle, because his bedding was hardly disturbed. Like his sire, he died free from any unsoundness or blemish of any sort, despite the severity of the labor he had done.

Because his stock were of such excellence and durability, Sherman was greatly in demand as a sire. During his lifetime he had gained a distinguished reputation and was universally regarded as New England's leading sire. According to John Bellows, his last owner, ". . . he yielded a handsome income to his possessor." The horse stood at fourteen dollars the season or eight dollars the single service, plus a dollar gratuity to the stud groom, a marked increase over the modest fee which had been charged for his sire's services.

As a group, the Shermans were famous for their docility. As an example, Linsley recounts the following tale: "Sitting one evening at the hotel in St. Johnsbury, Vt., and talking with a conductor of the Passumpsic Railroad, we said to him that we understood that he had a very smart little mare of the Sherman family. He said he had, and that she was out in the street before a cutter, and as the night was not very dark, proposed that we should go out and look at her. We went out upon the steps, but did not notice any animal about the premises. However, our friend commenced calling, 'Nelly! Nell! Nelly!' and sure enough the mare, who was standing on the opposite side of the street, and some six or seven rods from us, pricked up her ears, and immediately came over to the place where we were standing. We jumped into the sleigh and took a turn down the street, the mare proving herself as spirited as she was gentle."

Sherman was bred extensively and left at least 40 entire sons. They, in turn, were extensively bred from and travelled widely. Their stock was in great demand, both in the large cities and on the rapidly expanding frontier. Sherman's grandsons and great grandsons were taken to Canada, Ohio, Kentucky, Virginia, Iowa, Illinois and the Western Territories. His influence spread in ever-widening waves until it reached from coast to coast, and finally to lands beyond the seas. His descendants furnished the foundation stock for the American Saddle Horse, Standardbred, Tennessee Walking Horse and, to a much lesser extent, the Quarter Horse.

Sherman's greatest son was Black Hawk, who founded a dynasty of his own and will be discussed in a separate chapter.

Other entire sons of Sherman that left progeny included: Young Sherman (of which there were three so-called), Goss Horse, Wilson Horse, Morgan Tiger (two horses), Morgan Robin, Hammond Horse, Batchelder Horse, Newell's Gray, Eastman Horse, White Mountain Morgan, Pope Horse, Fisher's Morgan, Blanchard Horse, Sir Charles, Blinn Horse, Sherman Morgan (Kilburn's), Sherman Morgan (Adam's), Beloit Morgan, Willey Horse, Turk, Carpenter's Gray, Morgan Othello, Ward Horse, Sherman King, Dapple Gray, Dutch Prince, Fox, Mountain Traveller, Howard Morgan, Roebuck, Cock of the Rock, Flint Morgan, Eaton Horse, Silvertail and the Adams Horse.

Billy Root (Root Horse, Comet, Red Bird) was a dark chestnut son of Sherman. He was foaled in 1829 at the farm of Hezekiah Martin of St. Johnsbury. His dam was an excellent harness horse and was said to have been out of a daughter of Justin Morgan. She was also called a French mare from Montreal, another clue pointing toward the possibility that the Morgan Horse stood one or two seasons north of the border. At any rate, her endurance, build and willingness to do were typically Morgan, for on three occasions she was driven from Portland, Maine to St. Johnsbury, a distance of 120 miles, in a single day.

Billy Root was sold as a two- or three-year-old to Eldad Root, who kept him at Genessee Flats, New York for several years before taking him to Highgate, Vermont. Billy Root was a potent sire. In a six-year period he covered 600 mares, getting 450 of them in foal. W. H. Hoyt, who cared for the horse is quoted by Battell as saying, "I never saw so handsome a horse as he; never saw him make a false step." Many of his descendants were trotters of record. His blood comes down to us today through Cushing's Green Mountain. The Government Farm Stallion Troubadour of Willowmoor carried three crosses to him through the dam of Bob Morgan, the dam of Ethan Allen 3rd, and through Nell, who also traced to Billy Root through the Watson mare by Comet.

Another of Sherman's sons that left excellent stock was Royal Morgan (Crane Horse, Morgan Rattler), a stocky, 1,000 pound, 13:3 hand dark bay foaled in 1821. His dam was the Aldrich mare, also sired by Justin Morgan. She was a dark bay of compact build and great endurance. Royal Morgan was extremely long-lived and left many descendants. He was exhibited at the state fair at Burlington, still sound and vigorous at the age of thirty-seven. He was still getting foals even at this advanced age, having sired twelve the previous year. In one season he covered 114 mares. While in his late twenties he was described as looking like a colt. Because of their excellence, his stock was in great demand and brought correspondingly fancy prices. One gelded son was sold in Boston as a two-year-old for the then-unheard-of sum of $1,000. The purchaser was an English nobleman who shipped the horse to Liverpool.

Royal Morgan left a large number of entire sons, among them Morgan Tiger, Young Morgan, Green Mountain Boy, the Ramsay Horse, the Scott Horse, the Taylor Horse, the Chamberlain Horse, Young President, Blue Morgan, Buckskin Morgan, Sultan Morgan, Niles Horse, Ives' Morgan, Orleans Flying Morgan and Model Morgan.

Jonathan Shepard, the blacksmith who had owned the original Morgan Horse briefly before trading him and his smithy to James Hawkins for a piece of farming property, bred Wicked Will, a grandson. He was a 14:2 dark bay, foaled in 1823. He was handsome, compact, well-built and a good traveler, but inclined to be cross.

Vermont Morgan Champion (Knight's Horse) was another highly regarded son of Sherman. He was a 15:2 black, foaled in 1826 out of a mare called Fanny, said to be a full-blooded English hunter. He was an excellent roadster, fast, stylish, with a big, square, powerful trot. In those days a fast driving horse was greatly prized. Impromptu "brushes" or contests of speed were a common occurrence when two trotting cracks met on the road, in much the same spirit as drag racing today.

Champion was described as being kind and easily managed. His get, also, were remarkable for kindness and disposition. He was thought to have been one of Sherman's best sons. Although his stock was outstanding, commanded a high price and eleven sons were kept as stallions, with the exception of the Shedd Horse foaled in 1840 — "a perfect Morgan pattern" — they left few descendants.

7

Black Hawk

BLACK HAWK WAS SHERMAN'S GREATEST SON. THERE ARE FEW, IF ANY, Morgans living today that do not carry a preponderance of his blood. He was black with no marks, standing an even 15 hands and weighing 1,000 pounds. He was foaled in 1833 at the farm of Ezekiel Twombly of Durham, New Hampshire.

Black Hawk's dam was a large, good-looking black mare with flaring nostrils, handsome head, long neck and clean, sound legs. She stood close to 16 hands and weighed 1,100. She was said to be perfection at the trot. Although willing and courageous, she was so gentle and tractable that she was driven alone by an eighty-year-old lady.

Little is known of the mare's origin except that Benjamin Kelly, a Durham hotel keeper, had bought her from a peddler who said he had gotten her in Nova Scotia and that her dam was an imported English mare. Several variant pedigrees, none backed by definite proof, have been advanced. She was variously alleged to have been by Shark, by Quicksilver by Dey of Algiers, a horse from Germany with Appaloosa markings; by the Thoroughbred Captain Absolute, dam by Lofty by Saunder's Wildair; by Lofty; or by a Naragansett pacer. All authorities agree that she was an unusually fine animal. In foal to Sherman, she was traded to Twombly for another horse.

In the chill of early spring, the foal was dropped on the bare ground of a pasture behind Twombly's barn. The colt was so ugly, small, awkward and ungainly that it was not certain whether he was worth raising. A neighbor who stopped by at the time to buy some hay assured the dubious owners that the unpromising foal would grow into a useful animal and might, with a little luck, be worth as much as $100.

69

At a later date a story was circulated that, because of the colt's unlikely appearance a suit had been filed to recover a portion of the stud fee. The claim was based on the allegation that an inferior black stallion, Paddy, who stood at a seven-dollar fee had covered the mare, rather than Sherman who stood for 14 dollars. Although the tale was undoubtedly spurious, it gained such wide acceptance that John Bellows wrote a letter to the Boston *Cultivator* in 1855 in which he affirmed, speaking of the dam of Black Hawk, "She was covered in my presence and I have the original charge for the service, made in my hand writing now before me and will give you a copy of it as follows:

> 1832 — May 14. Benjamin Kelly of Durham, N.H.
> To Black Hawk at Warrant $14.00
> Groom money 1.00

Underneath is a minute made afterwards — 'This mare produced Black Hawk from this service' . . . I never owned Paddy after 1830."

The story of Black Hawk's dam being covered by Paddy, the teaser, is typical of the tactics used in the old pedigree wars to discredit a famous horse's lineage. Controversy over Black Hawk's origins and his influence on the American Trotting Horse was to rage for half a century. An anonymous writer lampooned the trotting horse enthusiasts who attributed all racing quality to Messenger and Hambletonian influence: [1]

Is it not a little tiresome the constant hammering on the one string that stretches back to Messenger? Let an old plug run, skip, jump, or trot under 2:30 and forthwith he is named Hamdalmessenger, and his pedigree is tabulated about as follows: By Skimmilk by Ethan, by Vermont Black Hawk, by Sherman, by Justin Morgan; first dam said to be by Hambletonian; second dam said to be by Abdallah; third dam by Bishop's Hambletonian; fourth dam by Messenger. This richly bred young horse traces back through fifteen lines to Messenger, the great progenitor of trotting horses that ever exhibited. Of course, there had to be a sire, but the small amount of Morgan blood was so insignificant that the glorious blood of Messenger floated it as easily as an ocean does a chip, and enabled Hamdalmessenger to win his race without an effort in 2:29¾ . . . We have always doubted that Messamdalger belonged to the Morgan family and now we have unearthed evidence that goes to prove that he is descended in a direct line from Engineer, son of Messenger. John Toadstool, now in his ninety-ninth year, has made affidavit that when he was a boy he remembers hearing Ananias Smith say that he held the greatgrandam of the black mare that was the dam of Messamdalger by the bridle when she was served by a horse that was said to have been sired by a son of Messenger, and that the colt looks exactly like the pictures of Messenger; that color is just like Messenger's and that he is a Messenger. With this evidence we must take Messamdal-

[1] in *Spirit of the Times* reprinted in the *Maine Horse Breeders' Monthly*, "Tired Out" (Aug. 1887, p. 142–43).

ger from the Morgan family and place him to the credit of Messenger, and what has the Morgan family left? . . . If our wiseacres have read thus far they may be ready to ask what is this fool after? This fool is but a representative of many other fools who are tired of paying for and reading or skipping the innumerable efforts to replace bad pedigrees with worse ones. We are tired of the incessant strumming upon the Messenger string. It is worn threadbare and has become discordant; give it a rest. We are tired of the constant disparagement of all families save one, which owes much of its greatness to what it has taken from others . . .

Ezekiel Twombly gave the black foal to his grandson Shadrack Seavy, who made his home with him. The boy had complete charge of the colt and, at the usual age, broke him to harness. The colt was kind and willing and was soon able to overtake and pass anything he might meet on the road. He was also adept at escaping from his enclosure, a talent that proved to be a nuisance. As a two year old he broke out of his paddock and visited a receptive neighbor mare. The result of the clandestine meeting was later sold for $175. A similar unplanned breeding occurred when the colt was four; the fine filly gotten in this chance manner brought $600 as a four year old!

When The Morgan, as he was then called, was four, young Seavy made a decision that, if carried out, would have been an incalculable loss to the breed. He decided the time had come to geld his colt. He made arrangements with a Mr. Whitten to perform the castration and keep the horse until he had fully recovered from the operation. Fortunately, when Mr. Whitten saw the quality of the black youngster, he strongly urged that he be kept entire. His horsman's eye saw beyond immaturity and poor condition. The Morgan was then far from his mature form, in a very rough state, long coated, muddy, and down in flesh, but with a bright, intelligent expression and an easy, open gait that has seldom been equalled.

In 1838, when the stallion was five, Seavy traded him to Albert Mathes for a cheap horse and 50 dollars. Mathes kept him but a short while, four to six weeks by his own recollection. He trained him, putting speed and finish into his trot, fed and groomed him well and so greatly improved his appearance that he resold him for $200 to William Brown and Benjamin Thurston of Lowell, Massachusetts. Soon after, Brown sold his interest to Thurston, who named the horse Black Hawk, as he was known thereafter.

For the next six years Black Hawk was used as a personal driving horse. Mr. Thurston, a professional horseman who often had as many as 35 horses at one time, described Black Hawk as the finest horse he had ever owned. Further, he said that if all the best qualities of all the numerous horses he had ever owned over a 25 year period — and he purchased only the finest — were combined, they could not add up to a horse to surpass Black Hawk.

Black Hawk, from Linsey's *Morgan Horses.*

It was during Thurston's ownership that the ugly duckling developed his great potential. Black Hawk was frequently driven 50 miles in a day and once went 63 miles in seven hours and fifteen minutes without visible sign of fatigue. Mr. Thurston often raced the horse in and around Boston, once for a stake of $1,000 a side. There is no record of his having been beaten. His mile record was a respectable 2:42 in the days before lightning-fast tracks and bicycle-wheeled sulkies.

In 1844 he was sold for $800 to David Hill of Bridgeport, Vermont, where he was kept until his death in 1856. Black Hawk was the first horse in the United States to stand for a stud fee of $100.

George B. Loring, who knew the horse well while owned by Thurston, said of him, "He was one of the strongest horses I ever knew. . . . He was admirably balanced. His stifles and gaskins were immense and beautifully formed. His back was short and strong. His shoulders and arms were very muscular. At the same time he was symmetrical and had no superfluous flesh. No horse ever had a handsomer head and neck than he had, and his

BLACK HAWK.

THIS CELEBRATED HORSE WILL STAND TO IMPROVE THE BREED OF HORSES, AT THE SUBSCRIBER'S IN BRIDPORT, VERMONT.

"The above cut shows some of the points of this noted horse, but as a whole, is very far from giving a just representation of his shape and proportions. The shanks are too long — the original being very short at this point — and the cut gives no idea of the easy and graceful movement which Black Hawk displays.

"This animal is widely known. In himself and his progeny, he has acquired a name from Canada to Texas. To give his biography is not the object of this article; but some general facts in regard to his origin and character, will not be out of place in this connection. He was bred by the late Wingate Twombly, of Greenland, N. H.; was by the horse known as the 'Sherman Morgan;' his dam, (owned by Mr. Twombly,) was said to have been in part of English blood, and from New Brunswick. 'Sherman Morgan' was by the first, or 'Justin Morgan,' so called.

"Black Hawk was for several years well known as a trotter. His full speed was never ascertained; but in several instances he trotted a mile in two minutes and forty-two seconds. But he is most remarkable for a combination of speed with strength and power of endurance. At the Cambridge Course, in 1842, he won a match of $1000, by trotting five miles in sixteen minutes, and has performed other feats equally as extraordinary. He was never beaten.

"His progeny partake of his properties in a high degree. No horse of which we have any account, has left his impress more strikingly, and his future rank will be among those most distinguished for the improvement of their species.

"The reputation of Black Hawk's Stock is such that they command a ready sale, and a large proportion of them bring very high prices. It would be desirable to know the whole amount of money which has been received for those of his progeny that have been sold, but this is impracticable. We have before us a list comprising a portion of those which have been bred and sold in the town of Bridport, Vermont, where he has been kept since 1844, from this it appears that 38 animals, and an interest in the 39th, to the amount of one-half, have brought the sum of $22,737, or an average of $590 (and a fraction) each! Their ages ranged from six months to six years. Most of them were colts, (entire,) but some were geldings and some fillys. This is wholly from actual sales in this town, and has no reference to stock on hand. It shows in a favorable light the estimation in which the stock is held where it is best known.

"Black Hawk stands the coming season at the stable of David Hill, Bridport, Vermont, at $100 the season, and is limited to fifty mares." — *Boston Cultivator.*

Gentlemen wishing to secure the services of this horse, must send in their letters at once.

Good pasturing will be provided for mares from a distance, at 50 cents per week, — and all ACCIDENTS, ESCAPES, and THEFT will be at the risk of the owner.

N. B. — Terms for the use of said horse will be, for the season, $100, payable in cash, or satisfactory note on demand, with interest.

·DAVID HILL, Agent.

BRIDPORT, VERMONT, APR. 2, 1855.
PLEASE POST UP.

Broadside advertising the services of Sherman's famous son, Black Hawk, the first stallion in the United States to stand for a fee of $100. (Courtesy Vermont Historical Society)

intelligence was great. . . . His gait was always level. . . . That a handsome, cheerful, powerful, well-made, good-gaited horse like this should have laid the foundation of a good family is perfectly natural."

Indeed, he did found a family, not only of Morgans, but of trotters. At the turn of the century, only Rysdyk's Hambletonian appeared more fre-

Champion Black Hawk. "Champion, the 'grace of all the Black Hawk' is the best representative of the sire we have ever seen." — *Ohio Farmer* from Linsley's *Morgan Horses.*

quently in Standardbred pedigrees. Black Hawk sired 25 trotters of record, four in 2:30. In 1892, 1,500 2:30 trotters traced to him, one-third through the direct male line.

Numerous sons and grandsons were taken to New York, Ohio and Michigan. The following account of the Seventh Annual Fair of Ohio appeared in the *Ohio Farmer* on Oct. 4th, 1856:

Vermont herself could scarcely produce more fine Black Hawk and Morgan horses than were exhibited at our State Fair . . . . Champion — the grace of all the Black Hawk — is the best representation of the sire we have ever seen. There is an indiscribable something in the whole family which always assures one of the certainty that it is a distinct race of horses, and of as much individuality as a Shorthorn, or a Devon. Nothing could be more palpable than was this, at the exhibition of the colts for the sweepstakes premium. Of the fifteen that were on the ground, the Black Hawk stamp was upon all. Champion's colts took the premium, and David Hill's the first and second as three years and the second as two years old . . . . The stock of Messrs. Ladd was fine; some of it being a cross with Black Hawk, and thoroughbred; but the finest head and neck was on Champion out of a Black Hawk mare, sired by Black Hawk . . . . The colt of the fair was Buckeye sired by David Hill and bred by Dr. Carpenter of Litchfield. He could out trot any on the ground in his class and compete with most of them of any age. He has the style of old Black Hawk.

Champion was graceful and David Hill lively and practical. Onderdonk showy and active, and Morril and Bullet swift and powerful.

The Black Hawks were considered a distinct breed. This stallion was owned by a Mr. Butternut of Coldwater, Michigan. From *Ohio Farmer.* (Courtesy Western Reserve Historical Society)

Ethan Allen

Ethan Allen, Black Hawk's most outstanding son, won national acclaim as a trotter.

Although early trotting matches had been under saddle, by the mid- and late-nineteenth century each county fairground had its trotting track and the races held there marked the high point of the year in sporting and social activity. Before the days of national advertising, the trotting horse acted as a magnet to draw crowds of spectators to the fairs, thus helping promote the other goods that were exhibited.

In those days, everyone was to some extent a horseman — by necessity

Ethan Allen, a national hero. In him the Morgan trotter reached its apogee. (Courtesy *Morgan Horse Magazine*)

July 18, 1849. Early trotting matches were held under saddle. Mac, winner in straight heats, is described as a "brown gelding raised by Mr. Samuel Frinch, in the State of Maine: sired by the Reyerson Horse of Messenger and Morgan blood." (N. Currier)

if not by choice. General interest in horses was very high. Outstanding trotting horses and their drivers achieved a degree of fame only approached by baseball, football, movie and television stars of our era. The horse was part of everyone's daily experience and enthusiasm for "a good 'un" knew no bounds.

Because they belonged to the established culture, differing only in degree by seeming to be larger than life, they were revered as authentic folk heroes. Whenever a second or a fraction of a second was cut from the world's record it was a matter of national importance. Often the event was immortalized by a print published by Currier and Ives, the acknowledged specialists in horse prints. The lithographers spared no expense in maintaining the best equine artists on their staff. Large folio prints (18″ x 27″), hand-colored, were sold at $1.50 to $3.00 by the firm's many agents, while small prints at 15 cents and 25 cents were sold at every crossroad, much as scenic post cards are today.

The appearance of a famous harness performer at any local track would bring spectators from miles around. Families loaded their children and picnic lunches into the buggy and set off to make a day of it. There was excitement, gaiety, horse trading and wagering; a fine time was had by all.

Ethan Allen, named for a hero, became, himself, a national hero and the idol of millions. He was the subject of many newspaper and magazine articles, prints and engravings. He was celebrated in a popular song and toys and weathervanes were made in his likeness.

A bright bay, just under 15 hands and weighing 1,000 pounds, he looked every inch the part. He was bred by Joel B. Holcomb, of Ticonderoga, New York, and was foaled in 1849. His dam was a gray mare of uncertain breeding, said to be of Morgan background. He had a wonderful disposition and, when a colt, was very much the family pet and would come to the kitchen window to beg for a treat. During most of his long life he was used both on the track and at stud. He changed hands fairly often — at the age of twenty-one for the remarkable sum of $7,500. He was taken to Lawrence, Kansas where he lived to be twenty-eight. A correspondent writing in *Wallace's Monthly* described him in his old age: "He still presented the outline of a noble horse. Twenty-six years of the most exhaustive labors both as a stock and turf horse had slightly bowed his back, and shrunken the muscles from his spinal column, but had not impaired the elasticity of his step, nor relaxed the sprightly play of his ears, nor dimmed, in the least degree, the brilliant lustre of his eyes. Never did the vital energy of a robust constitution battle more successfully with the wasting effects of labor and time."

Mr. Wallace, writing of Ethan Allen in his magazine said: "Of all the horses that have been favorites with the American people, no one has ever approxi-

Cassius M. Clay 164 (1/16) 16 h.h., dark bay or brown foaled in 1844, got by Henry Clay by Andrew Jackson; out of Jersey Kate, breeding unknown. A celebrated trotting stallion, in 1853 at the National Horse Fair at Springfield, Massachusetts, he won first premium over 56 competitors.

Cassius M. Clay was the sire of George M. Patchen (1/32) 2:23½, shown here. The winner of 20 races, the 16-hand bay was foaled in 1849. His dam was by *Trustee. (A Currier and Ives print; he is defeating Brown Dick and Millers Damsel.)

Ethan Allen and running mate. (Courtesy Chicago Historical Society)

mated the popularity of Ethan Allen. His remarkable beauty, his perfect action, and above all his kind and gentle disposition made him the admiration and pet of everybody."

Although long for his height, Ethan Allen was beautifully proportioned. His action was perfect and he was seldom defeated at the track. He was the world's champion trotting stallion and set two new records — 2:25½ and 2:15 when hitched with a running mate. President Grant rode behind the horse in 1874 and immediately ordered one of his aides to buy two broodmares and have them bred to the celebrated stallion.

One of Ethan Allen's greatest moments was his famous match race with Dexter in 1867, in which each side put up $2,500. Ethan Allen, who was eighteen at the time, was hitched with a running mate to a light skeleton wagon, while Dexter was to go in single harness. Dexter was considered to be invincible. Interest was at a fever pitch, and an estimated 40,000 people crowded into the grounds of the Fashion Course to witness the great event. Ethan Allen won in straight heats, despite breaking badly in the second and dropping several rods behind before hitting his stride again. The times were the record breaking 2:15, 2:16 and 2:19.

Ethan Allen was the sire of 72 trotters of record, ten in 2:30, and the grandsire of the fastest of all Morgan trotters, Lord Clinton, 2:10¼, by Honest Allen.

Among many outstanding horses sired by Ethan Allen, Daniel Lambert (Hippomenes, the Porter Colt) stands out. He was a light chestnut foaled in 1858, standing 15:2 and weighing 1,030 pounds. His dam was Fanny Cook by Abdallah by Mambrino — trotting blood. He is described as active, elegant, fine and finished, with a neat, bony head and large, well-set eyes. He was famous, not only for siring blazing speed but also great beauty. His get were pure, open-gaited trotters that needed neither boots nor weight to balance them or improve their way of going. Also they had typical Morgan kindness and cheerfulness, doing their best without being touched by the whip. Daniel Lambert sired 117 trotters of record, 37 to trot the mile in 2:30 or better.

The Morgans' success as trotters contributed enormously to the growth

The famous match race between Ethan Allen and running mate, and Dexter. (Courtesy Yale University Art Gallery)

Daniel Lambert. (Courtesy *Morgan Horse Magazine*)

of the breed, but it very nearly proved to be its undoing. For a time during the nineteenth century, Morgans were without rival the most popular and widely distributed breed of light harness horse in the world.

While New England's puritanical heritage frowned upon flat racing as being, no doubt, an invention of the Devil, harness racing was quite another matter. Trotters were seldom hedged about with legislative restrictions such as those which from time to time have all but wiped out Thoroughbred racing. Morgans were the racing trotters of early times, in the days before the emergence of the Standardbred as a distinct breed, just as Arabs were the breed of running horse before the Thoroughbred surpassed its parent stock in speed.

Morgan harness racers reached their apogee before the rise to prominence of the Hambletonians whose size, speed and length of stride they were unable to match. Some authorities suggest that an extreme degree of inbreeding caused the Morgan star to wane. It is certain that in the latter part of the nineteenth century numerous outcrossings in the hope of attaining greater speed caused the number of Morgans to decline.

In tail male descent Morgans have completely disappeared from Standardbred pedigrees, but are still an important influence in bulk. The Morgan furnished the foundation of stamina on which trotting speed could be built and the modern Standardbred's debt to the Morgan is great.

In addition to Sherman's influence through Black Hawk, Ethan Allen and Daniel Lambert, the other sons of Justin Morgan also influenced the American

Trotting Horse. The Woodbury strain got Hale's Green Mountain and Gold-dust, both important influences, while Bulrush is tail male ancestor of Morril, founder of a trotting family of his own; Fearnaught, who lowered the trotting record to 2:34¼ in 1868; and Bebbo, the first to trot a mile in 2:28. Mighty Grayhound 1:55¼, whom many consider to be the greatest trotter of all time, carried five crosses to Justin Morgan, while Titan Hanover 2:00, the first two-year-old to trot a mile in two minutes had 22 crosses to him.

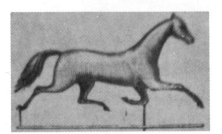

Weathervane in likeness of Ethan Allen. (Courtesy *Morgan Horse Magazine*)

8

Woodbury and His Descendants

WOODBURY MORGAN (OLD WHITEFOOT WOODBURY MORGAN, BURBANK Horse, Walker Horse) was bred by eighteen-year-old Lyman Wight and was foaled in May of 1816. The dam was owned by Lyman's father, who had loaned her to the youth for the purpose of raising a foal. She was a five year old at the time her famous son was born and had been bought the preceding year from Major John Moulton of Bethel, Vermont, who had brought her into the vicinity. She stood over 15 hands, weighed about 1,100 pounds, and was a dark bay, marked only by a small star. Although she had a beautiful head and an excellent chest, shoulders and quarters, she was rather strung-out and flat-ribbed. Her over-all appearance, however, was pleasing. She carried herself well, had a fine, flowing mane and tail and was a spirited driver. Considered to be fast in harness for the time she both trotted and paced and was also known as a fast walker. Her breeding is untraced.

As a weanling the colt was sold to David Woodbury for 50 dollars, according to Linsley, while Battell quotes David's daughter Sarah as saying that her father had traded a sleigh valued at 50 dollars for the colt. Woodbury kept the horse until he was mature, breaking him to drive and using him in harness. Later he sold him to his brother John, an excellent horseman under whose training the horse achieved a degree of local fame. He sold him to Ebeneezer Parkhurst, who in 1826 sold the horse to Simon Smith and William Walker of Hartland, Vermont, for $500.

At about the same time the partners also acquired another son of Justin Morgan, Bulrush. Mr. Walker had a positive passion for fine horses. He appreciated the excellent qualities of the Morgan strain which he hoped to propagate and went to great lengths to promote the breed. Unfortunately, his resources were limited, the financial venture was not a success and the partnership was dissolved with Bulrush going to Smith, and Walker taking Woodbury, which he shortly thereafter "sacrificed" for $400 to a Newbury lawyer, Peter Burbank, Esq. The horse was boarded at the stable of Jesse Johnson and Brothers, at Bradford, Vermont, where he and Bulrush were again stablemates.

Following Mr. Burbank's death in 1836, his twenty-year-old stallion was sold at public auction to Norman Baglee of Gainsville, Alabama. The horse was shipped from Boston on a small sailing vessel — rather the long way round from Vermont to Alabama. According to Linsley, the aging horse never fully recovered from the unaccustomed fodder aboard the ship and the rigors of the long, stormy voyage and died in 1838. Battell, on the other hand, states that he had it on good authority that the horse died as a result of breaking a leg while being unloaded from the ship. Whatever the cause and whenever Woodbury's death occurred, there is no record of any stock sired by him in Alabama.

Of the three principal sons of Justin Morgan, Woodbury was the tallest. He had more of the old horse's bold, fearless style. Brilliant under saddle, he was greatly in demand as a parade horse. "His style of action was bold and resolute, and his temperament was so nervous, that when taken out with a bridle it was almost impossible to keep him still. . . . He appeared to the best advantage under saddle. Militia colonels and generals were eager to ride him and no 'musters' or reviews could pass without his being seen; in his case to be seen was to be admired. His disposition was pleasant and playful. Martial music only roused him, the firing of guns in no way distracted him, waving flags and gay uniforms seemed hardly able to attract from him a single glance, and he moved about as if he was himself the principal object of attraction and the cause of all the attending excitement and display."

Woodbury was a dark chestnut with a right hind half stocking and a stripe in the face. As a colt his tail had been docked, but the remaining ten inches or so was full and wavy.

Eighteen of Woodbury's sons were kept entire. They averaged 15 hands in height. He was the first horse to sire three sons (Gifford Morgan, Morgan Eagle and Morgan Caesar) which each got a trotter on the 2:30 list.

Woodbury's son, the Gifford Morgan, bred by Ziba Gifford of Tunbridge, Vermont, foaled in 1824, was a liver chestnut standing 14:2 and weighing about 1,000 pounds. He was out of a mare said to be by Henry Dundas, a son of Woolsey(Cardinal Woolsey, the Hough Horse), a Thoroughbred, or near-Thoroughbred. Gifford changed hands often and traveled widely, standing at Barnard, Vermont; Walpole, New Hampshire; Woodstock, New Haven,

GREY HAWK

WILL STAND

The ensuing season at the Stable of the SUBSCRIBER,

On Mondays, Tuesdays, Thursdays and Fridays. On Wednesdays and Saturdays, at the Stable of G. ALLEN, BRANDON HOUSE.

COLOR OF GREY HAWK is a beautiful IRON GREY, is fifteen and a half hands high,—weighs 1070 pounds, is 6 years old in July; strong boned, of great action and spirit, and is a natural trotter and has proved himself a sure foal getter.

PEDIGREE.

This beautiful MORGAN HORSE was sired by OLD GREY HAWK who was sold in Chicago, two years ago for $6000: his grand sire old WOODBURY MORGAN. Grey Hawk's dame was B. Griffin's english mare Kate, sired by OLD DUROCK, brother to OLD ECLIPSE, Cook of the Rock, Blucher and Wellington; her dam an english mare, brought from Providence, R. I. by Abner Smith of Leicester. She was one of the fastest trotters of her day.

YOU WILL PERCIEVE THAT GREY HAWK is descended from the first stock of horses in the United States: and we offer his services to all who are desirous of improving the stock of that noble animal the horse. TERMS $10 to insure a foal. All mares disposed of before foaling will be considered with foal. Good pasture furnished mares from a distance.

B. GRIFFIN.

Sudbury, May 26, 1856.

WESTERN VERMONT TRANSCRIPT PRINT, BRANDON.

Advertisement. (Courtesy Vermont Historical Society)

Gifford Morgan in extreme old age. Atrophy in back muscles has given him a hollow-backed apppearance. (From the *Morgan Horse and Register,* Vol. I)

Middlebury, Stockbridge, Hancock, Bethel, Warren, Connecticut; and in Washington County, New York.

Gifford was a compact, stylish little horse very closely resembling the old Morgan Horse in every respect but color. His flair, presence and beautiful way of going made him much admired as a parade horse. He also had the breed's well-established quality of retaining vitality and good looks to an advanced age. An Albany *Cultivator* account of the 1847 New York State Fair states that "The old Gifford Morgan paraded in the van of the cavalcade with all the fine action and gaiety of a horse of six instead of twenty-three years." The horse was still in active service at the time of his death in 1850. He sired more than 1,300 foals, which were sold widely, going as far south as New Orleans. Several were exported to England, high tribute to the quality of his get, for, traditionally, England has always been the supplier of blood-stock to the rest of the world. Gifford's progeny were noted driving horses that "excel in great endurance, are full of noble and generous spirit, with such docility of temper that the most timid can drive them, but if put to their mettle, they are a handful for the best drivers," according to Battell. Gifford also sired many notable harness racers.

His most celebrated son was Green Mountain Morgan (Hale's Green Mountain, Young Woodbury) foaled about 1832. He was seal brown, almost black at certain times of the year and stood 14:2, weighing about 1,100. Little is known of his dam's pedigree, although she is believed to have been a daughter of Woodbury. Green Mountain Morgan lived to be thirty-one. He traveled extensively and was shown at several state fairs. He won the first premium at the Ohio, Kentucky and Michigan State Fairs in 1853, and at the Vermont State Fair in 1854. Several of his sons sold for $1,500 or more.

At the New York State Fair in Saratoga in 1844, Black Hawk by Sherman, Green Mountain Morgan and two other sons of Gifford were exhibited. According to an account in the *Spirit of the Times,* "The four bore a close family resemblance both in appearance and action . . . such promptness and fire, with such perfect docility, I never saw united in any other species . . . when moving I never saw such majesty embodied in horse flesh as was displayed by Green Mountain Morgan. His arched neck seemed clothed with thunder, and his floating mane, his eye of fire, his red distended nostrils, his open mouth with the rigid tendons about it standing out in sharp relief, realized more perfectly to my mind the originals of those fiery, magnificent coursers the Greek ideals of the war horse, to be found on the Elgin marbles than I ever saw elsewhere."

Silas Hale's Green Mountain Morgan, the prototype of the breed. It is his likeness that appears at the top of Morgan registration certificates. (From the *Morgan Horse and Register,* Vol. I)

It is the likeness of the Green Mountain Morgan, taken from an old daguerreotype, that appears on Morgan registration certificates and is used as the emblem of several regional Morgan clubs. He was considered to be Vermont's outstanding stallion and, like his sire, his get were widely distributed. In one season the horse bred 180 mares, getting 123 in foal, while the following year he covered 154 mares, with 133 live foals resulting. Silas Hale, who owned the horse for thirteen years, took 15 of his sons to the west to sell in Ohio and Illinois and, particularly, Iowa. Hale's Green Mountain was sold at the age of twenty one for $2,000 — a large price for an aged horse, then, or at any time.

Sultan by Colby's Young Green Mountain. (Courtesy *Morgan Horse Magazine*)

Fanny Jenks, a daughter of Gifford, trotted ten miles in 29:59, defeating Neptune and Misfortune. On another occasion, in a match against time, she trotted 100 miles in 9:42:57. Then, to prove her soundness and endurance, she trotted the 101st mile in 4:23. The average for the 101 miles was 5:35; truly a remarkable performance by any standard.

A famous son of Green Mountain Morgan, which did a great deal to popularize the breed in northeast Ohio, was Eastman Morgan (Sykes Horse, Old Morg, Syke's Green Mountain Morgan, Stockwell Morgan). A bay standing 15:1 and weighing 1,150 pounds, he was foaled in 1848 at the farm of Dorson Eastman in East Rupert, Vermont. His dam was also bred by Mr. Eastman and was by the Stoddard Horse. The second dam was described as

Morgan. He was kept at stud in Rupert for several years, where his services were in great demand and he did a lively business.

In the 1850's the Eastman Horse was sold to Hiram Sykes who brought him to Ohio, first to Marietta and later to Medina. Battell describes him as "a very perfect horse. He was shown one Fourth of July at Hinkley, Ohio with 125 of his suckling colts. His stock were blocky and of the Morgan type." He proved to be an unbeatable competitor as well as a sure foal getter and won in harness, both racing and pulling. At the 1856 Ohio State Fair he took the first premium for stallions in a roadster class of 117. *The Ohio Farmer* described him as follows: "Green Mountain is a good horse, very strong and muscular, fit alike for the plow and the carriage; and had very few superiors as a trotter."

Competition was keen and feeling ran very high. Fire was set to the barn where the Eastman Horse was kept in an attempt to eliminate what many thought to be unfair competition. The horse was rescued and a fireproof stone barn was built for him. Then an attempt was made to poison him. Fearful that the horse's enemies might eventually be successful, Mr. Sykes sold his stallion in 1866 for $1,000 to parties who took him to a settlement on the Mississippi River, either in Wisconsin, or Iowa. He later appeared in Clinton, Iowa, owned by Stillman Stockwell and was known as the Stockwell Morgan for the rest of his life. He died in 1875 at the age of twenty-seven, presumably from old age rather than the efforts of poisoners or arsonists.

Eastman Morgan left one trotter of record, Little Fred 2:20. He also sired the dam of George W. Davis 2:26 and the second dam of Sardis Ensign 2:30. He left several entire sons in the East, Cheney's Morgan and Harvey's Morgan, both of which eventually followed their sire West. Morgan Lion, bred in Granger Ohio, was taken to Illinois *in utero*. Frank Kellog was foaled in Hinkley in 1860 and was sent to Iowa.

The Eastman Morgan was an important factor in the improvement of horses in Ohio. For many years a photograph of him hung in the lobby of the Old Phoenix bank on the town square in Medina.

Woodbury also sired Morgan Eagle (Independence) foaled at the Royalton, Vermont farm of his breeder, a Mister Cheney. He sired Henderson's Morgan Eagle, Jr., sent to Utica, Michigan, where he got Magna Carta (Macomb Chief), which at the age of four in 1859 broke Ethan Allen's then world record by trotting the mile in 2:33½. He also had an unofficial record of 2:20½ made at a race in Madison, Wisconsin, in 1867. He sired 30 trotters of record and was the sire of the dam of many others.

Gifford Morgan, son of Woodbury, got the Barnard Morgan, sire of Ver-

This 1895 picture is of Old Nellie, a brown mare by Morgan Stranger by Billy by Eastman Morgan (Sykes Horse) by Hale's Green Mountain Morgan. Mare was twenty-seven years old at time of the picture. At foot is her five-month-old foal, Delmar. (Courtesy William Sykes, West Richfield, Ohio)

Uncle Dort, foaled 1894, bred by William B. Sykes. Sired by Eastmond by Colonel by Evermond by Harold, First dam, Old Nellie by Morgan Stranger by Billy by the Eastman Morgan (Sykes Horse) by Hale's Green Mountain Morgan; second dam by Eastman Morgan; third dam by Major Gifford by Gifford. (Courtesy William Sykes)

Old Morgan

Putnam Horse,

This Horse, so well known in Northern Vermont, where he has been kept for the last eight or nine years, in consequence of the value of his stock, has been purchased by the subscriber, and will stand for the use of mares the present season at the following places, viz : [illegible] East Randolph Thursday & Friday at West Randolph [illegible]

THE PUTNAM MORGAN

Is 17 years old this grass, was raised by Capt. DANIEL PUTNAM of Bethel, Vt., sired by the celebrated Old White Foot Woodbury Morgan, afterwards called the Walker and Burbank horse. White Foot Woodbury Horse was sired by the original Morgan Horse. He is of a beautiful chesnut color, weighing 1050 lbs., and was never in better condition than now. He is one of the purest Blooded Morgan horses now living, and is second in no particular to any of the Old Stock of Morgan horses.

The Dam of the PUTNAM Horse was a celebrated English mare, imported to Connecticut and brought from thence to Woodstock, Vt., and subsequently bought by a Mr. Hitchcock of Bethel, Vt., at the age of 20 years, for $100.

The stock of this horse is so well known in Vermont, it is hardly necessary to repeat their merits. They excel all other horses in great endurance ; and for beauty of form, speed and action, cannot be surpassed by any other stock of Horses in New England, and only need to be known to be from the PUTNAM MORGAN, to meet a ready sale in any market.

Among the many celebrated foals of this horse are a pair of Matched Gelding Horses owned by Horace Loomis, Esq., of Burlington Vt., for which he was offered $1250 last summer, but refused. Also a Stud Horse five years old, owned by Levi Whitcomb, of Richmond, Vt., which is valued at $1000, and has drawn the first premium in Chittenden County every year since he followed the mare. Also, the Hon. Milo Bennett, Judge of the Supreme Court, of Chittenden County, has a Stud Colt, three years old, which is said to be the best in the county. Also, Leonard Hodges, Esq. of Williston, Vt., has a Stud Colt, five years old, which is second to none. Also, the GAY HORSE, of Stockbridge, Vt., sold in March, 1847, for $400, to Gleason of Syracuse, New York, for which he has since refused $1200. Also the ABBOT Horse of Stockbridge, Vt., sold October, 1847, to Seymour of Brattleboro', Vt., for $450, for which he now refuses $1000, &c., &c.

PEDIGREE
OF THE ORIGINAL MORGAN HORSE.

Raised by JUSTIN MORGAN of Springfield, Massachusetts, and taken to Randolph, Vermont, in the fall of 1795 ; sired by the true Britton or Beautiful Bay, raised by General DeLANCY of Long Island, and sired by his imported Horse, Traveller. Dam of the original Morgan, was of the Wild Air Breed, sired by the Diamond who was raised in East Hartford, Connecticut. Diamond was sired by the Wild Air, known as the Church Horse. The Church Horse was sired by the Wild Air, imported from England by DeLANCY, and afterwards sent back to England. The Dam of the Church Horse was an imported Wild Air Mare, owned by Capt. Samuel Burt of Springfield, Massachusetts.

The subscriber holds documents to prove the above to be the Genuine Pedigree of the Morgan Horse.

Pasturing will be provided for Mares at a distance at a reasonable rate. All Escapes and Accidents at the risk of the owner. All mares parted with before the usual time of foaling will be considered in foal, and charge for the full service of the Horse.

TERMS---$3 the leap : $4 to warrant.

JOHN WAITE.

Braintree, May 15, 1848.

E. P. WALTON & SONS, PRINTERS, MONTPELIER, VT.

Stallion Poster. Note that pedigree of Justin Morgan given at lower right corner corresponds with Linsley and Battell. (Courtesy Vermont Historical Society)

Green Mountain Road Horse
"MORGAN JEWEL"

Morgan Jewel possesses more of the celebrated Morgan blood in greater purity than any other stallion now living. By Wier's Green Mountain Morgan; dam Flying Kate, by Ryla M. Adams' Flying Morgan of Burlington, Vt., the sire of Ethan Allen, a fact now proved, will serve a limited number of mares.

TERMS, THE LOW PRICE OF $15

$5.00 to be paid at the time of service, the balance if the mare proves in foal. Mares parted with before the usual time of foaling will be considered in foal. Pasturage furnished for mares from a distance at a reasonable rate.

ALL FOALS HOLDEN FOR THE SERVICE OF THE HORSE.   ACCIDENTS AT THE OWNER'S RISK

NO BUSINESS ON SUNDAY.

►●►PEDIGREE ●◄◄

Morgan Jewel by Wier's Green Mountain Morgan, by old Green Mountain Morgan or Silas Hale Horse, by Gifford, by Woodbury, by Justin Morgan---dam of Wier's Green Mountain Morgan by Sherman Morgan, 2d, by Sherman 1st, by old Sherman, by old Justin Morgan, grand dam John True's horse of Sutton, Vt., by old Sherman, by old Justin Morgan. Morgan Jewel's first dam Flying Kate, great roader weight puller, bred by Dares A. DeWolf, Walpole, by Ryla M. Adams' old Flying Morgan of Burlington, Vt., the sire of Ethan Allen. I kept and handled the horse at the time of service of flying Kate, by Hackett Horse, by Gifford, by Woodbury, by Justin Morgan; 2d dam Dares A. DeWolf's noted mare Old Kate, bred by him, big roader, by old Green Mountain Morgan or Silas Hale horse by Gifford, by Woodbury by Justin Morgan. 3d dam, William Chappell mare Kate Way by Francis Boardman horse, by Morgan DeForest or Derrick Hart horse, by Morgan Cock of the Rock, by old Sherman, by Justin Morgan, Chappell's Mare (Kate Way), dam bred by Timothy Eastman, Claremont, by Justin Morgan. The Boardman horse dam bred by Gen. James Wilson, Keene, by Woodbury, by Justin Morgan, her dam bred by Jotham Alls, Claremont, by Justin Morgan. Morgan DeForest dam bred by Dr. Leonard Jarvis, Claremont, by Justin Morgan. The above were all Bay or Chestnut color.

◄◆►DESCRIPTION ◆◄

Morgan Jewel is of my breeding, a natural trotting road horse; no one man can sit behind him long enough to tire him; eight years old this Spring, color bay, star, both hind ankles white; in size, shape, style and action in harness or under the saddle, is a fac simile of old Gifford Morgan, except color. His best recommendation his stock from Morgan mares, as they show the true Morgan stock. In his blood connection there is not a weak point. He shows the true trotting instinct of the Flying Morgan Family, so much admired; pure gaited.

Every one wants a Morgan, and nearly all claim their horses to be part Morgan, and I never knew any one counterfeit a broken bank. Morgans always excite the admiration of strangers, are always in demand. Breeders of fast trotters recognize the value of the Morgan blood for beauty, style, finish, purity of gait, and lasting qualities. Professional drivers admit that a dash of Morgan blood is most desirable in the trotter; they make them go faster at a loss of more valuable Morgan qualities.

I have been a breeder of the Morgan horse in its greatest possible purity for the past 57 years or more. A few inbred Morgan colts and fillies for sale.

F. A. WIER

Walpole, N. H., 1888.   PLEASE POST.

Stallion poster issued by F. A. Wier, one of the earliest students of the Morgan breed. (Courtesy Vermont Historical Society)

Golddust, from *American Morgan Horse Register,* Vol. I.

mont Morgan, sire of the fabulous Golddust 2:43. The dam of Golddust was thought to have been by the famous imported Arab, Zilcaadi, which figures prominently in Saddle Horse pedigrees, a gift of the sultan to the United States Consul, Mr. Rhind. Golddust was foaled in 1855 near Louisville, Kentucky. In spite of his short life span — only sixteen years — and the fact that most of his active years of service were during a time while breeding activity was at a low ebb in Kentucky due to the Civil War and the disorganization that followed it, he is an enduring influence upon the American Trotting

Morgan Hunter, by Gifford, out of a mare by Gifford. From the *Albany Cultivator.*

ETHAN ALLEN, 2D.

———:P:———

This Morgan Horse is no doubt the Purest Bred Morgan now Living.   Pedigree as follows:

He was sired by Peters Morgan; by Peters Old Vermont; by Wood Horse; by Hale's Old Green Mountain; by Old Gifford; by Woodbury; by Justin Morgan.

Dam of Ethan Allen, 2d, was raised by Stephen Dow of Woburn, Mass., and sired by Old Ethan Allen, out of his famous Morgan mare Jennie; she was sired by Hale's Old Green Mountain Morgan; her dam was owned by Dr. J. L. Wood of Boston, and was called Old Phebe. She was sired by Tom Morgan (or Perkins H). Phebe's dam was sired by a Horse S. T. B. Nondescript.

PEDIGREE OF PETERS' MORGAN.

He was by Old Vermont; by Wood Horse: by Hale's Old Green Mountain; by Old Gifford; by Woodbury; by Justin Morgan. Dam of Peters' Morgan was by Hunter, Jr. owned by Frank Goldthwait of Newport, N. H.; he by F. A. Weirs' Morgan Hunter of Walpole, N. H. Weirs' Hunter was by Old Gifford; by Woodbury; by Justin Morgan. Dam of Weirs' Hunter was by Old Gifford Morgan. Dam of Morgan Hunter, Jr. was sired by the Old Bean Horse, and he by old Sherman Morgan; by Justin Morgan. Grand Dam of Peters' Morgan was sired by Old General Hibbard; by Old Woodbury: by Justin Morgan. Great Grand Dam of Peters' Morgan was sired by Old Bullrush; by Justin Morgan. Dam and Grand Dam of Peters' Morgan were raised by Welcome Partridge of Croyden, N. H. Peters' Old Vermont was sired by Wood Horse; by Green Mountain by Gifford; by Woodbury; by Justin Morgan. Dam of Old Vermont was sired by Hale's old Green Mountain; by Old Gifford; by Woodbury; by Justin Morgan. The Dam of Old Vermont and the Grand Dam of Ethan Allen, 2d was one and the same mare.

For terms, enquire of

A. W. PETERS,
BRADFORD, VT.

September 25, 1898.

(Courtesy *Morgan Horse Magazine*)

Horse. In 1861 Golddust defeated Iron Duke in a match race for $10,000. As his name implies, he was a light, bright chestnut, golden in the sunlight. He was an animal of great beauty and refinement, noted for siring extreme speed. Although his stud career was curtailed by war and his own untimely death, he left 44 trotters of record, four of which won ten or more races, including the outstanding mare Lucille Golddust 2:16¼, winner of six races.

Gifford's son Green Mountain Morgan sired the Wood Horse, which got Vermont, sire of Peter's Morgan (Peter's Horse), sire of Ethan Allen 2nd, through whose line the family traces today.

9

Bulrush and His Descendants

BULRUSH MORGAN (BELKNAP HORSE, CHELSEA) WAS BRED BY MOSES Belknap of Randolph and was foaled in 1812 on the farm of Ziba Gifford of Tunbridge, who later bred the Gifford Morgan by Woodbury.

The background of Bulrush's dam is unknown, but it would seem that she had far less quality than the dam of either Sherman or Woodbury. She was described as a dark bay with a heavy mane and tail, a low, compact, large-boned individual with a long neck and good head which she carried rather low. Although a smart trotter, she was not spirited to drive. Mr. Belknap had acquired her from a teamster who used her in a six-horse hitch pulling freight between Boston and Montpelier. Although she was a willing worker, the teamster thought her rather light for such rough work and traded her to Mr. Belknap for a larger horse.

When in foal to Justin Morgan, the mare was sold to Mr. Gifford with the understanding that the foal was to be returned at weaning, or might be kept for an additional payment of $13. Rather than pay the added sum, Gifford returned the colt to Belknap, who kept the horse until he was a mature stallion of seven. He then sold him to Abel Densmore, who sold him to Darius Sprague, of Randolph, who kept him until March of 1826, when he was sold for $350 to the partnership of Smith and Walker. When the partnership was dissolved in 1839, due to financial adversity, Simon Smith took Bulrush. In 1833, he sold the horse to Jessee Johnson and Brothers, the establishment where Woodbury was also stabled while owned by the Newbury Lawyer, Peter Burbank. In 1837, the Johnsons sold Bulrush to Messrs. Blake and Foss of Chelsea, who kept him until 1842 when he was bought by Lewis Jenkins of Fairlee. His last owner was F. A. Weir of Walpole, who kept him until his death in 1848 at the remarkable age of thirty-six.

Bulrush was a deep bay with no marks except a few white hairs scattered in the forehead. He stood about 14 hands and weighed 1,000 pounds. His luxurient mane hung almost to his knees. Like Woodbury, while still a colt he had had his tail docked to a length of nine inches or so. He was large-boned, with broad, flat joints and tremendous muscular development. Although his back was not ideally short, it had no tendency to be low. His most outstanding characteristic was his phenomenal power of endurance. Although he was not as animated as Woodbury or Sherman, he was faster than either. Sixteen of his sons were used as stallions, of which thirteen were bay, one brown and two gray. This distribution strongly suggests that he was homozygous for bay patterning, as was the famous Thoroughbred sire St. Simon.

Randolph Morgan (Randolph Horse, Morgan Bulrush, Young Morgan Bulrush, Little Randolph, Little Bulrush, Western Horse, Edson Horse, Goss Horse, Buckminster Horse), a son of Bulrush foaled in 1820 was a dark bay standing about 14:2½ and weighing about 950 pounds. He was bred by Mr. Weston of Randolph from a mare of untraced background. The horse was sold as a five year old to John Goss. Like his sire, the Randolph Horse had a heavy mane, tail and foretop and was noted for his great endurance.

Randolph's son, the Jennison Colt, a bright bay standing nearly 16 hands was described by his breeder Abijah Jennison, "When . . . foaled, well, the best description of him I can give is that he was perfect and grew perfect." When only two, he sired Morril, the founder of the famous Morril Family of trotters which included Mountain Maid 2:26, Young Morril 2:31, Draco 2:28½, and Fearnaught 2:23 — the world's champion trotting stallion of his day.

Although the Bulrush male line is for all practical purposes extinct, his influence is felt through the dams of several outstanding horses. Major Gordon 2924 traced to Octoroon 302, whose second dam was by Bulrush. Richard Sellman, who bred more Morgans than any breeder before or since, used Major Gordon extensively for thirteen years. Nearly all his early broodmares were daughters and granddaughters of Major Gordon, as were many of the two carloads of mares Sellman sold to Rolland G. Hill of Gustine, California. Horses of Hill's breeding are distributed all over California and the Far West. The third dam of Peter's Morgan (see above) was said to be by Bulrush.

In the early years the three main Morgan families — the Shermans, the Woodburys and the Bulrushes — were kept more or less distinct and separate, both by geographical limitations and by the personal preferences of their owners. At the Vermont State Fairs in the 1850's separate classes were offered for Bulrush Morgans, Sherman Morgans and Woodbury Morgans. Line breeding within the families or, frequently, inbreeding of daughter's to sire, son to dam, or brother to sister, was practiced. Each family had its loyal enthusiasts who, such being the unfortunate frailty of human nature, had the tendency to disparage the qualities of the other families. Although the similarities between the three strains were more striking than their differences, each family had its own particular strong points and also certain limitations, which set it apart from the others.

In the first half of the nineteenth century, the Bulrush Family was most numerous along both sides of the Connecticut River which divides Vermont from New Hampshire. Almost without exception they were dark bay or brown and absence of marks was the rule. They had an abundance of bone which sometimes verged on coarseness, heavy mane, tail and leg hair. They were not as lively, animated or graceful as the others. They were noted for their exceptional power of endurance and remarkable soundness. Linsley quoted a jockey as saying, "A smart, active boy would wear out a wrought-iron rocking-pony, sooner than a grown man could break down the constitution of a Bulrush horse."

The Woodburys were most numerous in Central Vermont. They were the tallest of the three strains, having the deepest flanks and heaviest quarters. They were famous for their bold, lofty action and abundance of nervous energy, in spite of which they were very tractable. Their natural animation made them favorites as parade horses. They were either chestnut or bay in about equal number, usually marked with one or both hind stockings and a star or strip in the face. Their legs tended to be free of coarse hair above the fetlocks and their manes and tails were less full than the others, while the body hair was finer. The Woodburys had the most prominent, lively eyes with great width between.

The Shermans were concentrated between Newbury and the Canadian border and the adjoining portion of New Hampshire. As a group, they tended to be smaller than the others and slightly low-backed, a trait which in no way indicated weakness, since the backs were also short, wide and muscular. Chestnut was the most common color, marked with a stripe or star and one or two stockings behind. The Shermans excelled as harness horses. Not as fiery and animated as the Woodburys, they were the easiest of all to train. The legs were exceptionally good with clean, distinct tendons set well back.

Basically then, the Shermans excelled as buggy horses, the Woodburys as saddle horses, and the Bulrushes as enduring utility animals — fast at the trot and kind at the pull.

It was three full generations before there was much intermingling of the families. In the hundred years since Linsley set forth the characteristics of the three principal families there has been much crossing of strains, resulting in greater uniformity of breed type today.

In tail male descent, the Bulrush line existed for many years through Sun Down Morgan 7388, a brown stallion foaled in California in 1933. He was by Raven Chief, by Morgan Chief, by Julien Morgan, by Winnebago Chief, by Mountain Chief, by Morril. He was very typically Morgan in appearance, but was used principally on grade mares. He died in the early 1960's and it is doubtful whether he left any entire sons. Red Flash (Colorado–Louisa) a grandson of Raven Chief, at twenty-seven is still standing in California, but most of his years at stud were spent getting half-bred foals on Thoroughbred mares, culled from race-horse production.

For years the Woodbury strain was represented only by the horses bred by J. H. Peters and Son of Bradford, Vermont, and it came very close to dying out entirely. Ethan Allen 2nd, foaled in 1877, revitalized the strain. He was sired by Peter's Morgan (Peter's Horse) by the Wood Horse by Hale's Green Mountain Morgan. Ethan Allen 2nd (Peter's Ethan Allen) sired Ethan Allen 3rd, Headlight Morgan and Croyden Prince, each of which established a strong family of his own.

In direct line, Sherman's descendants, principally through Ethan Allen, far outnumber the others. Every Morgan living today traces in one or more lines through Ethan Allen and Mansfield, who was foaled 85 years after Sherman's death, carried over fifty crosses to him.

The nearly extinct Bulrush male line is carried on by Red Flash 8416 (Colorado–Louisa) foaled in 1940. (Courtesy Rhed Morgan, Oakdale, California)

PART IV
Widening Circles

10

Winning the West

THROUGHOUT THE ENTIRE HISTORY OF THE HUMAN RACE, UNTIL THE FIRST decade of the twentieth century, the horse has played a tremendous role in man's affairs. Tribes that had domesticated the horse were able to overrun and dominate those that had not. The horse made man more mobile. By easing his burden by doing much of the heavy work he enabled his users to reach a high level of civilization and to turn their leisure time to the arts and sciences. In addition to being man's servant, the horse has always been a source of pleasure and recreation.

From earliest Colonial days, horses were a necessary part of the development of North America. Today, when the horse has almost completely disappeared from the daily scene, it is difficult to realize how utterly and completely dependent everyone was upon horses little more than a generation ago. Our ancestors' way of life, particularly in pioneer days, very nearly approached a horse-culture. Not only was horse transportation the only overland means of getting from one place or another — except, of course, for "shank's mare" — horses also provided the power that cleared, tilled, cultivated and harvested the land. They pulled ploughs and cultivators, worked in treadmills and turned grinders and cornshellers. They added color and excitement to lives that were often lacking in both; for, wherever and whenever men and horses have co-existed, horse sports have been popular — from the Greeks' chariot races through backwoods matches to the highly organized pari-mutuel roulette of today.

In many ways the horse shaped the pattern which communities assumed. Along the turnpikes — toll roads that laced the new nation together — taverns were located a day's journey by horse from each other. They often became

101

Horses furnished the power for operating farm machinery such as this thresher. (From a wash-and-ink drawing by James E. Taylor, 1864; courtesy the Western Reserve Historical Society)

Country inns along the stage routes became the nuclei of new settlements. (Drawing, James E. Taylor; courtesy Western Reserve Historical Society)

Horse-powered grain crusher. (From the *Ohio Farmer;* courtesy Western Reserve Historical Society)

the nucleus of a cluster of buildings — a stable to supply replacement horses, a smithy, a small general store, and houses for the hostler, farrier, and grocer who served the travelers' needs. The small group of dwellings often grew into a village or town. Similarly, within the states, the counties were laid out so that the courthouse and the center of commerce that crystalized around it were no more than a day's journey by horse from any point.

The village livery stable was almost as ubiquitous as the corner gas station today and was the social and recreational center for young men and idlers who gathered to pass the time of day. There the peripatetic stallion made his one-day stands, well advertised in advance. A horse and buggy could be hired at any hour of the day or night. Reputations were made and broken. Endless arguments about the relative merits of various stallions, their sureness in getting foals and the quality of their get, raged back and forth. Rumors, tall tales, spurious pedigrees changed hands. Horses were swapped and opinions on all equine subjects were freely aired. According to Phil Stong, "There was as much talk about horse shoe caulks and fitting as there is now about automobile tires in a garage . . . Mares and wenches were discussed with equal simplicity."

Erasmus Fuller, a lifelong horseman, was quoted as saying, "The breed of horses we used mostly in our livery business was the Morgan . . . I ran a stage line from St. Albans to Richford from 1869 to 1872. . . . My horses were practically all Morgan. I kept using them because I could depend on them. They were lively, bright, cheerful and intelligent driving horses . . . all square trotters . . . You spoke to them and they were ready to start."

Although the blacksmith shop and livery stable are vanished parts of the American scene, there are many expressions in the vernacular today left-over from the times when we were a horse-oriented society: "feeling his oats," "kicking over the traces," "going in double harness," "long in the tooth," dark horse," "horse of a different color," "changing horses in the middle of a stream," "horse play," "whipping a dead horse," "Putting the cart before the horse."

The horse helped shape the land, but invariably changing needs and uses shaped the horse. In the South, where large plantations were worked by slaves, horses tended to become specialized: easy-gaited saddlers for oversee-ing the work, agile hunters for following hounds or swift footed runners for winning a wager. From earliest times breeding horses for sport was part of the Southern way of life. Height was of great importance and in describing his horse's size the Southerner would always mention his measurement in hands. In New England, however, where the horse was always more utili-tarian, the owner would describe his horse's size in terms of weight. Where land holdings were small, due to inhospitable geography, and were farmed by the owner and his immediate family, there was a need for an all-purpose horse. A visitor from England wrote home that in America landholders them-selves perform tasks which in other countries are performed by servants. The Morgan admirably met and filled the need for the versatile horse-of-all-work. He could grub out stumps, pull the stone boat, drag saw logs to the mill by day and furnish amusement by lantern light in front of the tavern by racing the other man's horse for a glass of rum. Hitched to the buggy, he pulled the family to church in brisk style, but was gentle enough for the womenfolk to handle. Almost every red-blooded young man belonged to a local troop or militia unit. Parades and military musters, in the days when amusements were few and simple, brought the citizenry out in great numbers. The erst-while buggy horse, log puller and match racer could easily be spruced up to make a brilliant showing on the parade ground.

In the early days before roads were sufficiently developed to allow wheeled traffic, all travel between populated areas was by horseback. Freight was carried by pack animals. Many roads were no more than a track hewn through the wilderness and it took a post rider nearly two weeks to reach Boston from New York. The journey was interrupted by any sizable body of water and, like the taverns, the ferries became the seeds of towns — such as Harper's Ferry and Martin's Ferry. Horses of the Narragansett Pacer type with easy gaits were favored in the days before improved roads. As a network of roads developed and vehicular traffic became possible, the smart trotter was sought after. By the 1850's the Morgan was the most numerous, widely distributed and popular breed of horse in America. Morgans brought the highest prices paid for utility (as distinct from racing) stock. Pleasure driv-

Road team having strong Morgan type — both descended from Black Hawk. (Courtesy Chicago Historical Society)

ing became an extremely popular diversion. A fast roadster or a handsome matched team were as great a status symbol as the steel and chrome offerings from Detroit a hundred years later.

Several American presidents owned Morgans. Shortly after taking the oath of office, Abraham Lincoln ordered a stylish matched pair of black Morgans to pull his carriage. They came from central New York State, where a reported $3,000 was paid for them. Franklin Pierce, a lover of good horseflesh, bred as well as owned Morgans and was driven around Washington during his presidency behind a fine matched span. As we have seen, President Grant was also an admirer of the Morgan and had ordered two mares purchased and sent to Ethan Allen's court. Another presidential Morgan fancier and owner was Benjamin Harrison. He had an excellent roadster team selected for his use by Proctor, his Secretary of War, a Vermonter who considered the breed developed in his home state to be second to none.

By 1870 an estimated 90 per cent of all horses in New York used on light carriages, railway street cars and coaches were of Morgan background. An authority of the time said, "Go where you will among livery stable keepers or horse railroad managers, ask them what type of horse they have found most profitable to use out on the road; they will invariably answer, 'The old fashioned Morgan.'"

Morgans became very popular in the Mid-West. Interest in horses in general and in Morgans in particular reached a high level in Ohio in the 1850's and '60's. In 1859 an estimated 5,000 persons attended a horse fair at Orwell, a tiny village far from the large population centers.

Morgans did a great deal to upgrade the horses already in the state. An article in the *Ohio Farmer* said, "If the improvement in horses progresses as rapidly for ten years to come, as it has for ten years past, Ohio will have as good horses as can be desired." In the County Reports for Medina, "The breed of horses have been improved very much during the last few years. The Morgan blood prevails." And in Erie County, "The Morgan Horse [is] preferred on account of his uncommonly hardy constitution."

Writers of the time seemed to try to out-do each other in describing the

Road teams were the status symbol of their day. Dam of Small Hope said to be **Morgan**. Lady Mac's dam said to be by Pilot which Battell claimed as Morgan. (Courtesy **Chicago Historical Society**)

Bob B (Bob Morgan–Black said to be by Kirby Boy), bred by James Baird, East Burke, Vermont. (Courtesy J. Cecil Ferguson, Greene, Rhode Island)

breed's good qualities. As an article in the *Ohio Farmer* said, "All unprejudiced minds speak well of the Morgan, the only difference is in the degree of praise." John Dimon writing in the *Cultivator and Country Gentleman* in 1873, said, "In fineness and softness of coat they resemble the thoroughbred though it is usually heavier . . . [and have] a head which cannot be found as fine and beautiful in any other breed of horses except the thorough-bred or Arab. . . . They are remarkably long lived and in age retain their spirit and vigor. The reputation of the breed is not the result of a temporary excitement got up by interested parties to assist their sale, but the result of a long and convincing trial of their powers."

Thomas Brown prefaced his remarks in regard to the origin of Justin Morgan and his famous descendants in the May 17, 1856, *Ohio Farmer* with this tribute to the breed, "The readers of the *Ohio Farmer* will be gratified in learning some few interesting items in relation to the valuable horses for which Vermont has become so celebrated and which lovers of the horse, in Ohio, are constantly seeking here to improve the level of that noble animal in the Buckeye State."

In the same year, another correspondent wrote, "Morgans possess the capacity of transmitting their peculiarities to their descendants with a degree of uniformity seldom equalled by horses claiming the purest pedigree."

Not everyone, however, was enraptured at the Morgans' rapid rise in numbers. They were all too numerous in the opinion of one reader of the *Ohio Farmer* who wrote to express his views in 1859. "Why is it that we see in the *Farmer* no advertisements of Thoroughbred horses kept in the vicinity of Cleveland? Will nothing but Morgans answer on the [Western] Reserve? For my part, although I think Morgans the best buggy horses in the world, I don't believe they are adaptable to all purposes."

Agricultural fairs held in each county were the high point of the year. The *Ohio Farmer* reported that at the Geauga County Fair at Burton in 1856, "The exhibition of horses formed the chief attraction . . . the favorite blood appears to be the Black Hawk Morgan . . . and the Green Mountain through Emperor."

The culmination of the fair season was reached at the State Fair. The larger cities competed with each other for the honor — and revenue — of playing host to it. In 1860, the Ohio State Fair was held in Dayton with over 450 horses competing for $2,000 in premiums. Classes were offered for thorough-breds, roadsters, horses for general purpose, draft horses, light harness, saddle and trotters. State fairs often featured a match race between two outstanding trotters, such as Lancet and Flora Temple.

The *Ohio Farmer* went to great lengths to explain the qualifications for each class. "The term 'thorough-bred' when applied to the horse has a different significance from what it has when applied to cattle. . . . A thorough-bred horse . . . is one whose pedigree can be traced for many generations each of which has signalized himself on the turf or as the progenitor of superior horses' . . . most of our roadsters, trotting stock, saddle and carriage horses contain a mixture of the thorough-bred. . . . The Morgan horses are a good illustration." The class for blooded horses was won by Napolean Morgan in 1852.

The article continued to describe the attributes of a roadster. "The Morgan horse is a good illustration of this class. . . . He need not be as large as the horse of all work, nor so strong; but on the road he should be his superior, travelling daily with light loads fifty miles, not for a single day but for weeks. . . . H. M. Reed of Sidney, Ohio has a steel-mixed Black Hawk from Hill's celebrated horse Hill's Champion Black Hawk. He shows many of the characteristics of his half brothers all over Ohio." It was the roadster class which Eastman Morgan had won in 1856 in a class of 117 while Black Hawk Bishop Onderdonk was second.

Big classes and keen competition were the rule at state fairs. "Horses for general purpose were represented by over 70 specimens of all ages. . . . A horse for all work is the farmer's horse; he can do anything; he is, in a certain sense, a draft horse, a farm horse, a roadster, a trotter, a family horse, and, like a 'jack of all trades,' can fill almost any place. Of the twenty-seven stallions in the ring . . . at least twenty were first rate horses: horses with muscle, bottom and not without beauty. It was finally decided that Abner C. Jennings of Urbana had the best one. . . . Mr. Jennings horse, 'St. Lawrence,' is of Black Hawk blood, large and very much admired."

Black Hawk Morgan Onderdonk, by Black Hawk, out of a flea-bitten gray mare by the Shoreham Morgan. Second dam by Messenger. He was a bay roan, standing 15 hands and weighing about 1,075 pounds. James M. Brown and associates bought him from his breeder, David Hill, of Bridgeport, Vermont, and brought him to Ohio in 1852. (From the *Ohio Farmer;* courtesy Western Reserve Historical Society)

Other outstanding Morgans bred in Ohio or brought to the state, where they stood one or more seasons were: Napolean Morgan (Massilon Morgan), Searcher, Colonel Hale, Major Gifford, Dolphus, Morgan Traveller 2nd, Champlain, Champion 2nd, Star of the West, Wild-Air, Telegraph, Robin Hood, Stockbridge Chief, Jackson's Flying Cloud, King Herod, Barre, Austin's Morgan Bulrush, Knowlton's Morgan, General Morgan, Case's David Hill, Nigger Doctor, Orr's Flying Cloud and Black Squirrel.

The Morgan moved West with the advancing frontier. Wherever there was hard work to do and rough country to tame, Morgans were there to get the job done. So great was the demand for them and such a steady stream of good horses were sent West that many people in Vermont feared their stock was being dangerously depleted — that they were being bled white to feed the needs of other parts of the country.

No lesser an authority on the western horse than Frederick Remington said that the Morgan was, for all practical purposes the best horse ever developed in the United States. Because of the breed's durability and the fact

Durable horses were needed on rough mountain roads. Here they are depicted transporting ore from the mines. (From David Alexander's *The History and Romance of the Horse;* courtesy Cooper Square Publishers, Inc.)

Winning the West. Horse is of strongly Morgan type. Lithograph by N. Currier, 1853, after a painting by Arthur F. Tait. (Courtesy Chicago Historical Society)

that the Morgan's useful years extended far beyond those of other types of horse, Morgan blood was especially sought-after. The compact build developed tremendous power in a small package — another point in the Morgan's favor, for pound for pound, the smaller horse is more efficient and can pull a proportionately greater load than can a heavy horse. The Morgan's small stature, for which he had often been adversely criticised, now became an asset, because he could survive where pickings were lean, and a larger, less thrifty horse would have starved.

The hardships of the frontier were vividly described by James Flint, who traveled through the Mid-West early in the nineteenth Century. "The poor animals are forced to range the forests in winter when they can scarcely produce anything that is green. . . . Want of shelter completes the sum of misery. . . . Horses are not exempted from their share in these common sufferings with the addition of labour." Joel Palmer who guided settlers on the Oregon Trail reported that horses were required to travel 40 miles a day, carrying 200 pounds, living off whatever forage could be found along the way. "I find that such horses will endure such labor for twenty-five or thirty days, resting of course on the Sabbath, upon this grass without injury to them."

According to tradition, Brigham Young's wagon was pulled by a team of Morgans, and the Moyle strain of horse is supposed to be descended from Morgan stock brought to Utah by the Mormon settlers.

In 1862 the Homestead Act was passed opening up vast areas of the West to settlers from the East. During the period that the act was in existence (1862–1935) homesteaders took title to 276,000,000 acres of land. The hardships of the frontier and the homesteaders' dependance upon their horses are beautifully described in Rose Wilder Lane's *Free Land*. Morgans were highly prized, for, ". . . they'd move as much as any team of Percherons." The demand for good horses was greater than the supply and Morgans brought top prices.

Horses were so much a necessity of life in the West that horse stealing was considered to be a crime of the highest magnitude. Because theft of a man's horse was likely to result in his death by starvation, the horse thief, when caught, was shown little mercy. In Indiana the penalty was 39 lashes — sometimes a virtual death sentence. In Nebraska, the punishment was shooting; and hanging was the rule anywhere further west. In Texas, horse thieves originally were branded with a "T," fined, or imprisoned; but when these milder measures did not prove to be a deterrent to horse stealing, the traditional rite of hanging was adopted, and "the trees began to bear strange fruit at all seasons," according to DeKoster, quoted by Phil Stong.

From Gold-Rush days on, many Morgans were taken to California. Be-

tween 1849 and the early 1880's more than 100 stallions, including McCrack-
en's David Hill 2nd were taken overland or by ship. Crossed with Spanish
mares they got a cow horse that has never been equalled. Wisconsin was a
stopover point on the overland way West, and several stallions made one or
two seasons there before continuing their journey. In California the Morgans
brought top prices. Three Black Hawk Morgans — "all jet black and beautiful" — were brought from Kenosha, Wisconsin, in 1860 by Nicholas Ehle
and sold for $14,200; the highest priced individual brought $7,000.

Unfortunately, few ranchers had the time or the inclination to keep breeding records of any sort. The period is in many ways comparable to the "Lost
Century" in Quarter Horse history when few records were maintained. Working hours were long, conditions were unbelievably hard, illumination ranged
from primitive to non-existent, writing materials were expensive and scarce,
and literacy was at a low ebb. Beside, the proof of the pudding was in the
eating, and if a horse could do an honest day's work, what need did he have
for a lot of fancy ancestors? Human records were scarcely more carefully
kept; the marriages, births and deaths were written on the flyleaf of the family
Bible. It was a wise child who knew his own father, and many, many good
Morgans completely dropped from sight, as such, while their good qualities
of speed, hardiness, endurance and, above all, savvy were passed along to
the using stock horse of the West.

11

Morgan Blood in Other Light Horse Registers

THE MORGAN PLAYED A TREMENDOUS PART IN THE DEVELOPMENT OF other light horse breeds in North America. With the exception of the Thoroughbred, which furnished the foundation stock for all American breeds except the Arab, Appaloosa and Albino, no other breed has had an influence that approaches the Morgan's.

The Standardbred

The Morgans had the greatest impact upon the American Trotter and were the harness racers of a century ago, before the Hambletonians' rise to prominence. As we have seen, the Morgan very nearly lost its identity in the breed it helped found.

Although Morgans have disappeared entirely from tail male descent, they continue to exert a great influence in bulk, just as the Leedes Arabian and the Darcy Turk outweigh the taproot Thoroughbred sires in sheer number of crosses, although their direct lines are no longer extant. Similarly, the Black Hawks, Fearnaughts, and Morrils continue to contribute to the Standardbred. Although the Hambletonians got speed, the Morgans contributed bottom, stamina, substance and purity of gait at the trot.

The American Saddle Horse

The American Saddle Horse is also heavily indebted to the Morgan. According to Joseph Battel, of the original list of stallions selected as the foundation sires by the National Saddle Horse Breeder's Association in 1899, Black Squirrel, Cabell's Lexington, Coleman's Eureka, and probably Tom Hal, Copperbottom and Davy Crockett were of Morgan descent. Today more than 90 per cent of all Saddlebreds carry Morgan blood, principally through Black Hawk's grandsons, Gist's Black Hawk and Indian Chief.

Peavine, by Rattler, by Stockbridge Chief, by Black Hawk, was foaled in Kentucky in 1863. A 16-hand, 1,150-pound chestnut with a heavy mane and tail, he was an outstanding show horse, roadster and race horse, a winner of eight races with a record of 2:35½ for the mile. He won first premium in a class of 63 at the St. Louis Fair. His get were fine roadsters, very much sought-after as stylish, fast-driving horses. A reported $3,000 was once turned down for a pair of his gelded sons. From him trace such notables as Edna May's King, Wing Commander and Rex Peavine.

Another strong influence, also through Black Hawk, was Indian Chief by Blood's Black Hawk. He sired many top roadsters, including the outstanding fine harness mare Lady de Jarnette who was undefeated in the show ring. He was also the great, great grandsire of Marvel King, Bourbon King, and Montgomery Chief.

The backgrounds of Cabell's Lexington and Coleman's Eureka were also Morgan; the former was a son of Gist's Black Hawk and the latter was sired by Young's Morgan, a grandson of Eureka by the Green Mountain Morgan. Another prominent Saddler sire of Morgan descent was Benjamin's Whirlwind, by Whirlwind by Indian Chief; out of Arabian Maid by Vermont Morgan, second dam by Imported Zilcaadi, also the sire of the dam of Golddust. Benjamin's Whirlwind has the usual distinction of being recorded in the American Saddle Horse Register, the Trotting Register, and the *Morgan Horse and Register!*

Some authorities believed that the Canadian Pacers were a cross between French horses and stallions from New Zealand. The original French stock brought to the New World, however, was of the Norman, or draft type. As we have seen above, several of the sons and grandsons of Justin Morgan were sent to Quebec. There is even a strong possibility that the old horse himself stood one or more seasons in Canada during the years when there is no record of his being either in Vermont or New Hampshire.

The eastern townships of the Province of Quebec were settled principally by Vermonters who undoubtedly took their hard-working, easy-keeping Morgans with them. Battell suggests that the tendency to pace was introduced through Naragansett stock also brought from the States either by the original settlers or by Yankee traders. The hardiness and compact build of the Canadian Pacer strongly indicated the presence of Morgan blood. "A Kentucky breeder," however, in a letter to the *Ohio Farmer* suggested that the indebtedness ran the other way, with the Morgan a product of Canadian stock.

According to Battell, Canadian horses of probable Morgan background that were taken to the United States included Pilot, Tecumseh, Davy Crockett, Corbeau, and Tom Hal.

Tom Hal, foaled in 1809 and brought to Kentucky in 1816, was variously described as a blue roan and as a strawberry roan. He is also said to have come from Virginia, but letters from people who remembered the horse agree that although his owner John T. Mason came to Bath County, Kentucky from Virginia, the horse had come from Canada, and was of Canadian Pacing stock. Although nothing definite was known of his background, Battell rather arbitrarily assigned him one-quarter Morgan blood (grandson of Justin Morgan) by virtue of his strongly Morgan type. Tom Hal was a vigorous individual, getting many fine foals and living to the remarkable age of forty-one.

Battell assigned the chestnut stallion Copperbottom one-half Morgan blood, making him a son of Justin Morgan — again on the basis of type and the locality from which he was said to have originated. Copperbottom was "very strongly built, with broad breast, round barrel, short back, good neck and head, handsome appearance. . . ."

Pilot and Davy Crockett are two more Canadians included in the *Morgan Horse and Register* that were American Saddle Horse progenitors. They were, according to Battell, of pronounced Morgan type and were assigned a fraction of one quarter.

The Saddler is indebted to the Morgan for its finish, animation, stamina, good disposition and perfection at the trot, while his size and refinement are of Thoroughbred origin. Between 1917 and 1931 every winner of the $10,-000 Championship Stake held at Louisville, Kentucky, traced to Justin Morgan in one or more lines.

The Tennessee Walking Horse

Walkers are also heavily indebted to the Morgan through the breed's foundation sire, Allan F-1, a horse of Morgan descent. The black stallion, foaled in Lexington in 1886, traced through his dam to Black Hawk. His son Roan Allen F-38 was out of a mare tracing to Gifford through her dam's sire. Roan Allen got Wilson's Allen, Mitch F-5, Merry Boy — the sire of famous Merry-Go-Boy — Brantley's Roan Allen, Major Bowes, Curlee's Spotted Allen, Hal's Allen and Wilson's Bullet F-65.

In 1949 all 25 of the breed's top-rated stallions traced in direct male line to Roan Allen, who was Morgan on both sides of his pedigree. Another son of Allan F-1, Hunter's Allen, carried probable Morgan blood through Copperbottom.

Quarter Horse

The period between 1780 and 1880 is known as the "Lost Century of Quarter Horse Breeding," because few records were kept during that time.

In the West during frontier days, selection of stock was largely empirical, relying on performance rather than pedigree. Phil Stong, without offering us any proof of his assertation, states that the mighty Steel Dust was a Morgan — a possibility which even as zealous a Morgan enthusiast as Battell had overlooked. The 14:2 hand bay stallion was foaled in Illinois about 1845 and appeared in Texas a few years later. The tales of his legendary prowess are certainly in the Morgan tradition. This is not the same horse as the gray stallion Steel Dust on page 307 of Volume II of the *Morgan Horse and Register,* although some writers have confused the two.

It is certain that multitudes of Morgans went West, worked, propagated and died without leaving a trace in the form of a written record. The degree of their influence upon the Quarter Horse is impossible to estimate with any accuracy, although, in view of certain similarities of type between the two breeds, it must have been far from negligible. In 1920 the King Ranch at Kingsville, Texas purchased the two year old bay colt Lucky(Hugo–Eunice) from the United States Government Farm for the purpose of upgrading the stock horses they were breeding.

The American Albino

The late Caleb R. Thompson of White Horse Ranch in Naper, Nebraska, developed a strain of pure white horses known as Albinos. They are not true albinos in the strictest sense of the word because they are not completely lacking in pigmentation. Although they have pink skins and milk-white coats, their eyes are brown, hazel or blue.

The foundation sire was Old King out of a mare said to be Morgan. His excellent disposition, good muscular development, intelligence and well-formed head tend to substantiate the possibility of his Morgan background. The mares selected as foundation stock for the new breed were Morgan, either as to type or breeding. The pale coat is thought to be due to an extremely rare dominant mutant gene which is lethal when homozygous. Albinos are noted for their tractability and the ease with which they can be trained as trick and circus horses. Silver Tip 330 was purchased by the Japanese consul for the Emperor of Japan. Renamed Fubuki(Snow), he became Emperor Hirohito's famous white charger.

The Moyle Horse

Another western type of probable Morgan origin is the Moyle horse of Idaho and northern Utah. The strain takes its name from the Moyle family, who for three generations have bred these hardy horses from stock originally selected by the Mormons for long-distance use, over a century ago.

The predominant color of the Moyle horses is bay. They have good heads, tough feet, exceptional intelligence and great willingness to do, qualities which strongly indicate the presence of Morgan blood.

In 1965 a mare of Moyle breeding completed the 24-hour Lake Tahoe to Auburn, California, 100-mile Ride carrying 204 pounds over some of the roughest imaginable terrain.

More prosaically Morgans were used to produce superior work animals. In the 1940's at the United States Government Experimental station in Georgia, Morgan mares were crossed with jacks to produce a high-quality, general-purpose farm mule. Morgan stallions on Belgian, Suffolk and Percheron mares got excellent farm chunks, or small draft animals. Pers Crowell praises them as being "good tempered, handsome, easy to raise and train, durable, and long-lived." The advocates of the Morgan–draft cross claim that the resulting animal has great stamina, an abundance of energy and greater ability to withstand extremes of heat than do larger purebred draft horses.

12

Morgan Exports

MORGANS NOT ONLY SHAPED THE DEVELOPMENT OF AMERICAN LIGHT horse breeds; their influence was felt abroad as well. Many outstanding stallions and mares were shipped to other countries with the object of improving the local strain of horse.

A team of Morgans, not designated by name, were sent to France on the Vanderbilt to be added to the carriage stud of the French Emperor. In 1858, three more Morgans were sent to France aboard the Ariel. They had been ordered and carefully selected for the honor of drawing the Emperor's carriage through the streets of Paris. A correspondent writing in the New York *Herald* reported, "This shows that Louis Napoleon must have been well pleased with his first purchases." The horses had come originally from the Boston area, but were purchased through a New York agent. One was brown and a matched team were of a somewhat lighter color. They weighed between 1,000 and 1,200 pounds and were, "in all respects creditable specimens of the equine family. The price of these animals has not transpired, but it is no doubt royal, if not imperial. A span of the Morgan breed have brought as high as $6,500."

Shepard F. Knapp 3320, bred by George Snell of Turner, Maine, was a 15:2 hand chestnut, foaled in 1857. Sired by the Eaton Horse, he descended from Sherman both by way of the dam of the Avery Horse, his grandsire, and through his own dam, Jenny Lind, by Sherman's son, Whalebone. Shepard F. Knapp carried 3/16 of the blood of Justin Morgan. He was sold for a record price of $10,000 to parties who took him to England, where he proved to be a sensation. He was the fastest trotter both in Great Britain and on the Continent. He won many races, including one at two and one-half miles in which all of the best horses of Europe competed. He won with ease in a time of 6:14. Hiram Woodruff wrote of him, "At the meeting of the Yorkshire Agricultural Society a prize was awarded to Shepherd F. Knapp, whose action was as beautiful as anything ever seen in this country. . . . For pace no English Roadster could touch him." His action was so high that he sometimes cut his elbows.

Shepherd F. Knapp (Avery Horse–Jenny Lind by Whalebone) Morgan trotting stallion taken to England. He and 16 descendants are included in Volume I of the Hackney Stud Book of Great Britain. (Courtesy Mrs. Charles C. Holloway, Three H Farm, Barrington, Illinois)

Shepherd F. Knapp was recorded in the appendix of the *Hackney Stud Book,* as were his sons Goldfinder, The Great American, Knapp, Shepherd F. Knapp (Ringer's); in the main volume are his sons Washington, Rapid Road, Norfolk Shepherd (not entered separately, but as the sire of Jerry), and Primrose, dam of Rising Star and Star of the East.

The good trotter Tom Allen was sent to France. By Ethan Allen and foaled in 1874, he was thought to be a full brother to Honest Allen. In France he won two important races in decisive style and, according to the *Spirit of the Times,* "Nobly maintained the Morgan tradition."

Trotting match between Shepherd F. Knapp and Morning Star. (From an original painting by E. P. Lambert)

In 1886 a pair of Morgan mares were sent to London as a carriage team. The following account of their reception in England appeared in the *Maine Horse Breeder's Monthly* (page 233) for December of that year, written by E. L. Norcross:

Lord Rothschild of England gave an order, last winter to the Hon. August Belmont of New York, for a team of American trotters. Mr. Belmont engaged Mr. Bishop to furnish said team. Mr. Bishop is one of those horsemen who consider the blood of Hambletonian an objection when a man wants a fine, goodlooking, pleasant road team; therefore he came to Maine. At Norridgewock he bought the white Fearnaught mare Nellie R., record about 2:35, then he found a black mare by Winthrop Morrill, out of a Knox dam that for size, style and speed, matched Nellie R. After driving them together they could show 2:30, and drove like one horse. In June Mr. Bishop took his team, with a Brewster top buggy, weight 180 pounds, and a fine pair of New York harnesses, to England. Upon his arrival he notified Lord Rothschild that he had arrived with the team, and that he had brought along a buggy and harness. His Lordship said, "I want no American trash to ride in. I want something safe." Mr. Bishop replied, "I brought this carriage and harness to show this team in London, not to sell." The next day Lord Rothschild sent his head clerk down eight miles where the horses were stabled, and Mr. Bishop gave him a ride. On the following morning his Lordship sent his head groom, requesting Mr. Bishop to drive the team up to his palace. They had got started and about halfway up, when they met his Lordship on horseback. Bishop saw him, and started the mares up to a fast clip, and went by him, and then turned around again and came back. Upon returning his Lordship had dismounted and motioned them to stop. They did so, and his Lordship told the groom to take his horse back to the stable and he would get in with Mr. Bishop. He did so and Bishop immediately gave his Lordship the reins; the street was like a floor, and Bishop clucked to the mares and they set sail. The exhilaration took away all fear, and the trotters from Maine just flew over the road, and Bishop said he never saw any man get the dimensions of a pair of trotters, like his Lordship. He drove them home into his own stable. There stood the coachman looking and feeling as though he owned the whole of London. His Lordship said to Mr. Coachman, "How do you like those?" After a very careful examination he pronounced them the best team he had ever seen. His Lordship said, "Mr. Bishop I lunch at one o'clock, you will be there." After lunch his Lordship called his head clerk in and asked Bishop what was the cost of those mares. Upon Mr. Bishop's reply he said, "How much did the carriage cost in your country?" Mr. Bishop gave the price. "How much for the harness?" Price given. "I wish for all expenses." It was given. "Now Mr. Bishop what kind of money do you wish?" "American notes if convenient." The money was forthcoming, and Mr. Bishop bid his Lordship good day, and returned to America. Some few weeks after Mr. Bishop received a box containing a magnificent English tandem harness stitched with silk and richly mounted, as a present from his Lordship. Maine should feel proud, as it has furnished the finest team in London and it is driven by the wealthiest man in London. The balance of the foreign news will be gratifying to the owners of Fearnaught stock as it was to me. At the great trotting race in Vienna, in September last, the sweepstakes of four thousand Francs open to all trotters, was won by the Fearnaught mare Gladys 2:23, beating a field of seven; report says it was a desperate struggle, as all went in to win.

Autumn 5056, bred by Joseph Battell and foaled in 1892, was sent to the Philippines for the improvement of native stock. The chestnut stallion was a son of General Gates 666 (Denning Allen–Fanny Scott by Revenue, Jr., a Thoroughbred) and out of Belle of Middlebury by Fire Fly, a son of Daniel Lambert.

Edmunds (General Gates–Polly B) was purchased by the Agricultural College of Puerto Rico in 1912. The following year two additional Morgans were shipped to the college, Navarre (Donlyn–Fanny P.) and Nadri (Troubadour of Willowmoor–Grief). All were bred by the United States Morgan Horse Farm.

In the spring of 1920, Dr. Issa Tanimura of Tokyo, acting as agent for the emperor's stud, purchased 11 Morgans which were taken to Japan. From Spencer Borden of Fall River, Massachusetts, he bought the nine-year-old mare Lucy McDonald (Donald–Lucille) and her suckling colt Stockwood by Jerome Morgan. He also acquired a mature stallion, eleven-year-old Donlyn (Donald–Chestnut by Billy Roberts) from the U. S. Government Farm; a nine-year-old broodmare, Bessie Baker (Dart–Bird) bred by J. B. Baker of Waverly, Iowa, and owned by C. C. Stillman; and a weaning colt, Trumpeter (Troubadour of Willowmoor–Jewel) from the United States Bureau of Animal Industry, along with his dam Jewel (General Gates–Minnehaha). The group of Morgans were reported to be doing very well in their new environment according to a 1923 bulletin.

During the twenties, South and Central Americans, who also recognized the Morgan's good qualities and wished to upgrade their own stock, purchased stallions and an occasional mare for export.

Bobbie Burns (Headlight Morgan–Jessie A by Major Antoine) was bred by Richard Sellman and foaled in 1915 near Rochelle, Texas. As a five-year-old he was sold by the A & M College of Texas to Raphael d'Avila Olivera of Rio de Janeiro, Brazil.

Quartermaster (Bennington–Carolyn) was sold as a yearling to Succesion J. Serralles of Puerto Rico by the Government Farm.

Nodaway (Donlyn–Sunflower Maid), also bred by the United States Morgan Horse Farm, was sold as a four-year-old to Señor don Samuel Alvarez of the Republic of El Salvador in Central America.

In 1926 Dr. Manuel Luiz Osiro took to Rio Grande do Sul, Brazil, two mares and a stallion, the two-year-old filly Rhyme (Mansfield–Leila), the six-year-old mare Grisette (Scotland–Beauty), and Sudbury (Bennington–Ruth), a yearling colt.

In 1927, J. C. Brunk of Cotton Hill Farm, Rochester, Illinois, sold the yearling colt Jubal (Allen King–Daisy Knox) to Manuel A Cardeñas of Cuba. Sir Ben (Bennington–Tootsie) went to Nicaragua as a yearling, transferred by his breeder, B. O. Wales, of Middlebury, to Manuel Zavala. The same year, Señor Zavala acquired from the Government Farm the three-year-old filly Sunapee (Bennington–Novice) and the yearling colts Uxbridge (Bennington–Quietude) and Use Me (Mansfield–Lady Lyndon). Herbert H. Robbins, of Middlebury, sold Dutchman (McMahon Morgan General–Viola), a four-year-old stallion, to the South Puerto Rico Sugar Company and Trading Corporation of Santo Domingo.

The trend continued during the thirties. Wimbleton (Bennington–Carolyn) was transferred from the United States Department of Agriculture to Colonel L. A. Beltran of Havana for use in the Cuban Army Remount Service, in

1931, when the colt was two. The following year the Department of Agriculture sold Baldwin (Bennington–Florette) to G. G. Fischer of Trinidad. In 1933 the Cuban Army Remount service purchased several mares from the United States Morgan Farm, the eleven-year-old mare Pink Rose (Bennington–Rose Leaf), the two-year-old fillies Bee (Bennington–Quietude) — a full sister to Uxbridge, which Senor Zavala had bought five years earlier — and Bernice (Mansfield–Peerless) and the twenty-one-year-old brood mare Jana (Alkadaza–Kitty E.), which the Government Farm had bought from J. C. Brunk as a three-year-old.

The Government-bred stallion Querido (Bennington–Artemesia) headed Roland G. Hill's large stud in California for many years. In 1937, when the stallion was fourteen he was sold to Alfred W. Carter, of Kamuela, Hawaii. In the same year, Hill also sold Aylmer F. and Lester B. Robinson of Kanai, Hawaii, the three-year-old filly Angela Bird (Querido–Angela).

In 1938, J. C. Brunk sold the five-year-old stallion King Copper (Hiro–Sentola) to A. B. Malcomb, of Nassau in the Bahamas.

In 1940, Benign (Bennington–Agatha), bred by Charles A. Stone, of Charlottesville, Virginia, was sold at nine to Francisco de Sola, of San Salvador. According to the *Morgan Horse Magazine,* the horse had sired 30 half-bred foals before his death the following year. In 1941 another Morgan of Stone's breeding went to Latin America — the four-year-old stallion Gingersnap (Virgil–Alda), purchased by the Ministerio de Agricultura in Caracas.

Linsley Romanesque (Romanesque–Jipsy L.), bred by Elmer Brown, of Halstead, Kansas, and foaled in 1939, went to the Parker Ranch in Kamuela, Hawaii. In 1945 Paul J. Furnas of Spring Hollow Farm, Media, Pennsylvania, sold two yearlings of his own breeding, the colt Pendennis (Upwey Mont–Penn–Curtain Time) and Pennelope (Upwey Mont–Penn–Alola) to Alfedo Volio of Cartago, Costa Rica.

World War II curtailed the exportation of horses temporarily. In 1947 the Chinese Ministry of National Defense purchased 26 Morgans including Magellan (Goldfield–Topaz), Ora (Mansfield–Ishtar), Jacqueline (Upwey King Peavine–Torch Glow), from the United States Morgan Horse Farm; Lady's Man (Lippit Mandate–Lady Field) from Marilyn G. Carlson; Red Rex (Red Man–Meta Knox), Veltayr (Jack Sprat–Angelak), Belle Gates (Red Vermont–Linsley Belle), Kitty Q. (Querido–Kitty C.), Joseayr (Jack Sprat–Josephine Romanesque), Anayr (Jack Sprat–Angela K.), from Mr. and Mrs. E. W. Roberts, of California; Senator Bain (Senator Graham–Monty) from Helen Brunk Greenwalt; Tifona (Juzan–Molly from Joseph R. Brunk; Black Bub (Sutterdon–Stareda) from Thomas T. Brunk; Dolly Hudson (Archy Hudson–Lady Russle), Brown Dolly (Rhythm Ramble–Dolly

Hudson), Rhythm Ramble (Dude de Jarnette–Airy), and Senior Don (Dude de Jarnette–Byrrh) from C. J. O'Neil.

In 1951 Mr. and Mrs. E. W. Roberts transferred a large group of Morgans to Lester B. and Aylmer F. Robinson of Hawaii who 14 years earlier had bought the Morgan Lady Bird from Roland G. Hill. The group included: Marguerita Sonfield (Sonfield–Bessie Ro), Mae Livingston (Blackman–Gojea), Lela Colonel (Colonel's Boy– Dam not listed in Vol VI), Karen (Gay Mack–Mary Blossom), Karen Jean (Gay Mac–Gojea), Fern Jekyll (Jekyll–Fanita), Elizabeth Blackwell (Blackman–Nell R F), Belgrade (Blackman–Gliderayr), Betty Romanesque (Blackman–Betty Contez), Allen White (Nathan Allen–Elizabeth Blackwell), Henry Nagel (Blackman–Nellayr), Angel Sprat (Jack Sprat–Angela K), Winayr (Monerayr–Angelayr), Reginayr (Homerayr–Queenayr), Princess Tonya (Sparbeau–Marietta), Patsyayr (Jack Sprat–Angela K.), and Myrlana (Redman–Dorethy Abbey).

In 1956 Generalissimo Rafael L. Trujillo Molina of the Dominican Republic bought Colette (Jubilee's Courage–Paragraph) from Mrs. Frances Bryant of Springfield, Vermont, and Windcrest Sabrina (Upwey Ben Don–Windcrest Kiss Me Kate) from Mr. and Mrs. Frederick O. Davis.

In 1960 Rock Hudson (Don Hudson–Dot S. Belle) was sold by his breeder, R. L. Brachlear, to Francisco de Sola of San Salvador, El Salvador, Central America. In 1963 Thomas Geddes (Robin Geddes–Lady Helen) was purchased by John Armstrong of Guatemala, Central America, from his breeder, Alexander G. Ruthven, of Ann Arbor, Michigan.

13

Morgans as Military Horses

DURING THE MEXICAN WAR, MORGANS WERE USED AS CAVALRY MOUNTS. So superbly were the American horses trained that they continued to gallop in pursuit of the retreating enemy even after their riders had been shot from the saddle.

According to some authorities, the use of cavalry reached its greatest heights during the Civil War. Other authorities, however, believe that with improved firepower, cavalry, as such, had already declined by the time of the War Between the States and had become mere mounted infantry. In any event, the use of horse soldiers was the decisive factor in many major battles.

In the beginning the South's cavalry was vastly superior to the North's and most of the early cavalry victories belonged to the South. The Rebels' superior riding skill was due, in part, to the Cavalier tradition, which venerated white womanhood and the blood-horse with almost equal reverence. The South was rural and agricultural; much of the North was already industrial. Training in horsemanship was part of the Southerner's upbringing. In the North it was not, and one Yankee troop of cavalry rode into its first battle with the soldiers tied to their saddles!

The great improvement and enlargement of the Union's mounted forces between 1863 and 1865 helped turn the tide of the conflict.

The most outstanding Northern cavalry officer to emerge from the war was General Philip Sheridan whose famous charger, Rienzi, was a Morgan. The gelding, of Black Hawk blood, was foaled near Grand Rapids, Michigan. Archibald Carpenter, an officer of the 2nd Michigan Cavalry, brought the horse with him when he joined the army. On May 25, 1862, Sheridan, who was then a colonel, assumed command of the regiment which was stationed

MILITARY HORSES: Many Union troops were mounted on Morgans. These matched chestnuts of the Sixth Pennsylvania (Rush's Lancer's) have the appearance of being Morgan. (Courtesy Company of Military Historians, Alexandria, Virginia)

The Patriot Scouts of '61!

"Fire when you see the whites of their eyes, Boys."--OLD PUT.

MILITARY HORSES: Civil War Recruiting Poster. (Courtesy Chicago Historical Society)

at Rienzi, Mississippi. Shortly thereafter, Carpenter, who was devoted to the horse but a little afraid of him, presented the beautiful black gelding to Colonel Sheridan in the name of a group of fellow officers.

In his memoirs, Sheridan described the horse, in part, as follows: "He was of Morgan stock and about three years old. He was jet black excepting three white feet, sixteen hands high and strongly built with great powers of endurance. . . . He was an animal of great intelligence and immense strength. . . . He always held his head high and by the quickness of his movements gave many persons the idea that he was exceedingly impetuous and fiery. This was not so, for he could at any time be controlled by a firm hand and a few words and he was as cool and quiet under fire as an old soldier. It is doubtful if a superior as a horse for field service was ever ridden by anyone. . . . He

Rienzi, from Sheridan's *Memoirs*. (Courtesy Chicago Historical Society)

was so active that he could cover with ease five miles an hour at his natural walking gait" . . . and he was never . . . "overcome by fatigue, though on many occasions his strength was severely tested by long marches and short rations."

According to Drennan, for 23 years Sheridan's confidential clerk, the General rode Rienzi from the day he was presented to him until the close of the war and was in nearly every engagement in which the General participated, including the Battle of Chaplin Hills, the Battle of Stone River, the Engagement at Eaglesville, the Engagement at Cowan Station, the Capture of Winchester, the Battle of Chickamauga, Missionary Ridge, the Wilderness and Appamatox Courthouse.

One of the decisive battles of the war was fought at Missionary Ridge near Chattanooga, Tennessee. The Confederates under Bragg were dug in on high ground and held the Union troops down in captured entrenchments at the foot of the mountain with a murderous crossfire of artillery and musketry.

The situation was frustrating. The Union position was untenable. With-

The Battle of Missionary Ridge was one of the most dramatic and inexplicable moments of the Civil War. (Courtesy the Library of Congress)

drawal after having come this far at great cost was unthinkable, yet to advance seemed suicidal. General Sheridan, always flamboyant in his behavior, appeared on the scene in full-dress uniform, astride his black charger. According to Bruce Catton in *This Hallowed Ground* ". . . he sat on his horse looking up the forbidding slope and drew a silver flask from his pocket to take a drink. Far above him a confederate artillery commander standing amid his guns looked down at him and Sheridan airily waved the flask to offer a toast as he drank. The Confederate signaled to his gun crews, and his battery fired a salvo in reply; it was a near miss, kicking up dirt and gravel and spattering Sheridan's gay uniform. Sheridan's face darkened; he growled, 'I'll take those guns for that!' and he moved his horse forward calling out to the men near him. . . . Then as if in response to one command, the whole army surged forward, scrambled up out of the captured trenches and began to move up Missionary Ridge."

Sheridan rode Rienzi up the face of the ridge in spite of "the terrible fire of musketry pouring over us from the guns on the crest." At the summit he was urged to dismount for the sake of his safety, for on horseback he presented too prominent a target.

The unauthorized attack cut Bragg's defensive position and demoralized the troops. The Confederates ran down the opposite side of the mountain in wild, disorganized retreat. The charge was one of the bloodiest engagements of the war. Sheridan described the conduct of his men as heroic.

One of the North's greatest victories was the defeat and destruction of General Jubal Early's forces in the Shenandoah Valley of Virginia. The campaign began in August of 1864, when Sheridan's cavalry began systematically destroying any supplies in the area which could not be consumed by his own army. Warehouses, graneries, barns and bridges were burned. Ordnance, military supplies and stores were either destroyed or reissued to the Union troops. 4,240 horses were captured. By August 20, Sheridan was able to

General Phil Sheridan on Rienzi during the Battle of Opequon. From James E. Taylor's Sketchbook. (Courtesy Western Reserve Historical Society)

Battle of Opequon. From a drawing by James E. Taylor. (Courtesy the Western Reserve Historical Soicety)

report, "I have destroyed everything that was eatable south of Winchester and they will have to haul supplies from well up to Staunton."

Sheridan's campaign in the Shenandoah was every bit as ruthless as Sherman's March in Georgia from Atlanta to the sea. He explained his theory of total war, "As war is a punishment, and death is the maximum punishment, if we can, by reducing its advocates to poverty, end it quicker, we are on the side of humanity."

The first major encounter between Sheridan and Early occurred on September 19 on the Winchester to Berryville Road near Opequon Creek. The day began badly for the Yankees; their first attack was repulsed and for awhile the tide of battle flowed in favor of the Rebels. Catton, again, describes the scene: "But Sheridan was all over the field in person, riding at a pelting gallop on his big black horse, his hat gripped in one hand and his starred battle flag in the other; he reorganized his lines, brought up his reinforcements, and

Miss Griffiths, and Jennie and Susie Meredith greet Generals Crook and Sheridan after Battle of Opequon. From James E. Taylor's Sketchbook. (Courtesy Western Reserve Historical Society)

at last drove home an irresistable charge, a whole division of mounted cavalry shearing in behind the Confederate flank, every man in action . . ." The hard riding Yankees, which included the famous 1st Vermont Cavalry, entirely mounted on their homebred Morgans, overran Early's position with sabre and pistol and forced them to retreat through Winchester, which was captured.

Sheridan described the clash as "a most stubborn and sanguinary engagement," which lasted from dawn until 5:00 P.M. It was the Union's first victory in the valley. Following the Battle of Opequon, Sheridan received congratulatory messages from President Lincoln, General Meade, with whom he

Sheridan's ride as depicted in an engraving by William Sartain after a painting by Christian Schussele, published in 1868 by Bradley and Company, Philadelphia. (Courtesy Chicago Historical Society)

Another version of Sheridan's ride: an aquarelle facsimile print by Prang, Boston, 1886. After a painting by Thur de Thulstrup. (Notice that the general is beardless and without his overcoat in this version.) (Courtesy Chicago Historical Society)

Rienzi awaits his master, General Sheridan, at dawn on the day of his famous ride. From "Sheridan's Ride," by Thomas Buchanan Reed. (Courtesy the Western Reserve Historical Society)

had frequently quarreled over policy, General Grant, and Secretary of War Stanton. At Washington, a 100-gun salute was fired in honor of the victory.

There were various minor skirmishes up and down the valley for a month, including the battle of Fisher's Hill, until the final decisive battle.

At 5:00 A.M. on October 19, the Confederates launched a surprise attack on Sheridan's troops, who were in a defensive position along Cedar Creek, about 20 miles from Winchester. Sheridan had been called to Washington for a conference. On his way to rejoin his forces he stopped for the night in Winchester, which was held by the Union. He was restless and slept badly. He arose early and with his escort mounted and rode off. As the men passed through the streets of Winchester, the women shook their skirts at them and made other derisive gestures. The General could hear the sound of distant artillery, which grew rapidly more distinct. On the road he found his men

"We must face the other way, boys!" From a drawing by James E. Taylor. (Courtesy Western Reserve Historical Society)

demoralized and in retreat. 1,300 men had been taken prisoner and 18 field pieces had been lost. Galloping to the scene of confusion, he cried out to his men, "We must face the other way!" This became a rallying cry. "We are going to lick them out of their boots," he told them. "Every mounted officer who saw me galloped out on either side of the pike to tell the men at a distance that I had come back. . ." The troops regrouped around their leader and his high-headed black horse. "My whole line as far as the eye could see was driving everything before it."

Before the day was over the Union troops had routed the enemy and captured 23 of their guns, in addition to recapturing their own abandoned guns and baggage. "The disaster was converted to a splendid victory." Rienzi had covered at least 75 miles during the long day. Sheridan's famous 20-mile ride to rejoin his men was immortalized by Thomas Buchanan Reed. Set to music by David A. Warden, it was a popular ballad of the time.

Following the Battle of Cedar Creek, the Confederates were pursued to

Wounded soldier recognizes Sheridan and waves encouragement. From James Taylor's sketchbook. (Courtesy Western Reserve Historical Society)

". . . the men rose from behind the barricades with cheers of recognition." Sheridan quoted in Taylor's Sketchbook. (Courtesy Western Reserve Historical Society)

"Now the big Black, White fetlocked 'Rienzi,' bearing the General, thunders by like a whirlwind. . . ." From James Taylor's Sketchbook. (Courtesy Western Reserve Historical Society)

Waynesboro, where they again sustained heavy losses of men and artillery. Although Early escaped, the remainder of his men disappeared and all organized resistance in the Valley came to an end.

In the spring of 1865, in spite of heavy rain and deep mud, which made the mountain roads almost impassible, Sheridan's hardy cavalry pushed on toward Charlottesville, continuing their mission of destruction. They had orders to destroy the Virginia Central Railroad, the James River Canal and to capture Lynchburg. The canal was destroyed, bridges and trestles blown up, track torn up, and canal boats burned. Military equipment, stores, ordnance and clothing were either destroyed or confiscated. Sheridan's cavalry took part in the final skirmishing in Virginia and were present at the surrender at Appamatox Court House. "It came to an end at last on Palm Sunday, April 9, 1865, when Sheridan and his cavalry and a whole corps of infantry got squarely across the road in Lee's front . . . the last long mile had been paced off. . . . There was a spatter of fighting as his advance guard tried the Yankee line to see if it could be broken. It could not." This is how Catton describes the final action of the Civil War.

Apparently, Rienzi had a charmed life, for although he was in many battles and was wounded in several, he carried his master through the final engagement of the war. He lived to be nineteen and was "attended to the last with all the care due the faithful service he had rendered." After his death, his hide was stuffed and displayed in the Smithsonian Institution, where the sun

Rienzi on exhibit in Smithsonian Institution. The hide was mounted green in 1879, so the taxidermy leaves something to be desired. (Courtesy of Smithsonian)

Battle of Cedar Creek. (Courtesy the Library of Congress)

faded his hair from glossy black to a dull yellow. General Lee's gray war horse, Traveller, suffered a similar indignity. Both his skeleton and hide were on display at Washington and Lee College where it was a fad for the students to autograph his bones!

Pink

In the Union Army, certain troops were superbly mounted. It was common practice for a sponsor to buy special horses, sometimes matched as to color, and then be reimbursed by the quartermaster at the going rate for remounts which ranged from $90 to $175. One such special troop was H Company of the 5th New York Cavalry recruited and commanded by Lt. Colonel John Hammond of Crown Point, Essex County, New York. Their mounts were all Morgans hand-picked and paid for by the Colonel's father, a breeder of fine horses, who underwrote the entire extra expense above the government allowance out of his own pocket. The 108 bays, blacks and chestnut horses, were a splendid group, and all were descended from Hill's Black Hawk. They were selected in Essex County, except for a few which came from across Lake Champlain, in Vermont. Every horse was examined and approved by John Hammond. Of the 108, only seven survived the slaughter, including Pink, the Colonel's personal mount. Purchased as a five year old, he survived 88 skirmishes and 34 major battles, including Winchester, and the Wilderness, and lived to the ripe old age of thirty. He was a grandson of Hill's Black Hawk, the eighteenth foal from a Hambletonian mare, dam of Katie Taft, owned by Commodore Vanderbilt.

General Hammond was high in his praise of his troop's Morgans. They often kept their place in ranks after their riders had been shot from the saddle. "In charging infantry, he will thunder straight at a man and knock him down." The hardships were very great and many horses dropped of exhaustion and were destroyed so that they would not fall into enemy hands. In a letter to his wife and children, Colonel Hammond described how they had arrived at Culpepper, Virginia, after a forced march of six days. For three and one-half days the horses were not unsaddled and no rations had been issued during the entire march. Pink was in sorry condition, sore-backed and sort-footed.

When the war was over, Pink went home to Essex County with his owner. At his death, a 12-foot-high granite marker was placed over his grave with the inscription:

THIS HORSE CARRIED HIS MASTER 25 YEARS AND WAS NEVER KNOWN TO SHOW FATIGUE, WHILE OTHER HORSES OF CAVALRY AND FLYING ARTILLERY WERE DYING FROM WANT OF FOOD AND EXHAUSTION.

Colonel John Hammond personally selected the Morgans used by "H" Company of the 5th New York Cavalry. (Photo courtesy of the Penfield Museum, Ironville, New York)

Pink, Colonel Hammond's personal mount, is buried under a monument near Crown Point, New York. (Courtesy of the Penfield Museum)

Major Eugene Hayward's Mink, by Othello by Black Hawk, was unbroken when selected for the company, but she soon developed into an outstanding military horse. Her owner wrote, "I had not at that time nor have I yet, seen the horse that would carry a man with such ease mile after mile, day after day, summer's heat or winter's cold, plenty of oats or none at all, a slow march or a fast one. . . . A twine string would guide her and while she would go anywhere she was reined, she was as wise in battle as a General and as full of fire as the canon." She was ridden in over 70 engagements. "She was never still a moment while under fire, and she always knew whether she was going towards the enemy or from him. She was famous as a jumper in the line of duty and many who would out jump her in camp refused to follow her over fences on the skirmish line."

Major Hayward once rode Mink 75 miles in one day. In the bitter Battle of the Wilderness she went without feed for three days. "She never failed me," he wrote. Mink survived the war, bore two foals and moved with her master to Davenport, Iowa, where she died of colic brought on by over eating oats.

The 5th New York and 1st Vermont Cavalry regiments serving under General Custer saw bitter fighting in the Battle of the Wilderness. (Courtesy the Library of Congress)

Billy (Hard Road by Black Hawk–Telegraph) was Colonel James A. Penfield's war horse. He survived the war, although wounded at Gettysburg, and lived to be thirty-two. (Courtesy the Penfield Museum)

Another H Company survivor was Colonel James A. Penfield's Billy. Sired by Hard Road by Black Hawk, he lived to be thirty-two.

Lieutenant Barker's Prince, raised by C. F. Hammond "had wonderful endurance and could carry a heavy load." In a clash with Mosby's raiders, his twenty-one-year-old rider charged a Rebel canon. They were peppered with grape shot, and both wounded, although the gun crew fled before the Yankee officer's sabre, after he had fired all the rounds from his pistol. Prince, with four balls in his chest, was mortally wounded and died a month later.

Sheridan's cavalry increased in efficiency, and after the bloody Battle of the Wilderness he wrote, "The enemy's cavalry was superior to ours in numbers; but the *esprit* of our men increased every day while that of the enemy diminished."

Also under Sheridan's command was the 1st Vermont Cavalry which he

Rush's Lancers were mounted on horses of Morgan type. (*From Annals of the Sixth Penn-sylvania Cavalry;* courtesy the Historical Society of Pennsylvania)

praised highly as being among the best. They were mounted entirely upon Morgans.

George Austin, who assisted the Quartermaster in selecting horses for the regiment, said that they were the finest horses in the entire Union Army and outworked and outlasted all others. Eleven hundred Morgans were procured in Northeast Vermont and in the counties in New Hampshire along the Connecticut River.

Of 55,000 horses in Vermont at the start of the war, 10,000 had been taken for Army use by September of 1862, according to a contemporary news item in the Rutland *Herald*. In *Vermont in the Civil War,* G. G. Benedict states that the horses "were between 15 and 16 hands high, as required by the government standard, and between five and nine years old, sound, well knit and serviceable, though as untrained as the men. They were originally assorted by colors, each company having horses of one color, but the vicissitudes of the service soon disturbed this arrangement, and the attempt to maintain any uniformity of color was abandoned."

The Vermont boys caused a sensation as they rode off to battle. According to the Newark, New Jersey, *Advertiser,* "The horses are small, compact and sinewy and evidently capable of great endurance. It was the general remark that so splendid a body of animals had never been seen together in this city." A Washington correspondent for the Boston *Journal* called the Vermont horses the best cavalry mount that had yet been seen in the capitol.

The 1st Vermont saw action in 75 battles, some of the bloodiest of the war, including Gettysburg, Cedar Creek, Cold Harbor, the Wilderness, the Shenandoah Campaign and the final action at Appomattox Courthouse. Throughout the war they performed with distinction.

Of the 1,100 Morgans which left Vermont only 200 lived through the war. A few were taken back to their home state. Official reports made to the War Department stated that the Vermont Morgans were better able to withstand the hardships of war than any other horses. Reese says that, "Their short, strong legs, round, full-muscled bodies, and beautiful heads called forth universal admiration. Hardiness and endurance always have been and continue to be the prime essentials of a cavalry horse, and it is doubtful whether any breed excels the Morgan in the proper combination of all the characteristics demanded in such a horse."

Little Sorrel

Many officers and men in both armies rode Morgans. Their courage, hardiness and ability to live off the land if necessary made them ideal military horses. The distinguished stallion Napolean (Massilon Morgan), by Flint Morgan by Sherman out of a mare by Cock of the Rock, had a long career at stud both in his native New Hampshire and in Ohio where he won the sweepstakes and first premium for blood-horses at the 1852 State Fair before being taken to Memphis, Tennessee. When last heard of he was carrying an officer in the Confederate Army into battle when well into his twenties.

Ill-fated Stonewall Jackson's favorite mount was Little Sorrel, also called Fancy, a Morgan, so thrifty it was said he could exist on a diet of corn cobs.

The little chestnut gelding had been captured at Harper's Ferry in a trainload of supplies bound for Union troops stationed near Washington. Henry Kyd Davis in *I Rode With Stonewall* described Little Sorrel as, "stocky and well made, close coupled, good shoulder, excellent legs and feet, not fourteen hands high, of boundless endurance, good appetite. . . ." Apparently the pony's only shortcoming was a rather large, plain head. General Jackson ". . . never rode another one in battle. The endurance of the little animal was marvelous

General Jackson's Little Sorrel was a Morgan, captured at Harper's Ferry. (From a painting by Elder, "Heroes of the Valley: Jackson, Ewell, and Ashby." Courtesy Chicago Historical Society)

. . . he never seemed to change in looks or condition . . . he could eat a ton of hay or live on cobs."

Jackson was riding Little Sorrel during the tragic confusion at Chancellorsville. In the woods and gathering darkness he was fired upon by his own men and fell from the saddle, mortally wounded. Little Sorrel bolted toward the Union lines where he was captured. Later he was recaptured and sent to Mrs. Jackson at her home in North Carolina. He lived out his days — to twenty-two or twenty-three years — as a pensioner at the Virginia Military Institute in Lexington, and, later, at the Confederate Soldier's Home in Richmond. In his old age he was called Old Sorrel. Douglas S. Freeman wrote of him, "His skill in letting down draw-bars with his teeth was amazing. In the same way he could take rails off a fence until it was low enough for him to jump. Worse still, he learned how to remove the peg from the stable door hasp and daily, unless watched, he would go to the stables, release all the other horses and then lead them one behind the other into pleasant pastures."

After the American Civil War the use of cavalry steadily declined. It was

General Custer on a horse of Morgan type, passing John Brown's fort, Harper's Ferry on his way to the front. 1st Vermont and 5th New York Cavalry Regiments served under Custer. (From a drawing by James E. Taylor; courtesy the Western Reserve Historical Society)

"The Woodstock Races": General Custer doffs his hat to the Confederate forces before a cavalry charge that pursued the rebels for 26 miles. (From a drawing by Taylor; courtesy the Western Reserve Historical Society)

the last great conflict in which the United States Cavalry forces were used primarily for offensive purposes. Greatly improved artillery and the breech-loading rifle which increased the infantryman's fire power immeasurably made the offensive use of cavalry too costly to continue.

Even in the Civil War the losses had been staggering. The Federal Army alone required more than 500 horses a day to replace the casualties. The Army of the Potomac, during the first three quarters of 1864, used up an average of two remounts per man, or an estimated 40,000 horses.

The last successful massed cavalry charge took place during the Franco-Prussian War at the cost of appalling losses. Opposing foot soldiers with fast-loading rifles simply held their ground and mowed down the advancing horse troops at close range, until they were overrun.

In World War I cavalry was used only sporadically. A squadron of the American 2nd Cavalry fought in the Saint Mihiel and Meuse-Argonne operations. The cavalry's greatest asset had been its mobility, its element of surprise featuring quick raids and rapid withdrawals. Its tactical effectiveness was in pursuing and destroying retreating enemy forces. Strategically, it was used in scouting out enemy positions, as "the eyes of the infantry." Although there were a million cavalry men in Europe in 1916, the conditions of that war pointed up the impracticality of their use, for the enemy was not scattered but entrenched. Millions of American horses — Morgans included — saw action as the motive power for artillery, ambulances, ordnance and supplies.

Civil War Poster. (Courtesy Chicago Historical Society)

Because of the enormous demand for artillery horses, cavalry mounts were quickly converted to this use. In many areas the mud made vehicular travel impossible. Horses were not only used to drag the guns into position, they were also required to pack the ammunition from the depot to the emplacement in order to supply the weapons. The effectiveness of the artillery depended greatly upon the horses' steadiness under fire. The pack animals supplying the artillery suffered terribly. Ruts in the muddy roads were often two feet deep, and the animals were weighted to capacity. Because of the harsh conditions, thousands died of exhaustion.

The Army Horse Breeding Program

The Remount Service, a branch of the Quartermaster Corps, was charged with the purchase of military horses and the supervision of the Army's horse breeding plan. One of its functions was to procure animals suited for use as cavalry mounts from breeders and dealers. The animals were received, conditioned and issued by the personnel at the Remount Depots. The depot also carried on a limited amount of breeding, both to produce superior animals for special purposes (Olympic competition, for instance) which could not have been purchased for the modest price limit set by the Quartermaster Corps, and also to instruct remount personnel in stud-farm management so they, in turn, could supervise and instruct civilian agents in breeding procedures. New stallions were tested for fertility at the depots before being placed with agents.

Except for parade and ceremonial purposes the Remount Service did not purchase white or gray horses. They presented too conspicuous a target in battle, easily seen even in faint light. With few exceptions this practice was also followed by the United States Morgan Horse Farm and probably accounts for the decline in number of gray Morgans.

A plan to encourage farmers in certain localities to increase light-horse production by offering them the use of superior stallions at a nominal fee was begun in 1913. For several years, light-horse production in the United States had declined and the War Department was concerned at the diminishing supply of potential military horses. The project was assigned to the Department of Agriculture, in cooperation with the War Department. The plan consisted primarily of placing selected stallions with civilian agents. The government purchased only outstanding individuals, registered in a recognized stud book. They were picked for soundness and for conformation to saddle or artillery type. Any stallion that failed to get high-quality offspring or to settle a reasonable percentage of mares was castrated.

Under the terms of the breeding agreement, the mare's owner gave the government an option to purchase the resulting colt at the age of three for a price of $150. In the event of a sale, no stud fee was charged. If the mare's owner wished to be released from the option, a fee of $25 was then owing, but if the colt was purchased, or if the colt was offered for sale to the government and rejected, no fee was charged. The breeder was charged no fee for foals that were deformed or seriously injured, or that died. Breeders were permitted to retain fillies for breeding purposes without paying the stud fee. Stallions were rotated every four years, so that the fillies bred from the original stallion might be bred to another remount stallion of similar type to permit a system of upgrading. Mares which had certain unsoundness — bone spavin, ringbone, heaves, stringhalt, roaring, periodic opthalmia, and other types of blindness — which were thought to have an hereditary basis were not accepted for breeding to the Government stallions.

In the original group of stallions purchased for the Army Horse Breeding program were the Morgans Daniel Webster Lambert (Lambert B.–Aggie), Madison Lambert (Lambert B.–Jessie T.) and Donlyn (Donald–Mare by Billy), which was later purchased by Issa Tanimura for the Japanese Emperor's stud. At a later date, five more Morgans from the United States Morgan Horse Farm were added to the program. They were Bennington (General Gates–Mrs. Culvers), Castor (General Gates–Babe by Bob Morgan), Red Oak (General Gates–Marguerite), Snoqualmie (Troubadour–Sarah) and Troubadour of Willowmoor (Troubadour–Mare by Bob Morgan).

Other Morgan stallions that saw service with the Remount were Dewey (General Gates–Mrs. Culvers by Harrison Chief), Magistrate (Sealskin–Folly by Bennington), Melvin (Scotland–Sunflower Maid by Headlight Morgan), Langley (Hugo–Eudora by General Gates), Meredith (Sealskin–Helen Gates by General Gates), Oakwood (Troubadour of Willowmoor–Folly by Bennington), Orient (Troubadour of Willowmoor–Gertrude by General Gates), Page (Troubadour of Willowmoor–Dewdrop by General Gates), Scotland (General Gates–Highland Mary by Lambert Chief) and Linsley (General Gates–Sunflower Maid by Headlight Morgan). The agent who leased Linsley requested permission to show him at the 1921 Kansas State Fair. He won the Morgan class and his enthusiastic attendant telegraphed the War Department that the "Kansas State Fair considers him the finest Morgan Horse in all America."

The first three seasons of the program produced 3,089 foals, of which 174 were purchased by the War Department, while 111 fillies were retained by their owners. Many of the rejected colts were turned down for being undersized or of an undesirable color.

Civilian agents to whom the government stallions were loaned had first to pass inspection to make certain that they had the proper facilities for carrying on a horse-breeding operation. The stallions could be used without fee upon the agent's own mares. Hawk Jim (Linsley–Lady Spar) was leased to Merle Evans of Massilon, Ohio, whose herd of registered Morgans is now the world's largest.

For years the Remount Service wavered between Morgan and Thoroughbred, but finally — desiring a larger, faster horse — decided overwhelmingly

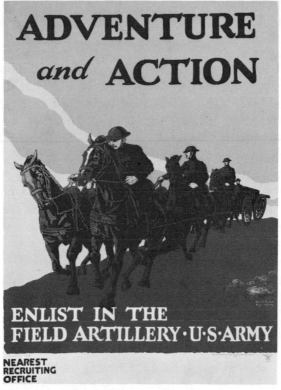

World War I Recruiting poster. Many horses of Morgan breeding saw action in France with the Artillery. (Courtesy Chicago Historical Society)

Bennington with the Remount Service. (Courtesy Department of Agriculture)

Three-year-old colt sired by government stallion. (Courtesy Department of Agriculture)

on the latter. In 1939 there were 644 Thoroughbred stallions at stud — at the Depots at Front Royal, Fort Reno, Fort Robinson and Pomona — or placed with civilian agents; by comparison there were only 18 Morgans. In 1943 the figures were 569 Thoroughbreds to 11 Morgans. It has been said, however, that the Remount Service was a home for unwanted Thoroughbreds, which through an excess of optimism had been left entire, yet whose record on the turf had not earned them a chance at stud in the highly competitive field of breeding for racing. In spite of its vacillation, the United States Government retained an active interest in breeding Morgans as late as 1940 when the stallion Haven (Delmont–Topaz) was transferred by Earl B. Krantz to the Remount Service.

All active cavalry units were mechanized early in World War II and converted to armored units, recon or mechanized infantry. Mounted troops last saw action in the Bataan Campaign when the 26th Cavalry Regiment (The Philippine Scouts) was annihilated by the Japanese.

In 1949 all remaining cavalry horses were sold, except those over seventeen years of age; they were retired to Fort Riley, Kansas, to live out their days. As of 1966, there is one survivor, Chief, a thirty-four-year-old gelding, in excellent condition in spite of his advanced age. At Fort Meyer, which adjoins the Arlington National Ceremony, 27 black and gray horses are maintained for pulling the caissons in military funerals. They are used on the average of twice daily.

With the dispersal of the United States Cavalry horses, a long and colorful tradition came to an end. While no one could mourn the passing of the use of horses as canon fodder, the Cavalry and its School had furnished the rest of the nation with high standards of horses, horsemanship and horsemastership. The body of knowledge — the skilled trainers, riders, instructors, stud grooms, farriers and highly trained horses — have almost completely disappeared from the scene. With the horse's sudden and dramatic return to popularity the gap is being sorely felt today.

14

The Register

IN ORDER TO ESTABLISH AND PRESERVE AN ACCURATE RECORD OF MORGAN breeding, Colonel Joseph Battell undertook the monumental task of compiling the first volume of the *Morgan Horse and Register*. Relying on the assumption that before an animal has itself produced progeny, the best guide to the sort of progeny it is likely to produce is an examination of its ancestors, Battell wished to have as complete as possible a record of the antecedents of the Morgan Horse.

The groundwork for the *Register* had already been laid by Linsley's premium essay on the breed which included the pedigrees of about 240 stallions — sons, grandsons and many of the great grandsons of the original Morgan Horse — as well as the probable origins of the foundation sire. Although Battell discovered a few inaccuracies and discrepancies in Linsley's work, including the charming tale of the two-year-old castoff, in the main he found him to be a reliable guide.

Active work for the *Register* was begun in 1884. The project was advertised in various agricultural journals. Readers were asked to submit the backgrounds of their Morgans insofar as they were known. Response was immediate and material began to flow in from all over the country.

Colonel Battell was uniquely qualified for the task to which he had set himself. He was a man of great means with the necessary leisure time and funds to carry the project through to the end. He also was a person of extraordinary drive, determination and selflessness. He pursued each clue, examining it with the most meticulous care to leave no detail uncovered. Nearly a hundred thousand letters were written. He personally visited most of the states — some of them more than once — and made numerous trips to the provinces of Canada adjacent to New England. He also went to Mexico.

"Neither trouble nor expense was spared to learn all the pertinent facts concerning every pedigree." Battell held thousands of conversations with old timers, listening to their often divergent recollections of early Morgans. He poured through old newspapers, farm journals and tax records to pinpoint exact dates on which a particular stallion had stood at a certain inn or tavern or livery stable. Scrupulously honest as well as painstaking, Battell set down as fact only what he had checked and proven to his own high standard of authenticity. Whatever he was unable to ascertain exactly, he qualified with the phrase "said to be." Material of doubtful authenticity was discarded, but occasionally, in his enthusiasm and desire to include every outstanding road horse of the day, he attributed Morgan blood to some horses whose background he was not able to verify. He allowed himself to jump to a few unjustifiable conclusions on scanty evidence and wishful thinking. Examples of this are the pedigree he ascribes to True Briton and the inclusion of the following doubtful sires in the Register: Copperbottom 66, Tom Hal 31, Pilot 104, St. Clair 48, Davy Crockett 603, Engineer 300, European 361, Columbus 1156, Tecumseh 811, Tom Thumb 875, Corbeau 3463 and Hamiltonian (Andrus) 6298. These occasional lapses should in no way detract from the worth of the volume.

The rule was established that any meritorious stallion which traced in direct male line to Justin Morgan and which carried as much as 1/64 of his blood would be eligible for inclusion in the *Morgan Horse and Register*. Because of the fact that very little attempt had been made to keep records of Morgan pedigrees prior to Battell's efforts, it was considered probable that a horse strongly Morgan in type carried numerous unrecorded crosses of the blood, especially if he derived from a Morgan region. Further, colts which were kept entire had been chosen as stallions because they showed breed character to a marked degree. The right was reserved, however, to reject any and all animals not regarded as meritorious.

W. H. Bliss, a Middlebury lawyer, worked closely with Battell on the project which covered eight years of the most careful research. The result was a 995-page tome, profusely illustrated with engravings, paintings and photographs. Pedigrees and detailed descriptions of thousands of horses were given. For notable horses, a complete life history, including the name of his breeder, every owner, and each crossroads at which the horse's services had been available were included. Trotting records and other achievements were listed, along with copious quotations from letters, posters, advertisements, newspaper articles, poems and eyewitness accounts. There were listings of trotters of record sired by the horse, their best times and the number of races won. In some instances the material on a single famous horse filled many pages.

Because of its sheer bulk and all-inclusiveness, Volume I of the *Register* is somewhat unwieldy. Horses are arranged by line of descent rather than alphabetically or chronologically, which makes it difficult to locate a particular individual.

In 1905, Volume II of the *Register* appeared. It included all the horses in Volume I, plus quite a few additional old-time horses, about which information had been received since the original publication. The Vermont Morgan Horse Breeder's Association had adapted a rule that admitted to registration all animals tracing through the dam to Justin Morgan and having 1/32 of the blood. These, too, were listed in the new book. Horses with both sire and dam in the *Register* were automatically eligible for registration.

Joseph Battell died on January 23, 1915, shortly before the publication of Volume III; he had been in failing health for some time. His death at 75 was attributed to the combined effects of overwork and the infirmities of old age. He left his considerable estate, including the *Morgan Horse and Register,* to Middlebury College which had carried out the issuing of Volume III — the major portion of which Battell had completed before his death.

The Morgan Horse lost a devoted friend with the death of Joseph Battell. His lifelong devotion to the breed saved it from oblivion. His enthusiasm was no empty thing, but was backed by the most persistent tenacity. No expense was too great in carrying out what he believed in, and his generosity was as great as his perseverence. He bought huge tracts of land to prevent their being despoiled by ruthless lumbering. He bequeathed over 30,000 acres of forests to Middlebury College, which he had attended. He also gave 500 acres of land, with extensive farm buildings, to the United States Government for the establishment of a Morgan Horse Farm.

In addition to the *Morgan Horse and Register,* Colonel Battell also published a five-volume work entitled *The American Stallion Roster, Including All Stallions Prominent in the Breeding of the American Roadster, Trotter, and Pacer.*

In Volume III of the *Morgan Horse and Register* all horses registered to date were listed in alphabetical order, a great convenience in locating a specific horse. Animals from the earlier volumes carried page references indicating where detailed material concerning them could be found; where new information had come to light, it was included. Numbers were assigned to each stallion, with "1" going to Justin Morgan, a fraction, in parentheses, followed the horse's name indicating the approximate percentage of the foundation sire's blood he carried, and a number in brackets showing the rule under which he had been admitted to the Register. For instance:

"BILLY ROOT (3-8), 9, [I.] Vol. I., p. 291 and Vol. II., p. 25."

AMERICAN MORGAN HORSE REGISTER

REGISTRATION CERTIFICATE

THE MORGAN HORSE
•The pride and product of America

This Certifies that the Morgan STALLION

Named LIPPITT MORO ALERT *No.* 11588 *Foaled* June 10, 1954

Color Chestnut *Marked* Prolonged star, snip, left hind pastern white.

Bred by ROYAL W. KNIGHT
NATICK FARM

Address 486 EAST AVENUE, WARWICK, RHODE ISLAND

SIRE LIPPITT ROB ROY No. 8450 *14,611 %*	**Sire** LIPPITT SAM 1532 No. 7857	SIRE ASHBROOK 14.625 NO. 7079	SIRE CROYDON PRINCE 5325	A	14.648
			NANCY 03553	B	14.721 %
		DAM LIPPITT SALLIE 16.027 NO 04565	SIRE BILLY HOFFMAN 6043	C	19.091 %
			DAM MARY ALLEN 03443	D	12.963
	DAM ADELINE BUNDY 13.867 No. 04584	SIRE ROB ROY 12.958 NO. 4483	SIRE ETHAN ALLEN 2d 406	E	13.671
			DAM Chestnut by Starlight	F	12.304
		DAM ROSE OF SUTTON 14.746 NO. 02232	SIRE BOB MORGAN 4549	G	14.453
			DAM Chestnut by son of STREETER HORSE JR. 675	H	15.034
DAM LIPPITT GLADYS MORO No. 05293 *14.687 %*	**Sire** LIPPITT MORO No. 7622 12.066	SIRE MORO 14.947 NO 7467	SIRE WELCOME 5702	I	15.441
			DAM POLLY ROGERS 02109	J	14.453
		DAM CROYDON MARY 9.785 NO. 02900	SRE CROYDON PRINCE 5325	K	14.648
			DAM Kate by Radway Horse	L	20.322
	DAM NE KOMIA No. 04489 16.912	SIRE ASHBROOK 14.685 NO. 7079	SIRE CROYDON PRINCE 5325	M	19.608
			DAM NANCY 03553	N	14.721
		DAM BRIDGET 19.140 NO. 02852	SIRE BOB MORGAN 4549	O	14.453
			DAM Chestnut by MOUNTAINEER 676	P	23.855

LIPPITT MORO ALERT 11588
14.650 %

is registered in the American Morgan Horse Register

Given under my hand and seal at New York, this
27th *day of* JULY *19 56*

_____
Registrar

High-percentage pedigree: percentages prepared by Dr. C. D. Parks. (Courtesy John D. Mahoney)

shows that Billy Root carried 37½ per cent of the blood of Justin Morgan, had the registration number 9, was admitted to the *Register* under Rule I, and that detailed information concerning his background and life history could be found in both earlier volumes.

On November 29, 1919, the administration of Middlebury College sold the *Morgan Horse and Register* to C. Chauncey Stillman, who had been secretary of the Morgan Horse Club since its organization in 1909. The name was changed to the *American Morgan Horse Register,* and it was incorporated according to the laws of the State of New York. An office was established at 3 East 44th Street in New York City and breeders were encouraged to register their Morgans. Mr. Stillman bore all expenses of maintaining the Registry and office.

In 1921 the new organization published Volume IV of the *Register,* listing new registrations made between 1915 and 1921. A table catalogued by number all Morgans registered up to that time. Mares and geldings were assigned numbers preceded by "0." Mares were given numbers on an alphabetical rather than a chronological basis from ABBIE 01 to ZODAK 02644, followed by a few miscellaneous names and then another series from ABBIE J. 02674 to ZULIKA 03872. This procedure was somewhat confusing, for a mare might have a lower registration number than either her first or second dam by virtue of her position in the alphabet. There was a great deal of duplication of names, with numerous Babes, Beauties, Belles, Helens, Julies, Kates, Mauds and Nellies. The Ladies were legion. For the first time transfers of ownership were recorded in a separate table, and there was also an index of owners.

On January 1, 1921 the following requirements for registration became effective:

RULE I: The produce of a sire and dam both registered in the American Morgan Horse Registry.

RULE II: To register any horse in the American Morgan Horse Register which is not the produce of a sire and dam both registered therein, application with full particulars should be made to the Executive Committee of the Morgan Horse Club . . . whose decisions will be final.

In the fall of 1926, Mr. Stillman died unexpectedly. His death coincided with a decline in breeding Morgans. The club had shrunk to 30 members, many of the earlier supporters having already died. Registrations had reached their lowest point.

Mr. Stillman's brother appealed to Charles A. Stone, president of the engineering firm of Stone & Webster — a long-time member of the Morgan Horse Club, and an owner and breeder of fine horses — for help in disposing of the *Register*. Mr. Stone agreed to help temporarily and all the assets of the *Register* were moved to his offices at 90 Broad Street. The temporary arrangement lasted rather longer than anticipated. The Stone family maintained the *Register* at their expense for over 30 years!

In his will, Mr. Stillman had provided that the stock and assets of the *Register* be offered to the Morgan Horse Club, which prior to that time had been an informal association of owners and breeders. Under Mr. Stone's direction, the Morgan Horse Club was incorporated according to the laws of the State of New York, enabling it, as a membership corporation, to accept and hold stock in the Register Corporation. Immediately upon its incorporation on October 13, 1927, the newly reorganized Morgan Horse Club, Inc. received the *Register* and its assets from the Stillman estate and the American Morgan Horse Register was dissolved.

In the tradition of Linsley and Battell, Charles Augustus Stone was another in the series of devoted admirers of the Morgan Horse, without whose extraordinary support the breed could not have survived. He had acquired his first Morgan while a student at the Massachusetts Institute of Technology in 1887. Later he bred Morgans both in New Hampshire and at Morven Stud near Charlottesville, Virginia.

Frank B. Hills, an expert in agriculture and animal husbandry, was employed by the Stone family as the manager of their estates for 35 years, during which time he devoted a large measure of his efforts to the Morgan Horse Club, Inc. He had a photographic memory for horses, faces and names and was thoroughly familiar with approved stud book procedures, having been employed for two years as assistant secretary of the American Guernsey Cattle Club. He supervised the registration of Morgans with scrupulous attention to detail during his tenure as breed secretary.

On the 150th anniversary of the birth of Justin Morgan, Volume V of the *Register* was issued by the recently reorganized Morgan Horse Club, Inc. The book's thinness reflected the low ebb to which annual registrations had fallen. For a long period, fewer than 100 horses were recorded each year. Volume V covered the eighteen-year period which had elapsed since Volume IV was issued and contained only about 2,000 names. It listed breeders and owners alphabetically with the registration numbers of Morgans owned or bred by them. For the first time animals admitted under Rule II were so designated by an "X" preceding their registration number.

During the lean years of the twenties and early thirties, the Morgan's continued existence was dependent upon the efforts of a mere handful of breeders. The largest of these was Richard Sellman of Rochelle, Texas. In a twenty-year period he registered 474 mares; many colts were not registered. Other principal breeders of the time were Elmer Brown of Halstead, Kansas; J. C. Brunk of Springfield, Illinois; Roland G. Hill, of the Horseshoe Cattle Company, Gustine, California; Robert Lippit Knight of Providence, Rhode Island; and the United States Department of Agriculture, both at the Vermont Farm and at the Miles City Experiment Station in Montana.

After this low ebb, there was a marked upswing in the number of Morgan registrations in the late thirties and forties. Volume VI, issued in 1949, was a noticeably fatter book than its immediate predecessor; although it covered only eight years it contained 3,200 registrations. As of January 28, 1937, a total of 12,984 Morgans had been recorded. The annual number of entries increased from an average of 100 or less prior to 1934 to nearly 700 in 1947. During the period covered by Volume VI the greatest growth in numbers took place in California.

A temporary setback followed the new high of 697 in 1947. According to Mr. Hills, as quoted in Kay's *The Horse,* this was due to an overly rapid buildup in California. "In the early days of the last World War, there was a lot of spare cash in the hands of what is known as the 'drugstore cowboy' group in California. A great many of them decided to buy a horse and a fancy saddle, and did. This created an artificial demand and stimulated breeding and registration of Morgans. When the cost of living caught up with these people, all of their horses with their expensive tack became surplus and the whole market collapsed, with the result that breeding was abandoned in many instances and registrations were sharply curtailed."

The reverse was temporary. With increased prosperity and greater leisure there was a general increase in interest in riding, reflected in accelerating light-horse production. Mr. Hills, who assembled and published Volumes V through VIII, had the satisfaction of seeing average annual registrations rise from less than 100 to more than 1,000 between 1926 and his death in 1961.

After the death of Charles A. Stone in 1941, his son Whitney Stone continued to maintain the *Register* at Stone & Webster's offices at 90 Broad Street. Whitney Stone is a lifelong active horseman who has shown and bred extensively. His annual consignment to the Saratoga Thoroughbred yearling sale is always one of the choicest offerings. In addition to being an officer and director of the Morgan Horse Club, Inc., he is or at one time has been, a member of the Jockey Club, a member of the Executive Committee of the American Horse Shows Association, and president of the United States Equestrian Team.

At last, with increasing interest and activity, the Morgan Horse Club, Inc. was on a sound and independent financial basis. Its offices were moved from

Pinto Morgan Stallion: Chief Paint (Chief Justin Morgan–Painted Girl by Warhawk). Horses with white marks above knees or hocks, except on face, are no longer eligible for registration as Morgans. Owned by Ab Cross, Du Bois, Wyoming. (Courtesy Aaron G. Olmstead)

Foal with natural white mark on body is not eligible for registration. (Robert A. Boyajian photo)

Foal with stocking extending above hocks and knees is not eligible for registration. (Robert A. Boyajian photo)

New York to West Hartford, Connecticut, with Seth Holcombe ably filling the job of secretary. In 1964, the Directors met in Denver and voted to set aside $125,000 in a trust fund to guarantee the *Register* for future generations.

Throughout the years, measures had been passed to tighten and restrict registration requirements.

Effective January 1, 1948: Only the progeny of a sire and dam both of which are already registered in the *American Morgan Horse Register* will be accepted for registration.

This amendment rescinded Rule II under which foals with only one registered parent could be registered. The "X" before a registration number became a thing of the past.

Effective April 7, 1962: No horse shall be eligible to registration which has a walleye (lack of pigmentation in the iris) or natural white markings above the knee or hock except on the face.

This rule was designed to exclude the registration of pintos, of which there are a scattering in the Registry due to recent outcrossings.

Effective January 1, 1963: No animal shall be eligible for registration which has passed the 3rd December 31st subsequent to the actual foaling date. That is: all animals must be registered by postmark on or before December 31st of their two year old year. All birthdays are computed on a January 1st basis in accordance with American Horse Show Requirement Rules.

It was further required that each and every transfer (change in ownership) must be recorded with the Morgan Horse Club, Inc. and be personally validated by the Registrar.

Effective July 1, 1962: It is the responsibility of the seller to complete *personally in full*, including the actual date of transfer and the name and address of the purchaser, each Application for Transfer. Provided, that where a horse is consigned at a regular auction sale, it shall be the duty of the sale manager to insert on Application of Transfer the complete name and address of the purchase including the actual date of transfer.

No one, therefore, can register a foal out of a mare unless he is her owner of record. These controls help curtail spurious registrations.

In 1965 a rule was passed that upon the death of an animal its registration certificate must be returned to the Morgan Horse Club, Inc.'s offices for cancellation, a measure to prevent the continued use of a horse's name on registration applications long after it has gone to greener pastures.

As in everything else, there have been fashions in naming horses. In the early days, horses customarily went by the name of their breeder or owner, as the Goss Horse, Fenton Horse, Hawkins Horse and Woodbury; or by its possible origin as the Old Dutch Horse, the Canadian Horse, or a location where the horse stood as Chelsea. Mares were known by their owners, as the Aldrich Mare or simply by their sires, as Mare by Sherman or Chestnut by Bob Morgan or Bay Mare by Ethan Allen 3rd. Often the sire's name was used as a sir name, a trend that has come down to modern times: Flora Eastman, Daisy Lambert, Lucie McDonald, Bessie Baker, Polly Forrest. Sometimes mares were simply given their sire's name, as was my grandfather's driving mare, Dandy Lambert, an elegant bay. Frequently, in a most confusing manner, sons were named for their sires, often without the benefit of "young," "second," or "junior." The names of famous horses were used repeatedly, with or without actual kinship. There are pages of Black Hawks — 171 horses in Volume III — Green Mountains and Ethan Allens.

At a later date, horses were given names that implied strength, boldness, or invincibility with a strongly masculine flavor. Tiger, Hawk, Highwayman, Lion, Eagle, Revenge were popular. Horses were also named after people, not necessarily an owner, but often an admired friend or national hero such as Ben Franklin, Ethan Allen, Henry Clay, Cassius M. Clay, General Sherman, General McClellan, General Scott, General Grant.

The era of romantic names, many of which would have suited gaited saddlers, was ushered in by Troubadour of Willowmoor. In the same tradition are Dawn of Wiltshire, Sealect of Windcrest, Upwey King Peavine, Becca Pepper of Willow Lane, Gay Maid of Wenloch, Black Hawk of Lone Pine, Jubilee de Jarnette, Flame of Sundown, Green Dream Lady Lee, Easter Twilight, Royalton Ashbrook Darling, and Kane's Spring Delite. At the other end of the scale are such appellations as Oh, Ugly, Jinx, Terror, Debt, Alkali, Rain in the Face, Free Legs, and Boo. The names of Western Morgans have a practical working ranch flavor — Yellow Dude, Zoro (and Zorro), Gay, Foxy, Jaquima W., Bar S Star, Stormy H, Redman and Spar K.

The modern trend is toward the addition of a prefix, which avoids duplication and serves as advertising for the ranch or farm which bred the horse. Upon application and payment of 25 dollars, a breeder can register a prefix for his future distinctive and exclusive use in naming Morgans foaled on his property. A name with a registered prefix cannot be changed and in showing, the full registered name must be used. Names are limited to 20 letters and spaces. Some famous Morgan prefixes are Lippit (Robert Lippit Knight), Devan (Merle D. Evans), Townshend (Mrs. Roger Ela), Windcrest (F. O.

Davis), U V M (Vermont Agricultural College) and Broadwall (Mr. and Mrs. J. Cecil Ferguson).

PREFIXES RESERVED AS OF FEBRUARY 23, 1966 FOR NAMING MORGAN HORSES FOR REGISTRATION

AA — Mr. and Mrs. Charles R. Adams, Westmoreland, N. H.

ACE HIGH — James Douglas, East Dixfield, Maine

ALBA — Mr. & Mrs. James D. Aley, Rt. 1, Hartstown, Penn.

ALDOT — Mr. & Mrs. Afred J. Martell, Box 265, Claremont, N. H.

ALEZAN — Hazel L. Wilbur, 145 N. Broad St., Norwich, N. Y.

ALLENDA — Mr. & Mrs. Charles R. Olsen, 3338 W. Orangewood, Phoenix, Ariz.

AMBER'S — Harold B. Stricker, 145 E. Mitchell Ave., Cincinnati, Ohio

AMBLESIDE — Mr. & Mrs. J. Warren Hale, 325 Arata La., Windsor, Calif.

ANNEIGH — Mrs. Ann L. Stedman (deceased), RFD 5, Box 196, Norwich, Conn.

APPLEVALE — Gordon Voorhis, Voorhis Farm, Red Hook, Dutchess Co., N. Y.

ASHLAND — Mr. & Mrs. Lawson W. Glidden, Box 87, Ashland, N. H.

ASHWINDS — Mr. & Mrs. M. D. McCarthy, Lake Whittemore Dr., Spencer, Mass.

AZUREWOOD — W. Dayton Keyes, Jr., Rt. 1, Raymond, Ill.

B & P — Mr. & Mrs. Paul J. Goeltz, Brook 'n Pine Farm, Morrisville, Vt.

BAR-T — Stephen P. Tompkins, Long Hill Road, Rowley, Mass.

BAYBERRY — Mr. & Mrs. Louis N. Hock, Allentown-Ellisdale Rd., Allentown, N. J.

BAYVIEW — Mrs. Charles I. White, Bay View Rd., Dover, N. H.

BECKRIDGE — Mr. & Mrs. Leo Beckley, Box 250, Mount Vernon, Wash.

BEN LOMOND — Mr. & Mrs. J. A. Shandrew & Family, Willard, Utah

BIG BEND — Mrs. William W. Barton, 1806 National Ave., Rockford, Ill.

BIRCH HILL — Dr. John C. Tate, 76 Birch Hill Rd., Agawam, Mass.

BLACKACRE — Mr. & Mrs. T. E. Pittenger, Peninsula, O.

BO'DOT — Mr. & Mrs. R. J. Milne, 821 164th S. W., Alderwood Manor, Wash.

BRIARWOOD — John P. Corley, M.D., Depot Rd., Colchester, Vermont

BRIDLESWEET — Parmley Harris, Mineral Point, Wisconsin

BRIDLE VALE — John & Anita Hoitsma, 871 Summit Ave., Franklin Lakes, N. J.

BROADWALL — Mr. & Mrs. J. Cecil Ferguson, Broadwall Farm, Greene, R. I.

BROOKWOOD — Mr. & Mrs. Norman Hodgkin, 4040 Kilmer St., Tucson, Ariz.

BRO-ROCK — Mr. & Mrs. David L. Brockett, Appleton Farms, Ipswich, Mass.

BURKLAND — Dr. & Mrs. S. Robert Orcutt, Main St., Rowley, Mass.

BURRWOOD — Ronald L. Mielke, Rt. 2, Box 29, Austin, Minn.

BUZZJACK'S — F. E. Schlimm, West Creek Rd., St. Mary's, Pa.

CAMBRIDGE — Edward T. Young, Jr., 2233 So. Jackson St., Denver, Colo.

CAMELOT — Thomas H. White, Jr., Rt. 1, Box 343, Fort Lauderdale, Fla.

CANTERBURY — Mr. & Mrs. Paul R. Reiss, RR 1, Box 363, Westfield, Ind.

CARIDEL — Mr. & Mrs. C. E. McLean, Route 1, Valleyford, Wash.

CAROUSEL — Russell J. Roe, 3606 Summitridge Dr., Doraville, Ga.

CATSKILL — Aubrey D. James, RD 1, Delhi, New York

CAVALIER — Dr. Ann E. Pressman, 238 Swigert Ave., Lexington, Ky.

CAVEN-GLO — Mrs. Larry Oakley, Caven-Glo Farm, 1301 W. Magnolia, Burbank, Cal.

CEDARCREST — Glenn Klapel, 31 Marquette Rd., Rockford, Illinois

CENTAUR — Mrs. Susan A. Tilton, 10563 Davis Rd., W. Manchester, Ohio

CHAFFIN'S — G. E. Chaffin, 1049 Maysville Ave., Zanesville, Ohio
CHAR-EL — Mr. & Mrs. Charles L. Akes, Rt. 3, Box 45A, Milton Freewater, Oregon
CHASLEY — Charles L. Rutherford, 1365 Government St., Mobile, Ala.
CIRCA'S — Dale Allen, 11 Marquis St., Granby, Quebec, Canada
CIRCLE H — Hunewill Land & Livestock Co., Bridgeport, Calif.
COLBROOK — Mr. & Mrs. Graham Bockus, Foster, Quebec, Canada
COLUMBINE — Mr. J. C. Connors, 2729 S. Broadway, Englewood, Colo.
CORINTHIAN — Mrs. Geraldine Hicks, Baer Creek Rd., Fairview, Penn.
COUNTRY — Mr. & Mrs. Robert A. Brunelle, Sunset Hill Rd., Thompson, Conn.
CRESTWOOD — Mr. Loren Bentley, Box 1228, Weed Heights, Nevada
CRISLAND — Walter R. Christensen, 5780 So. Lakeside Dr., Salt Lake City, Utah

DANE — Miss Anne Bentzen, Folly Farm, Woodstock, New York
DARTMOOR — Irene S. Gudewicz & George E. Grimshaw, E. Freetown, Mass.
DAWNCREST — Harold J. Allbee, RFD 1, Windsor, Vt.
DEE-CEE — Milford & Jane Fox, Rt. 1, Box 205, Middlefield, Ohio
DERBY — Paul R. Rexford, 16 School St., Newport, Vt.
DEVAN — Merle D. Evans, Massilon, Ohio
DICANNA — Mr. & Mrs. Richard Mathiot, RR 5, Box 57, Rockford, Illinois
DOVERDALE — W. Irving Dunn, West Dover, Vermont
DRUMCLIFFE — Dr. George F. Budd, 515 E. Ford St., Pittsburg, Kansas
DYBERRY — Dr. C. D. Parks, Bethany Rd., Honesdale, Penn.

ECHOBROOK — Harold A. Terry, 66 Central St., Randolph, Vt.
ECHO'S — Mr. & Mrs. Bill Dansby, Rt. 2, Box 29A, Galena, Mo.
ECO — Dr. Henry P. Boyd, 680 N. San Pedro Rd., San Rafael, Calif.
EEDAHOW — Mr. & Mrs. Edwin K. Buel, Box 96, Murtaugh, Idaho
EETHREE — Howard C. Eberline, Box 682, Santa Fe, New Mexico
E-JAY — Mr. & Mrs. John W. Jones, & Mr. & Mrs. Jack A. Emerson, Rt. 7, 4004 Leckron Rd., Modesto, Calif.
ELM CREST — Mr. & Mrs. George Feulner, 6800 West 3500 South, Salt Lake City, Utah
ELM HILL — Dr. Blanchard W. Means, Elm Hill Farm, Brookfield, Mass.
EMERALD'S — Mr. & Mrs. Orwin J. Osman, Box 613, Manteno, Illinois

FAIRLEE — Dr. William K. Woodard, 7000 Cutler N. E., Albuquerque, N. M.
FANFARE — Mr. & Mrs. William C. Haveran, Foote Rd., So. Glastonbury, Conn.
FWF — Mrs. Ruth H. Gay, & Mr. & Mrs. Whitney Haddock, Far Well Farm, Swanzey Center, N. H.
FIELDAY — Mr. & Mrs. J. Donald Foust & Family, RR 1, Plainville, Ind.
FIREPRIDE — Mr. & Mrs. Melvin H. Mandigo, Glover, Vermont
FLEETWOOD'S — Mrs. Earl W. MacMichael, Fleetwood Acres, Reeseville, Wis.
FLORABROOK — Mr. & Mrs. Irvin J. Flora, 8651 Troy Rd., #2, New Castle, Ohio
FLYING K — Kenneth R. Smith, Rt. 2, Box 29A, Galena, Mo.
FOLLY — W. Ronald Seay, RR 1, Grenville, Quebec, Canada
FORECAST — Mr. & Mrs. L. J. Schauer, 3128 Penny Creek Rd., Bothell, Wash.
FUNQUEST — Stuart G. Hazard, 1308 College Ave., Topeka, Kansas
FURBRUK — Mr. & Mrs. Frank D. Lathrop, Rt. 1, Pittsford, Vt.

GAYETIME — Miss Florence C. Williams, RFD 2, Box 132, Bedford, N. H.
GAYLYN — Dr. Charles P. Nelson, Madigan Lane, Harvard, Mass.
GEM — Mr. & Mrs. Gerald H. Moline, Rt. 1, Box 426, Fort Collins, Colo.

GIFT — O. C. Foster (deceased), 1330 S. Grand Ave., Los Angeles, Calif.

GLAMORGAN — Dr. Alden B. Starr, RD 2, Syracuse, New York

GRA-VAND — Albert H. Acken, Jr., 36 Northeast Ave., Tallmadge, Ohio

GREEN DREAM — Ralph D. Booth, Jr., Dover, N. H.

GREENGATES — Mr. & Mrs. Paul S. Osborne, RR 1, Box 486, Batavia, Ill.

GREEN MEADS — Mr. & Mrs. Darwin S. Morse, Green Meads Farm, Richmond, Mass.

GREEN TRIM'S — Mr. & Mrs. Adam Young, Webster Highway, Temple, N. H.

GREEN VALLEY — Alfred T. Gilman, 2002 Ranch Rd., Los Angeles, Calif.

H BAR — George A. Cross & Son, Dubois, Wyoming

HD-L — Edward H. Hopfensperger, Rt. 1, Fremont, Wisconsin

HEDLITE — Mrs. Mary H. Smith, 100 Pancho Rd., Camarillo, Calif.

HELICON — John H. Hamlin, RFD 2, Bennington, Vt.

HEL'S — Hugh H. Logan, Box 111, Glendale, Calif.

HERITAGE — Mrs. Urban V. Kerr, 6487 Town Line Rd., Rt. 2, Tonawanda, New York

HICKORY — Mr. & Mrs. Ben Malone, Rt. 1, Box 90, Fairburn, Ga.

HI-GAIT — Edward & Diane Kamis, 33 Farmcliff Dr., Glastonbury, Conn.

HIGHLAND — Clayton B. Conn, Walnut Hill, Chester, N. H.

HIGHOVER — Dr. & Mrs. Charles C. Thompson, New Durham, N. H.

HIGH PASTURES — Mrs. Harriet J. Hilts, RR 1, Box 220, Windsor, Vt.

HILLCREST — Mrs. Gardner Smith, Rt. 3, Box 538, Snohomish, Wash.

HILLTOP — Samuel W. Smith, Rt. 2, Box 221, Sandpoint, Idaho

HI MEDDO — Miss Linda L. Hall & Mrs. S. Souard, West Hill, Ludlow, Vt.

HI-MIST — Vernon E. Albert, RR 2, Box 274, Baraboo, Wisc.

HIP HEATH — Mr. & Mrs. J. G. Wolcott, Underhill Center, Vt.

HI-PRIDE — Mr. & Mrs. Ned Wilde, Box JJ, Arco, Idaho

HI-VALE — Mr. John Bennett, RFD 2, Killingly Ave., Putnam, Conn.

HI-WINDS — Mr. & Mrs. Walter R. Ford, RD 2, Claysville, Penn.

HLM — Mr. & Mrs. Henry L. Metzger, 445 Sand Run Rd., Akron, Ohio

HOBBY HORSE — Dr. George E. Taylor, 130 W. Main St., Cuba, N. Y.

HOLLANDIA — Jack Holland, Box 295, Fairburn, Georgia

HOLLYDALE — Mrs. Delvina B. Patterson, 9737 53rd Ave., College Park, Md., Mrs. Jacqueline P. Wilson, 9611 Glenn Dale Rd., Lanham, Md.

HOLZLAND — Howard A. Fohrhaltz, 580 Hancock Rd., Pittsfield, Mass.

HOOSIER — Mrs. Rachael & Miss Camille Centers, RR 2, Portland, Ind.

HORSESHOE — Robert J. Hudson, Horseshoe Farm, Chester, Vt.

HY CREST — Mr. & Mrs. Milo Measel & Mr. & Mrs. Richard Measel & Mr. & Mrs. John Measel, 8960 Hyne Rd., Brighton, Michigan

IMPALA — W. A. Lorenzen & Son, 8724 Hilmar Rd., Turlock, Calif.

INDIAN RUN — Harold E. Martin, Indian Run Farm, Exton, Chester Co., Pa.

IRIS FARM — Ross N. Coffin, Franconia, N. H.

IRONSTONE — Mr. & Mrs. Clifford Hitz, 15521 Minnetonka Blvd., Hopkins, Minn.

JEHU'S — Leroy Jehu, Portland, Penn.

J'S — R. T. Menuez, Box 16, Benton, Ohio

JUST-A-NOD — Mr. & Mrs. William O. Noble, RD 1, Dalton, Penn.

KAMROCK — Mr. & Mrs. Kenneth C. Smittle, E. 2001 Wellesley, Otis Orchards, Wash.

KANE'S — Walter & Rheda Kane, 22221 Pontiac Tr., So. Lyon, Mich.
K & E — Kirk & Erma Clarkson, K & E Morgan Farm, Applegate, Mich.
KASEY'S — Howard W. Kaseberg, Rt. 1, Box 689, Granite City, Ill.
KEDRON — Dr. Ina M. Richter, RR 4, Box 56, Bolivar, Mo.
KENNEBEC — Miss Margaret Gardiner, RFD 3, Wiscasset, Maine
KENNY B'S — Mr. & Mrs. Kenneth J. Bailey, 1850 Saltsburg Ave., Indiana, Pa.
KEYSTONE — E. Barclay Brauns & Rolf Eskil Families, Box 132, Wenatchee, Wash.
KULSHAN — Donald T. Anderson, 1716 Pease Rd., Burlington, Wash.

LARIGO — Mr. & Mrs. R. O. Schneider, Rt. 3, Deer Park, Wash.
LAURELMONT FARM — Mr. & Mrs. Donald C. MacMulkin & Family, Federal Hill
    Rd., Milford, N. H.
LEDGE HILL — Mr. & Mrs. Wm. E. Rogers, Marston Rd., Gardiner, Maine
LEDGLANS — Robert V. Olson, Box 684, Danielson, Conn.
LIBERTIE — Marita M. Clark, Box 231, Chappell, Nebraska
LIPPITT — Robert L. Knight (deceased), Box 542, Providence, R. I.
LONG HILL — Mrs. Harold M. Wilson, Long Hill Farm, Bolton, Mass.

MAD RIVER — Mr. & Mrs. Alfred C. Drowne & Mr. & Mrs. Gilbert E. Williams,
    Sandy Creek, New York
MAJO — Peter L. Wentz, 1 N. La Salle St., Chicago, Ill.
MAPLAIRE — Robert D. Anderson, Rt. 1, Box 82, Maple Plain, Minn.
MAPLE — Mr. & Mrs. Truman Pocklington, RR 2, Shipman, Inn.
MAR-LO — Mr. & Mrs. Milo Dugan, Rt. 2, Box 316, Loveland, Colo.
MARVIN'S — Ray L. Marvin, RFD 3, Littleton, N. H.
MAR WIN — Mr. & Mrs. Irwin Froman, 16625 Bovle, Fontana, Calif.
MATILIJA — Dr. & Mrs. John G. Bee, Box 817, Ojai, Calif.
MEADOWCREST — Mr. & Mrs. George E. Charlton, Box 70, Oshawa, Ontario,
    Canada
MEADOWBROOK — Hugh C. Smith, Box 151, China, Maine
MEADOWOOD — Jackson Kemper, 75 Meadowhill Rd., Barrington, Illinois
MEADOWROCK — Mrs. Doris V. Dem, Rt. 1, Box 107, Shepherdstown, W. Va.
MELDON — Erle M. Martin, St. Basile de Portneuf, Quebec, Canada
MELODY — George N. Brunk, 1929 Lowell Ave., Springfield, Ill.
MEREDITH — Mrs. Margaret van D. Rice, Rockbottom Lodge, Meredith, N. H.
MERRIEHILL — Mr. & Mrs. Martin Staehnke, Box 488, Winfield, Ill.
MERRY — Mabel Owen, Box 87, So. Dartmouth, Mass.
MIDNIGHT — Mr. & Mrs. Howard E. Splane, 1080 Kubli Rd., Grants Pass, Ore.
MILHOLM — J. Holman Waters, 5111 Cottonwood La., Salt Lake City, Utah
MILLONA — Mr. & Mrs. Millard M. Watson, 7120 N. Smith, Spokane, Wash.
MOHINI — Russ & Velma Loar, 1507 Jones Rd., R. 1, Richland, Wash.
MONARCH'S — Doris M. Laidlaw & Mrs. L. G. Lindsey, RD 2, Theresa, N. Y.
MON HEIR — Ira J. Cochran, Route 4, Walla Walla, Wash.
MORGANLANE — John L. Carter, Box 158, Atlantic Ave., North Hampton, N. H.
MORGAN LEGEND — Mr. & Mrs. Robert Rodricks, 875 King St., Chappaqua, N. Y.
MORO HILL'S — Mr. & Mrs. Chester Treftc, Big Lake, Cariboo, B. C., Canada
MORO'S — Miss Jean Cox, RFD 2, Box 184, Brewer, Maine
MORTANA — Jackson Morgan Horse Ranch, Harrison, Montana
MOUNTAIN MEADOW — Shirley Locke, West Brattleboro, Vt.

NATICK — Royal W. Knight, 486 East Avenue, Apponaug, R. I.
NEL-J — Mr. & Mrs. John C. Trushel, 822 Fox Ave., Paris, Ohio

OAKMOOR — Paul J. Birkmeier, Box 349, Delphos, Ohio
OAKRIDGE — Mrs. Marion E. Butts, 6449 Stanley Ave., Carmichael, Calif.
OAKWOOD — Richard N. Poux, 118 W. Main St., Titusville, Penna.
OCTOBER — Mr. & Mrs. James Cole, RFD 1, Box 468, Leesburg, Virginia
OLDTYME — Mr. & Mrs. Joseph M. Trudeau & Family, RR 1, 136th Ave., Wayland, Mich.
OLDWICK — Mr. & Mrs. Richard M. Colgate, Home Farm, Oldwick, N. J.
ORCLAND — Mr. & Mrs. W. Lyman Orcutt, Jr., & Family, Orcland Farms, W. Newbury, Mass.

PAMA — Major Donald L. Nichols, 1150 Parkinson Ave., Palo Alto, Calif.
PARK-LEA — Mr. & Mrs. Lloyd M. Parker, Marlboro Rd., Sudbury, Mass.
PEPPER (as suffix) — Mr. & Mrs. C. W. Rodee, 7 Aurora St., Moravia, New York
PETALBROOK — Philip W. Jackson, RD 1, Chelsea Rd., Wappingers Falls, N. Y.
PIANKESHAW — Charles A. Perkins (deceased), Piankeshaw Place, Hoopeston, Ill.
PIEDMONT, Hearst Organization, California
PILL PEDDLER — Dr. & Mrs. Eugene M. Holden, 14 Harrison Rd., Canton, Mass.
PINELAND — Joe L. Young, Box 522, LaGrange, Georgia
PINEVIEW — Frank L. Moore, 230 Pleasant St., E. Bridgewater, Mass.
PIONEER — Mr. & Mrs. Robert Zimmerly, Ridgefield, Washington
PORTLEDGE — Harold J. Allbee, RFD 1, Windsor, Vt.
PORVENIR — Wallace C. Bell, Porvenir Rt., Montezuma, New Mexico
POTHOOKS — Claude Goetz, Shepherd, Montana

RD'S — Mr. & Mrs. Ralph T. Danielson, Rt. 2, Box 115, Waitsburg, Wash.
RED CREST — Russell C. Jackson, 2700 N. Hayden Rd., Scottsville, Arizona
RED FOX — Robert Morgan, 15150 Via Colina, Saratoga, Calif.
REED'S — Everett A. Reed, 2025 Jamaica St., Aurora, Colo.
REX'S — Mrs. F. W. Waer, 18208 Modjeska Rd., Orange, Calif.
RIMROCK — Raymond W. Macy, 1230 W. 6th, Loveland, Colorado
RIO GRANDE — Mr. & Mrs. Hans J. Voss, 3851 B Alabama, Los Alamos, N. M.
RIVERBEND — Mr. & Mrs. Ken Berlekamp, Rt. 5, Fremont, Ohio
ROANOKE — Clayton A. Ewell, Roanoke Rd., Wyoming, N. Y.
ROBINHURST — Athur T. Winters, 306 Main St., Worcester, Mass.
ROCKLAND — Mr. & Mrs. Earl R. Herring, Box 471, Chico, Calif.
RO-MA — Jim Roe, 1529 Cedar Drive, Lorain, Ohio
ROSCREA — William G. Downey, Jr., Rt. 4, Box 260, Fairfax, Va.
ROVIRA'S — Barbara Rovira, Valley of Enchantment, Crestline, Calif.
ROYALTON — Dana Wingate Kelley, Justine Morgan Horse Farm, Woodstock, Vt.
R.R. — Mrs. Ayelien Richards, Box 172, Pine City, N. Y.
RU-LEE — Mr. & Mrs. Rodolphe H. Morais, South China, Maine

SADDLEBACK — Lawrence Appley, Saddleback Farm, Hamilton, N. Y.
SAN-KAYS — Mr. & Mrs. Clarence Richcy, 91 Williamson Rd., Greenville, Penn.
SHAKER — Mr. & Mrs. T. D. Ulrich, 225 W. Main St., Lebanon, Ohio
SHAR-LYNN — Mr. & Mrs. Joseph Kean, Mt. Lebanon St., Pepperell, Mass.
SHAWALLA — Mr. C. E. Shaw, Route 1, Box 286, Walla Walla, Wash.
SHERIMILLL — Vincent J. Rogers, RD 2, Martin Rd., Akron, N. Y.
SHERMAN'S — Mr. & Mrs. A. L. Sherman, 9143 Noble Ave., Sepulveda, Calif.
SINN FIEN — Dr. & Mrs. John J. O'Loughlin, 12 Shawandasse Rd., Waterford, Conn.
SKAGIT — Louise D. Bates, Rt. 2, Box 263, Arlington, Wash.

SKIPAREE — Robert Fowler, North Pownal, Vt.

SKYFIELD — Mr. & Mrs. Gerald Fahrni, Box 1141, Abbotsford, B. C., Canada

SKYLARK — Mr. & Mrs. Robert A. Peck, Sr. & Mr. & Mrs. Lewis W. Johnston, Elbridge, N. Y.

SPARFIELD — Patrick J. Dennison, Box 288, Halsey, Ore.

SPECIAL ACRES — Mr. & Mrs. W. E. Robinson, Bangor, Maine

SPENMAY — Mrs. Bryant O. Spencer, 44 Sunset Rd., Weston, Mass.

SPRINGBROOK FARM — Mr. Gerald F. Taft (deceased), 45518 W. 8 Mile Rd., Northville, Mich.

STAR CREST — Mr. & Mrs. Ralph L. Linton, Box 326, Plymouth St., N. Carver, Mass.

STARR B — Mr. & Mrs. Byard Bennett, Box 326, Escondido, Calif.

STIAHTA'S — Mr. & Mrs. Howard H. Browns & Family, RR 1, Greenwich, Ohio

STILLMEADOW'S — Mr. & Mrs. Warren W. Wagner, Rt. 1, Bedford, Ind.

STILLWATER — Peter J. Gaar, Salisbury, Conn.

SUNCREST — Arthur N. Peterson, 902 Foshay Tower, Minneapolis, Minn.

OF SUNDOWN (as suffix) — Mr. & Mrs. M. S. Maxey, Sundown Valley Ranch, Cholame, Calif.

SUNSET — Mr. & Mrs. Norman Dock, RD 1, Bethel, Maine

SUNUP — Mr. & Mrs. W. E. Buck, RR 2, White Pigeon, Mich.

SUPER-REY — Mr. & Mrs. Chester S. Reynolds, 513 Fair Ave., Erie, Pa.

TAMALAINE'S — Edwin Banias, Box 118, New Vernon, New Jersey

TAMARACK — Mr. & Mrs. John W. Mann, 494 Essex St., Hamilton, Mass.

TAMARLEI — Mr. & Mrs. Leigh C. Morrell, RFD 1, Brattleboro, Vt.

TANGLEWOOD — Miss Mary Meyette, Garden St., West Newbury, Mass.

TAPNOR — Mr. & Mrs. Ronald Hayward, RR, Kingston, Illinois

TARA'S — Dr. & Mrs. V. Watson Pugh, 1618 Oberlin Rd., Raleigh, N. C.

TEJAS — W. P. Thornhill, Route 4, Bentonville, Arkansas

TIPTOP — Mrs. Edward E. Rucinski, 573 Birnie Ave., W. Springfield, Mass.

TOPLANDS — Vernon E. Fish & Son, Toplands, West Rutland, Vt.

TOP RAIL'S — Mr. & Mrs. Richard S. Nelson, RFD 3, 513 E. Pleasant St., Amherst, Mass.

TOPSIDE — Mrs. Harry W. Nichoalds, 2003 Crestridge Dr., Littleton, Colo.

TORR-CONN — Mr. Michael A. Machuga, Winsted Rd., Torrington, Conn.

TOWNE-AYR — Mr. Roderick Towne, RD 3, Montpelier, Vt.

TOWNSHEND — Anna D. Ela, Townshend Morgan-Holstein Farm, Bolton, Mass.

TRAHREBE — John P. Eberhart, 177 Oakville Dr., Pittsburgh, Penna.

TRAILWOOD — Mr. & Mrs. Frank S. Hallett, Box 65, Castle Rock, Wash.

TRILBROOK — Harrison E. Miles, RFD 1, Windsor, Vt.

TRIPLE S — Mr. & Mrs. Robert L. Painter, Rochford, South Dakota

TRITON — Robert Morgan, Green Mountain Stock Farm, Randolph, Vt.

TROY — C. M. Bronson, Box 442, Globe, Arizona

TWIN-IDA — Mr. & Mrs. Roy Jesser, Route 3, Twin Falls, Idaho

UPWEY — Owen Moon (deceased), South Woodstock, Vt.

UU — Mr. & Mrs. M. C. Williams, Rt. 1, Box 107, Romoland, Calif.

VAL — Mrs. Virginia C. Fletcher, 1737 Ardleigh Rd., Columbus, Ohio

VANDALEER — Mr. & Mrs. Charles A. Paull, Box 433, Moscow, Idaho

VICTORY — Mary C. Woolverton, 5500 S. Steele, Littleton, Colo.

VIKING — Mrs. LaVonne Houlton, 2701 Church St., Rt. 1, Modesto, Calif.

VILLA NOVA — Albert J. Armanasco, Rt. 2, Box 137, Gilroy, Calif.
VONA — Mrs. Joseph Vona, Joselene Hills, Frederick, Md.

WAER'S — Mr. & Mrs. F. W. Waer, 18208 Modjeska Rd., Orange, Calif.
WALES FARM — Mr. & Mrs. Leonard S. Wales & Sons, Middlebury, Vt.
WASEEKA — Mr. & Mrs. E. Keene Annis & Mrs. Davieson D. Power, Waseeka
   Farm, Ashland, Mass.
WEDARE — Dr. Edgar B. Butler, 36 Gillette St., Hartford, Conn. & George Carter,
   Lancaster, N. H.
WELMORE — Mrs. Harriet H. Hamilton, Box 706, Pebble Beach, Calif.
WENLOCH — E. B. Rickard, Wenloch Farm, 4300 Saline Rd., Ann Arbor, Mich.
WESTCREST — R. G. Morgareidge, Box 1223, Casper, Wyo.
WESTFALL — Charles G. Mortimer, RD 1, Port Jervis, N. Y.
WESTRIDGE — Mr. & Mrs. Ellsworth W. Reed, Hewitt Rd., Claremont, N. H.
WEST WIND — Mr. & Mrs. Gary L. Sober, 8255 Stow Rd., Webberville, Mich.
WHIPPOORWILL — Mrs. Alex Vasiloff, Whippoorwill Rd., Old Lyme, Conn.
WHITE RIVER — Don D. Berlie, Chadron, Nebraska
WILDAIR — Dr. M. Terry Mills, Worcester St., Southbridge, Mass.
WILDE — Mr. & Mrs. J. R. Kipp, 8181 Turin Rd., Rome, N. Y.
WILDWOOD — W. F. Honer, RR 2, St. Joseph, Minnesota
WILLBROOK — Dr. & Mrs. John H. Williams & Family, 22132 39th Ave., Bothell,
   Wash.
WILLOW GLEN — Charles E. Sutfin, 6627 Stanley Ave., Carmichael, Calif.
WILLOW'S — C. Thomas Fuller, Catasauqua, Penna.
WIL-O-MOR — Dr. John R. Boswell, 16049 Prospect Rd., Strongsville, Ohio
WINDCREST — Mrs. F. O. Davis, Windsor, Vt.
WIND GATE — Mrs. Estelle Williamson, Box 192, Rock Valley Rd., W. Holyoke,
   Mass.
WINDMERE — Mr. & Mrs. W. C. Byers, 619 Pueblo Solano, N. W., Albuquerque,
   N. M.
WINDMILL — Mr. & Mrs. Robert J. Taylor, Rt. 1, Box 332, Louisville, Colo.
WINDROW — Mr. & Mrs. Robert F. Hill, Swayze Mill Rd., Hope, N. J.
WINDSONG — Mr. & Mrs. Fred H. Schwarz, RD 1, Alexandria, Ohio
WINDSWEPT — Mr. & Mrs. O. N. Burroughs, Box 113, Knightsen, Calif.
WINDY HILL — Mr. & Mrs. Ernst Rodenbach, Pluckamin, N. J.
WINDY MAIN — Donald A. St. Pierre, 143 Main St., Essex Junction, Vt.
WOOD HILL — Mr. & Mrs. Donald H. Wood, Alstead, N. H.
WOODSIDE — Jo Ann Stewart & Pat Swift, Olema, Calif.
WYLOWOOD — Mr. & Mrs. W. Lester Wyatt, Wylowood, Box 192, Oxford, Mass.
WYNWOOD — Mr. & Mrs. Jack Wigen, Wynndel, B. C., Canada
WYOMING — Reed Allen, Jr., Box 44, Popo Agie Rt., Lander, Wyo.

Distribution of Registration Number
by Volume of *Register*

Volume III	Stallions	1–6399 (approximate)
(1915)	Mares	01–02699 (”)
Volume IV	Stallions	6400 (approx.)–7199
(1921)	Mares	02700 (approx.)–03999
Volume V	Stallions	7200–8099
(1939)	Mares	04000–05199
Volume VI	Stallions	8100–9499
(1949)	Mares	05200–06999

Volume VII	Stallions	9500–11299
(1956)	Mares	07000–09099
Volume VIII	Stallions	11300–12599
(1960)	Mares	09100–010799
Volume IX	Stallions	12600–14999
(1965)	Mares	010800–013499
Volume X	Stallions	15000-18499
(1969)	Mares	013554-017099

Numbers beginning with 0 indicate mare or gelding; "X" preceding the number indicates registration under Rule II, rescinded January 1, 1948.

Abbreviations:
A. S. B.	*Arab Stud Book*	
A. S. H. R.	*American Saddle Horse Register*	
A. T. R.	*American Trotting Register*	
TH.	*Thoroughbred*	

Number of Registrations by Year

Year	No.	Year	No.	Year	No.
1921	64	*1937*	179	*1957*	554
1922	154	*1938*	186	*1958*	630
1923	133	*1939*	252	*1959*	870
1924	96	*1940*	311	*1960*	1069
1925	127	*1941*	402	*1961*	1135
1926	93	*1942*	304	*1962*	1364
1927	94	*1943*	410	*1963*	1411
1928	116	*1944*	427	*1964*	1511
1929	106	*1945*	471	*1965*	1629
1930	105	*1946*	599	*1966*	1901
1931	92	*1947*	697	*1967*	1961
1932	80	*1948*	469	*1968*	2134
1933	78	*1949*	480	*1969*	2280
1934	127	*1950*	479	*1970*	2378
1935	126	*1954*	458	*1971*	2757
1936	172	*1955*	452	*1972*	3177
		1956	482		

The Half-Morgan Register

The Half-Morgan Register, a division of the American Part-Blooded Horse Registry, was begun in 1940. The registrar and founder is J. C. Abbett, retired racing secretary general of the Oregon Racing Commission, Morgan owner and member of the Morgan Horse Club, Inc.

Horses are eligible for registration which have one fully registered parent, with the other parent of such type, breeding and quality as will meet the requirements of the Registry. A three-quarter bred is one whose parents are a fully registered animal and a half-bred of the same breed. Similarly a seven-eighths bred has one pure bred parent and the other a three-quarter bred of the same breed.

15

The Morgan Horse Magazine

OWEN MOON, JR. WAS A DIRECTOR AND PRESIDENT OF THE MORGAN HORSE Club, Inc. and one of the earliest members of the Green Mountain Trail Association which developed a system of bridle paths throughout Vermont and organized the first 100 Mile Ride which became the model for similar competitions throughout the United States. In 1941, Mr. Moon began to publish the Morgan magazine. Since 1911 he had been a breeder of Morgans at his Upway Farm near Woodstock. In 1939, in celebration of the 150th anniversary of the birth of Justin Morgan, Mr. Moon organized the first all Morgan horse show which was held at his farm following the fourth annual 100 Mile Ride. The show later became known as the National Morgan Horse Show, the largest all breed show in the United States.

Mr. Moon personally bore all the expenses of the magazine which first appeared in October 15, 1941. *The Morgan Horse News Bulletin,* as it was then called, consisted of eight mimeographed sheets. It was mailed free to the 132 members of the Morgan Horse Club, Inc., plus a few non-members who were Morgan owners. The following issue, which came out in December was printed rather than mimeographed and had grown to twelve pages. Folded and mailed without an envelope, it carried a picture of the Justin Morgan Statue on the back page which became the cover. This format persisted until 1947.

At Mr. Moon's death in 1947, the magazine and its assets were donated to the Morgan Horse Club, Inc. by Mrs. Moon.

Printed today in Leominster, Massachusetts, by the Eusey Press, the *Morgan Horse Magazine* is now a slick paper publication, lavishly illustrated with photographs. In addition to news items from local clubs, it runs feature articles by such noted authorities as Marilyn Childs, Charley Hamilton,

Dr. D. C. Parks, Barbara Cole, Janet Dakin, Anna Ela, Dr. E. W. Ensminger, Mary Turgeon and Mabel Owen. From its modest beginning it has grown to be one of the most outstanding breed publications. The 1966 March Stallion Issue contained 162 pages, nine feature articles, an editorial, a message from President Dr. Henry P. Boyd, four regular features, news from 23 affiliated regional clubs and hundreds of photographs.

16

Breeding Morgans at the
U. S. Government Farm and
Principal Private Studs

"In . . . preserving and perpetuating the Morgan breed of horses, it must be borne in mind that we believe it is the true interest of breeders to foster and preserve those qualities that render them so valuable as business horses, and to make no effort to adapt them to those kinds of service for which fashion or utility demand a different kind of animal. They have not height enough to suit fashionable people in the large cities who want horses to roll their princely equipages through the streets. They have not the natural paces that persons generally think best suited for the saddle; and if we were to attempt breeding horses to supply that demand, we should prefer a different breed." — DANIEL CHAPMAN LINSLEY

JOSEPH BATTELL NOT ONLY HELPED SAVE THE MORGAN FROM EXTINCTION by compiling and printing the *Register,* he also contributed heavily to the breed's preservation by helping establish the United States Morgan Horse Farm, and by furnishing the government stud with a stallion which for many years headed its breeding operation.

In 1907 Colonel Battell gave a tract of about 400 acres in Weybridge Township, near Middlebury, Vermont, to the United States Department of Agriculture which in 1906, in cooperation with the Vermont State Experiment station, had assembled a small band of Morgan mares. He donated an additional 35 acres in 1908. By purchase of an adjoining tract from Middlebury College in 1917, the Department of Agriculture acquired 550 acres, four barns and two houses, bringing the total to about 1,000 acres of gently

173

rolling land. The farm's limestone subsoil made it ideally adapted to the production of horses. All buildings were repaired, low lying fields were tiled to promote good drainage and woven wire fences were put up.

The primary purpose of the farm was to conduct research in nutrition and genetics that would aid all horse breeders, while perpetuating and preserving the good qualities of the Morgan. It was also planned to develop an improved type of road horse.

In 1907 the chief of the Bureau of Animal Industry stated, "The aim of the study at Middlebury is to preserve the Morgan type at its best, keeping the splendid conformation, spirit and endurance for which those horses are famous and eliminating the tendency to pace and mix gaits. Size will be increased carefully by selection, but it is not our purpose to make the Morgan a big horse. A size ranging from 15:1 to 15:3 hands is sufficient, with about 15:2 the ideal. However this will not by any means disqualify a 15 hand horse or one even somewhat smaller provided he has desirable characteristics of conformation, quality and action."

In 1907 the original breeding stock, which consisted of seven mares and two fillies acquired in Vermont and two mares from Kentucky, were moved from the station at Burlington to the farm at Weybridge.

Colonel Battell presented the farm with its herd sire. According to Mabel Owen, he "demanded road horse ability, trotting speed and fine looks. In that irrevocable order. He was first and foremost a horse user. He was later a horse breeder, but never once lost sight of the usability factor in his breeding program. He selected for it more assiduously than has any Morgan breeder since. If it was necessary to send a man to Arkansas — or go himself — for a good stallion or a fine mare then it was done and that simply. For he believed, as men have come to agree almost a century later, that performance not only could be bred into a horse, but that it had to be. Toward that end he studied performance records much more carefully than he did pedigrees, for he truly believed that only when the former was present was the latter of any value."

In 1907, when foundation stock was being selected for the Government Farm, the Bureau of Animal Industry report echoed his sentiments. "They should be bred along Morgan lines, but registration in the American Morgan Register will not be necessary for purchase." George M. Rommel of the Bureau added in 1910 that the test of the worth of a pedigree was the animal it produced and that the farm proposed to breed horses, not pedigrees. Reese says, "Those in charge of the U. S. Morgan Horse Farm have spared no effort in tracing the descendants of the best of the Morgans sold in the early days and sent from New England to other sections of the country. They have obtained stock in Kentucky, Kansas, Texas, New York, Washington, Iowa,

Troubadour of Willowmoor (Troubadour–Fanny) saw stud duty in the Remount service and at the U. S. Morgan horse farm. Justin Morgan statue is in background. (Courtesy *Morgan Horse Magazine*)

Rhode Island, New Hampshire and Illinois as well as the native State of Vermont . . . the whole effort being to get into the Government stud the very best Morgan blood in the country."

There was a great deal of adverse criticism, however, of the so-called improved Morgan as compared with the ancient Morgan type. Colonel Battell, the Department of Agriculture and the animals they had chosen were subjected to public censure for not adhering rigidly to traditional Morgan families in their breeding program. Among the detractors were C. A. Benton and C. C. Stillman, although the latter reversed his opinion at a later date and lent the support of his considerable fortune to hiring riders to condition Government Farm Morgans for the competitive rides.

In 1890, Colonel Battell's preoccupation with performance caused his attention to focus upon the fastest Morgan trotter ever to be developed. The horse had won over 60 heats at 2:30 or better and already had a record of 2:10¼. He was later to trot a mile in 2:08¾ and was once separately timed in a non-winning heat at 2:08 in a race won by Alix in a record breaking 2:07¾. In addition to being a superlative racer, Lord Clinton became a handsome carriage horse after he had let down from hard training and had

PEDIGREE OF TROUBADOUR OF WILLOWMOOR 6459.

Jubilee Lambert 1476. .... Daniel Lambert 62. .... Ethan Allen 50. .... Black Hawk 20. .... Sherman Morgan 5. .... Justin Morgan 1.
.... Abdallah. .... Mambrino. .... Imp. Messenger 1.
Harvey mare. .... Chestnut, by American Star. .... Duroc.
Taft horse 1296. .... Black Hawk 20. .... Sherman Morgan 5. .... Justin Morgan 1.
Indian Chief 538. .... Bloods Black Hawk 89. .... Black Hawk 20. .... Sherman Morgan 5. .... Justin Morgan 1.
Lou Berry. .... Ned Forrest. .... Imp. Grand Bashaw.
Young Bashaw. .... All Fours. .... Imp. Whip.
Jersey Messenger. .... Imp. Whip.
Belle. .... Lewis Warfield. .... Dave. .... Virginia Whip.
Littona Warfield. .... Cracker. .... Boston.
Mare by. .... Skinner's Tom Hal. .... Davy Crockett 603. (Blackburn's.)

Blood Chief 91. .... Bloods Black Hawk 89. .... Black Hawk 20. .... Sherman Morgan 5. .... Justin Morgan 1.
Miss Duncan. .... Scotts Highlander. .... Hunts Highlander.
Prospect 122. .... Mare by. .... Director.
Susan Jones. .... Ashland Chief. .... Mambrino Chief. .... Timoleon.
Kate. .... Bloods Black Hawk 89. .... Black Hawk 20. .... Sherman Morgan 5. .... Justin Morgan 1.
Blackwood. .... Queen. .... One Eyed Copperbottom. .... Sir Archy.
Alexanders Norman 2350. .... Morse Horse 627. .... European 361.
Bay mare. .... Mambrino Chief.

Lady Blackwood. .... Superb 1839.

Lady Harper. .... Boar 2057. .... Ethan Allen 50. .... Black Hawk 20. .... Sherman Morgan 5. .... Justin Morgan 1.
Mischief. .... Harris Hamiltonian. .... Bishop's Hamiltonian.
Young Columbus 1834. .... Columbus 1156.
Mischief. .... Harris Hamiltonian. .... Bishop's Hamiltonian.
Wilful. .... Daniel Lambert 62. .... Ethan Allen 50. .... Smith's Liberty. .... Justin Morgan 1.
Fanny Cook. .... Black Hawk 20. .... Sherman Morgan 5.
Colonel Moulton 1472. .... Chestnut mare. .... Abdallah.
Bigelow's Black Hawk 1068. .... Black Hawk 20. .... Justin Morgan 1.
Mare by. .... Gifford Morgan 30. .... Woodbury Morgan 7.
Green Mountain Morgan 42. .... Simonds Horse.
Wood Horse 402. .... Green Mountain Morgan 42. .... Tom Morgan. .... Woodbury Morgan 7.
Jennie. .... Phoebe. .... Gifford Morgan 30. .... Woodbury Morgan 7.

Peters Vermont 403. .... Morgan Hunter 341. .... Colby Horse 779. .... Justin Morgan 1.
.... Mare by. .... Woodbury Morgan 7.
.... Gen. Hibbard 29. .... Bulrush Morgan 6. .... Justin Morgan 1.
Chestnut mare. .... Bay mare by. .... Sherman Morgan 5. .... Justin Morgan 1.
.... Gifford Morgan 30. .... Woodbury Morgan 7.
Chestnut mare. .... Gifford Morgan 30. .... Woodbury Morgan 7.

Ethan Allen 2d 406. .... Ethan Allen 50. .... Black Hawk 20. .... Justin Morgan 1.
Chestnut mare. .... Green Mountain Morgan 42. .... Sherman Morgan 5. .... Justin Morgan 1.
Green Mountain Morgan 42. .... Gifford Morgan 30. .... Woodbury Morgan 7.

Brown mare. .... Bay mare. .... Sherman Morgan 5. .... Justin Morgan 1.
.... Bailey Horse 38. .... Justin Morgan 1.
Crane mare. .... Hubbard Horse 1719. .... Justin Morgan 1.
Billy Root 9. .... Justin Morgan 1. .... Justin Morgan 1.
Royal Morgan 11. .... Green Mountain Morgan 42. .... Gifford Morgan 30. .... Woodbury Morgan 7.
.... Wilder colt. .... Simond's Horse. .... Woodbury Morgan 7.
Wood Horse 402. .... Green Mountain Morgan 42. .... Tom Morgan. .... Woodbury Morgan 7.
.... Phoebe.

Peters Morgan 405. .... Morgan Hunter 341 342. .... Morgan Hunter 341. .... Gifford Morgan 30. .... Justin Morgan 1.
.... Mare by. .... Colby Horse 779. .... Justin Morgan 1.
Chestnut mare. .... Gen. Hibbard 29. .... Bulrush Morgan 6. .... Justin Morgan 1.
.... Bay mare by. .... Woodbury Morgan 7.
Ethan Allen 50. .... Black Hawk 20. .... Gifford Morgan 30. .... Justin Morgan 1.
Chestnut mare. .... Green Mountain Morgan 42. .... Gifford Morgan 30.
Green Mountain Morgan 42. .... Gifford Morgan 30. .... Woodbury Morgan 7.

Green Mountain 403. (Cushings.) .... Bay mare. .... Tom Morgan. .... Justin Morgan 1.
.... Sherman Morgan 5. .... Justin Morgan 1.
Billy Root 9. .... Royal Morgan 11. .... Daughter of.

Ethan Allen 2d 3967. .... Black Morgan 810. .... Green Mountain Bashup 16. .... Royal Morgan 11. .... Justin Morgan 1.
.... Sherman Morgan 5. .... Justin Morgan 1.
.... Hubbard Horse 1719. .... Justin Morgan 1.
.... Mare by. .... Green Mountain Bashup 16. .... Sherman Morgan 5. .... Woodbury Morgan 7.
.... Gorham mare. .... Batchelder Horse 17.
Peters Vermont 403. .... Daughter of. .... Sherman Morgan 5. .... Justin Morgan 1.
.... Royal Morgan 11. .... Sherman Morgan 5.
.... Billy Root 9. .... Daughter of.
.... Royal Morgan 11. .... Hubbard Horse 1719.
.... Mare by. .... Mare by.

Charlie Watson 813. .... Comet 682. .... Morgan Hunter 341. .... Wilson Horse 723. .... Royal Morgan 11.
.... Mare by. .... Batchelder Horse 17.
Bay mare. .... Chestnut mare. .... Black Hawk 20. .... Sherman Morgan 5.
.... Mare by.
Brown mare. .... Tiger 3438. .... Mare by. .... Goldplus 787.
.... Dr. Abel Brown Horse 1729. .... Billy Root 9.
Mare by. .... Justin Morgan 1.
.... Woodbury Morgan 7. .... Justin Morgan 1.
Green Mountain 403. (Cushings.) .... Green Mountain Morgan 42. .... Gifford Morgan 30. .... Sherman Morgan 5. .... Justin Morgan 1.
Bay mare. .... Billy Root 9. .... Daughter of. .... Hubbard Horse 1719. .... Justin Morgan 1.
.... Crane mare. .... Royal Morgan 11. .... Mare by. .... Bailey Horse 38. .... Justin Morgan 1.
.... Daughter of.
Nell. .... Comet 682. .... Billy Root 9. .... Mare by. .... Sherman Morgan 5. .... Justin Morgan 1.
Watson mare. .... Royal Morgan 11. .... Hubbard Horse 1719. .... Justin Morgan 1.
.... Royal Morgan 11. .... Sherman Morgan 5. .... Justin Morgan 1.
.... Bailey Horse 38. .... Woodbury Morgan 7. .... Justin Morgan 1.

(Left margin labels, bottom to top:)
TROUBADOUR 6459.
Jubilee de Jarnette 3354.
FANNIE 2D.
Bird Pepper.
Bob Morgan 4846.
FANNIE 2D.
Bay mare.

put on weight. His gait at the trot was typically Morgan, square, balanced and elastic.

On his sire's side, Lord Clinton's Morgan background was as impeccable as his road horse ability. He was a son of Denning Allen by Honest Allen by the incomparable Ethan Allen. Denning Allen was out of Rena, a dark brown daughter of Ward's Flying Cloud, a son of Black Hawk. The dam of Flying Cloud was said to be by the Hackett Horse by Gifford by Woodbury. Flying Cloud left many descendants in the trotting Register. Honest Allen was out of a mare by the Brooks Horse by Sherman.

In 1893, Denning Allen was awarded first premium for Morgan stallions of five or over at the Chicago World's Fair. The German sculptor Max Lansberg selected him as one of eight horses for a model of American horses to be used in the German agricultural schools.

Fanny Scott (Sally Scott), the dam of Lord Clinton, was something else entirely. She has been the subject of argument, disagreement and generally adverse criticism from her time to this. Only after a great deal of research was Battell able to determine her background. He finally established to his own satisfaction that her sire was the Thoroughbred Revenue, Jr., by Revenue by *Trustee. Revenue Jr. was out of Nannie Harper, an exceptionally well bred mare by the great English-bred horse *Glencoe, winner of the Two Thousand Guineas and the first three-year-old to win the two and one-half mile Goodwood Cup which he won with such consummate ease that he was fresh enough to gallop home first in a race the following day. *Glencoe had an active stud career on both sides of the Atlantic; it extended over twenty-two years, and his name led the American sire list for an unprecedented eight seasons. At the advanced age of twenty-four he was still serving a full book. No small measure of immortal Lexington's success as a sire was due to his use on *Glencoe mares. *Glencoe was a major influence on the development of the Thoroughbred in North America. Although his direct male line has almost completely died out, he is a strong collateral influence through Domino, Hanover and Stockwell. The 1957 Kentucky Derby winner, Iron Liege, was a descendant of *Glencoe — as was every other horse that ran in the race! In fact, there are few Thoroughbreds in this country that do not trace to *Glencoe in one or more lines, the majority in several.

Nannie Harper's dam was Fannie Hill by Monarch out of Allegante by *Young Truffle, and out of Phantomia by Phantom. The dam of Fanny Scott was said to be of Copperbottom breeding, perhaps by a grandson, and out of a mare said to be by Stump the Dealer, but by which of at least six horses by that name, is uncertain! Battell firmly believed that Copperbottom was of Morgan breeding, assigning him the registration number of 66 and the fraction, one-half, which designates him as a son of Justin Morgan.

Extended pedigree of Troubadour of Willowmoor shows 71 authentic crosses to Justin Morgan through many of the outstanding Morgans of their day. Purchased as a yearling for future stud duty at the government farm from breeder J. W. Clise, of Redmond, Washington.

Denning Allen (Honest Allen–Rena by Ward's Flying Cloud), sire of General Gates. (Courtesy *Morgan Horse Magazine*)

Thoroughbred blood is not antithetical to the Morgan heritage. The Thoroughbred Stump the Dealer descends from *Diomed and Wildair, horses whose names appear on the probable pedigree of Justin Morgan. The word "Thoroughbred," however, evokes in the minds of many people, the picture of an animated hat rack, more whippet than horse, and brittle and brainless to boot! Nothing could be further from the truth. People not familiar with the breed, who have never seen a fully developed horse, are likely to confuse immature individuals in racing condition with what is representative of the breed. The best examples of mature Morgans, Arabians and Thoroughbreds in prime condition are remarkably similar — which is hardly surprising in view of their common ancestry.

All things taken into account — his performance, courage, speed, beauty and breeding — Lord Clinton seemed ideally suited to head a stud dedicated to breeding superior road horses. Except for one small detail: Lord Clinton was a gelding.

General Gates 666 (Denning Allen–Fanny Scott by Revenue, Jr.) donated by Joseph Battell to the U. S. Morgan Horse Farm at Weybridge. (Courtesy Morgan Horse Club, Inc.)

After locating and looking over Denning Allen and Fanny Scott with the greatest of care, Colonel Battell bought both mare and stallion and had them taken to his Breed Loaf Farm in Vermont. The breeding that produced Lord Clinton was repeated and in 1894 a full brother, General Gates, was foaled.

General Gates was smaller, more compact and more typically Morgan than Lord Clinton. He was black and stood just under 15 hands. Old timers who saw him said that he very closely resembled the original Black Hawk. In many respects he was the ideal military horse as well as the ideal road horse. Several of his sons and grandsons saw service with the Remount. His descendants were so well placed on endurance rides sponsored by the U. S. Cavalry that he won the unique honor of being publicly commended by the War Department, an honor never before or since bestowed upon any other stallion.

On July 1, 1907 General Gates was presented by Battell to the United States Morgan Horse Farm at Weybridge.

The proof of a sire is in the quality of his descendants. In this respect General Gates was above reproach. The outstanding Morgans sired by General Gates went a long way toward quieting his detractors.

The sons of General Gates founded sire lines of their own and have had

General Gates was the ideal-type Morgan road horse. Many old-timers recalled that he greatly resembled the celebrated Black Hawk. (Courtesy *Morgan Horse Magazine*)

far reaching influence both upon Morgan and upon grade stock throughout the United States, particularly through the efforts of the Remount breeding program.

Red Oak by General Gates out of Marguerite by White River Morgan was bred by Colonel Battell and foaled in 1906. At the County Fair in Middleburg in 1908 he won first premium in a class of 20 other two-year-olds. Shortly thereafter he was purchased by the Government Farm where he was kept until 1911 when he was sent to the State Agricultural College at Amherst, Massachusetts, to be used in their breeding program. He was later sold to Richard Sellman of Rochelle, Texas, then the world's largest Morgan breeder. In 1922, Red Oak was shown at the Southwestern Exposition and Fat Stock Show in Fort Worth, and was first in the aged stallion class. The judge remarked that "The grand champion Morgan Horse Red Oak is the finest animal I have had my eyes on in twenty years of judging. He could win first prize at any horse show in the world." In 1924 Red Oak was transferred to the A & M College of Texas. He was a major influence in the West, both in Texas and in California through his daughters purchased from Sellman by Roland G. Hill.

General Gates also sired Vermont, Scotland, Dewey and Linsley.

Mrs. Culvers, a mare of roadster type sired by the registered American Saddle Horse Harrison Chief, was also the object of a great deal of adverse criticism. Her background was, in part, Morgan and many people felt that she deserved to be included in the *Register*. Her dam, Belle(Billie), was a daughter of the Morgan Cabell's Lexington, one of the original Saddle Horse foundation sires, by Gist's Black Hawk, by Blood's Black Hawk by Black Hawk — Old Polly by Sherman. Again, the proof of the broodmare is her produce and her son. Bennington by General Gates was an outstanding example of the breed. He was foaled in 1908 and lived to be twenty-eight. He was used primarily in the Remount Service for fifteen years before he was returned to the Government Farm. It was later felt that it was a pity he had not been used more extensively on Morgan mares and that a great deal of time had been lost in not doing so.

Bred to the Morgan mare Artemesia (Ethan Allen 3rd–Chestnut by Bob Morgan) Bennington got Mansfield Ulysses, Querido, Canfield, Redfern, Willys, Topsham and Artiben. The first four became noted sires: Mansfield at the Government stud; Ulysses with Dr. W. L. Orcutt, the Remount Service and Government Farm; Querido at Roland G. Hill's Horseshoe Cattle Company in California and Parker's Ranch in Hawaii; and Canfield at the University of Connecticut and the farm at Weybridge. Redfern and Willys were mares; Topsham and Artiben were gelded.

Of the quartet, Mansfield, foaled in 1920, was perhaps the most outstanding as an individual, as a sire of horses of uniformly high class and as a sire of sires. He headed the Government stud until his retirement from active service at the age of twenty-four, getting a total of 146 registered foals. Many of his sons became outstanding stallions that founded dynasties of their own, including Lippitt Mandate, Captor, Monterey, Sonfield, Fillmore, Tiffany, Gay Mac, Bayfield and Lippitt Mormon. His last public appearance was in 1942 at the Morgan Horse Show in South Woodstock where, at the age of twenty-two, he won the Justin Morgan Performance Class which consists of a half-mile trotting race in harness, a half-mile running race under saddle, a saddle class at walk, trot and canter, and pulling the stone boat with a minimum weight of 500 pounds.

Ulysses is best known for siring the great Ulendon out of Allenda by Captain Morgan, a show horse and sire of show horses. Ulysses also got the Government Farm sire Delmont out of the Saddlebred mare Ladelle (Brook-

Bennington (General Gates–Mrs. Culvers) taken at the United States Morgan Horse Farm in 1925 at the age of seventeen. (United States Department of Agriculture Photo)

Three brothers by Bennington out of Artemesia–Ulysses, Mansfield, and Canfield. (Department of Agriculture photo)

Topsham (Bennington–Artemesia), a full brother to Mansfield. Age twenty-two. (Courtesy Mrs. Fred Flowers, Elyria, Ohio)

Mansfield, at age five. (Department of Agriculture photo)

Another view of Topsham. (Courtesy Mrs. Fred Flowers)

Harvey (Mansfield–Carolyn), Morgan gelding. Foaled in 1937, he is shown here at the age of twenty-seven. (Courtesy Betty Plauth, Blue Spruce Farm, Altmont, New York)

Troubadour of Willowmoor (Troubadour–Fanny). (Courtesy the Morgan Horse Club, Inc.)

wood King–Morgan Fanny), who was another controversial purchase of the Department of Agriculture.

Another outstanding stallion at the Government stud was Troubadour of Willowmoor (Troubadour–Fannie 2nd by Bob Morgan) purchased as a yearling in 1911 from his breeder J. V. Clise of Redmond, Washington. His pedigree contained the names of many famous Morgans — Billy Root, Royal Morgan, Ethan Allen, Green Mountain Morgan, Davy Crockett, Tiger, the Hubbard Horse, Comet, Peter's Morgan, Daniel Lambert, Lady de Jarnette, Indian Chief — and traced to Justin Morgan in 71 authentic crosses through all three principal sons, Woodbury, Sherman and Bulrush.

All breeding stock at the Government farm was worked regularly. Troubadour of Willowmoor was routinely driven into town to pick up supplies, while Scotland took the farm children in a surry to school in Middlebury. Bennington hauled a daily load of silage from the main barn to the sheep barn. The mares, too, were used for driving and for farm work. The stock was kept outdoors as much as possible, and although the young stock was allowed ample feed of the best quality in order to insure proper growth and development, there was no attempt to keep the young stock in show condition. This common sense management program resulted in an average proportion of mares foaling of 67.3 per cent as compared with a national average of less than 50 per cent.

Magellan (Godlfield–Topaz). All horses were tested on a measured track and checked for pulse, respiration, etc. Cart with auto axle and wheels was developed at farm. (Courtesy *Morgan Horse Magazine*)

In general, the Government stud's objectives remained fairly constant with those set forth in 1907 except that, due to the rapid growth of the automobile, which supplanted the road horse as a means of private transportation, emphasis was shifted from harness to saddle type.

In addition to the Saddle Horse outcrosses, Nonius stock, imported from Hungary, was introduced in the thirties. The strain had originally been developed in Austria from Arabian stock. Apparently the cross was not an overwhelming success, for it was discontinued at the U. S. Morgan Farm at Weybridge in 1937 when all the Nonius and Nonius-Morgans were shipped to the Livestock Range Experiment Station at Miles City, Montana.

Under the direction of Earl B. Krantz, the Government Farm established measures of merit and performance. Horses were tested in harness pulling 60 per cent of their own weight, and under saddle carrying 20 per cent. If necessary, dead weight was added to bring the weight to the exact proportion. These tests were performed on a one-eighth mile track and on a cross-country course. Horses were scored on various points of action, length of stride, manners, ease of handling and ease of gaits from the rider's standpoint. They were also carefully checked as to temperature, pulse and respiration, both before and after exertion. Signs of fatigue were noted, and animals rated accordingly. Several testing and training devices were developed, notably a rig to facilitate harness breaking and a special cart mounted on automobile axle and wheels.

Detailed breeding records were maintained, which showed among other things that a mare's best producing years were between the ages of eleven and fourteen. Nutritional studies were also carried out, and all horses were weighed and measured twice a year — sucklings and weanlings at monthly intervals.

Willow (Bennington–Poinsetta) foaled in 1929. (Courtesy *Morgan Horse Magazine*)

Torch Gow (Mansfield–Poinsetta) foaled in 1929. (Courtesy *Morgan Horse Magazine*) *Magazine*)

On June 30, 1951, The U. S. Morgan Horse Farm was closed as a Federal enterprise. When the project was abandoned, some of the stock was sold by sealed bid, including Panfield and Riviera. Some mares were sent to land-

Revere (Mansfield–Folly) at the Range Experiment Station, Miles City, Montana. (Department of Agriculture photo)

grant colleges, with the University of Massachusetts getting Damsel, **Optic**, and Narissa; Penn State received Quaker Lady. Silkolene went to the University of New Hampshire where, to the cover of Ulysses' son Ulendon she produced Astronaut, now their senior sire. The University of Connecticut got Mentor, a son of the ill fated Goldfield, who had died at eight before achieving the great promise of which he seemed capable.

All other assets and livestock were transferred to the University of Vermont, including twenty mares and fillies, four virtually untried stallions and colts, and five foals.

At the Morgan Horse Farm in recent years there has been increasing emphasis on saddle performance (show) type with mild outcrosses to Upwey Ben Don and Orland Vigildon. The Morgan Horse Farm, dominated by the Justin Morgan statue erected in 1921, continues to be a mecca for horse loving tourists who number more than 30,000 a year.

In addition to maintaining the farm at Weybridge, the United States Department of Agriculture bred Morgans at the Range Livestock Station at

Miles City, Montana. Thirty-one purebred Morgans, including the stallion Revere(Mansfield–Folly), were obtained for the station in 1925. Another son of Mansfield, Monterey out of Scotanna, was also used as herd sire.

The purpose of the project was to study the management of saddle horses under range conditions. Morgans were also crossed with other types — Thoroughbred, Standardbred, Belgian and grade animals — with the idea of producing a hardy farm utility horse. Young animals were used in nutritional and developmental investigations, experimenting with several methods of feeding and management. In ten years the purebred herd had been almost completely replaced by crossbreds.

Several Indian agencies and schools bred Morgans. One of the largest herds was owned by the Chilocco Agricultural School. Others were the Pine Ridge Indian Agency, Unitah Indian School, Fort Washakia School, the Oglala Community School and the Wind River Indian Agency. Purebreds were produced and also the Indians were helped and encouraged to upgrade their herds.

Private Breeders

It would be impossible to list all the private breeders who contributed to the preservation and development of the Morgan, therefore only a few of the principal breeders will be mentioned.

For many years the largest individual Morgan breeder was Richard Sellman, who bred using horses at his beautiful Mountain Vale Ranch near Rochelle, Texas. Mr. Sellman's first Morgan was the six-year-old stallion Major Gordon by Young Octoroon, dam untraced. Young Octoroon was by Octoroon, a son of Comet, dam by Drennan by Davy Crockett; second dam by Bulrush. Sellman described Major Gordon as having "Fine style and action," and used him extensively at the ranch for thirteen years until the horse's death in 1899 at the approximate age of nineteen. His daughters and granddaughters became the foundation mares of Sellman's stud.

In the early years of the twentieth Century, Sellman purchased three colts for use as herd sires: Major Antoine (Meteor Jr.–Molly Lee by General Lee) foaled in 1901, Gold Medal (Meteor, Jr.–Bay by General Lee) foaled in 1902, and the Admiral (Jubilee de Jarnette–Brown by Winnebago Chief) foaled in 1903. Mr. Sellman had discriminating taste in horses and the means to indulge it. He was extremely selective in his choice of stock, buying nothing but the best. His most outstanding stallion was Headlight Morgan (Ethan Allen 2nd–Lady Stratton by Vermont Morgan; second dam said to be by Green Mountain Morgan) foaled in 1893 and bred by the Morgan Horse Company of Carpentersville, Illinois. Sellman purchased him in 1913. He sired

Red Wing, Red Tom, Dixie Dan, Dicksell, Dan, Clarendon, Casey Jones, Redwood Morgan, Sunflower Maid, and Joe Bailey the sire of Montcrest Sellman, sire of Red Man, prominent California sire.

Mr. Sellman's last major purchase was Red Oak (General Gates–Marguerite). He had his greatest success at stud when bred to the daughters of Headlight Morgan.

Much credit must go to Richard Sellman, not only for keeping the breed alive when its numbers were declining, but for always maintaining the highest possible standards of quality. His stock has had persistent and far reaching influence. Of the 1,200 mares listed in Volume IV of the *Register,* only 186 have living descendants. Of the mares with extant families, 61, or approximately one-third, were of Sellman's breeding. Over a twenty-year period he registered 474 mares. Many colts, especially those which were gelded, were not recorded. In Volume V, one-seventh of all mares listed were bred by Sellman.

Sellman put Roland G. Hill of the Horseshoe Cattle Company of Gustine, California, in the Morgan breeding business. Mr. Hill had been for many years a horse show judge and had raised stock horses of other breeds before buying his first Morgan, the stallion Redwood Morgan (Headlight Morgan–Bonnie A by Major Antoine) in 1922. He had sent a ranch hand to Texas to select the horse and was so delighted with him in comparison to the animals he had been raising that he personally went to Rochelle a few months later. He came back with a boxcar load of mares, mostly four-year-old daughters and granddaughters of Headlight Morgan and The Admiral. He went back for a second carload of mares two years later, this time, principally young daughters of Red Oak.

Mr. Hill kept Redwood Morgan for only a year because he considered him to be too closely bred to the Sellman mares to use on them. He sent to J. C. Brunk of Rochester, Illinois, for a colt, Pat Allen (Allen King–Patrona). He later replaced him with the Government Farm product Querido (Mansfield–Artemesia) whose daughters became the foundation of the Horseshoe Ranch breeding program. Querido's daughters crossed especially well with Sonfield (Mansfield–Quietude by Troubadour of Willowmoor). Mr. Hill registered almost 300 mares whose descendants are scattered the length and width of California, the state which today has the greatest number of registered Morgans.

William Randolph Hearst purchased mares of Sellman breeding from Hill. In addition to producing high class purebred Morgans, Hearst started a strain known as the Morab by using his Arabian stallions Ksar (Letan–Fasia) and Ghazi (Rodan–Guemura) on Morgan mares. The cross was not made the other way because Hearst did not own Arabian mares. According to long-

time California breeder W. T. Carter, the program fell apart because of lack
of seriously interested help. In 1937 the Hearst estate was dispersed at auction. The Morgans averaged $336 with the ten-year-old stallion Uhlan (Ben-
nington–Poinsetta) bringing the top price of $600.

J. Roy Brunk of Rochester, Illinois, is still raising Morgans on the farm
once owned by his grandfather George Brunk who first came to Illinois from
Ohio in 1817, walking all the way from Miami County. When the farm house
was completed George Brunk brought his mother and stepfather to live with
him. With them they brought a Morgan mare called Mousey, breeding unknown.

His son Joseph Chase Brunk went into the breeding business in a large
way with the purchase of ten mares and a stallion, Chetco (Ben Franklin–
Nellie B. by Harry Allen, Jr.), from the estate of Frank McGavock of Nash-
ville, Tennessee.

Ben Franklin 2:29, was a son of Daniel Lambert out of Black Kate by
Addison, by Black Hawk, foaled in Vermont in 1873 and sold to Mr. Mc-
Gavock for $8,000. At the same time a carefully selected band of fillies was
assembled which represented the best available Vermont bloodlines. Among
them were Daisy (Bodette Horse–Bay by Billie Floson), Flora Temple (Ethan
Allen 2nd–Chestnut by Starlight), Gentle Annie (Ethan Allen 2nd–Chestnut
by Bodette), Gyp (Clark Jones Horse–Chestnut by Ward's Lion) and Jenny
Lind (Chase Horse–Chestnut by Morgan Lion).

Joseph Brunk's son J. Roy Brunk started showing Morgans at the age of
eleven at the 1904 St. Louis World Fair and in his own words has "been at
it ever since." He judged the Morgans at the Ohio State Fair in 1965. At
their Cotton Hill Farm, the Brunk family have bred such outstanding sires as
Allen Franklin (Jasper Franklin–Daisy by Billy Bodette), Penrod (Allen
Franklin–Black Bess), Jubilee King (Penrod–Daisette), Juban (Jubilee King–
Jeanne), Red Vermont (Jubilee King–Daisy Knox), Juzan (Jubilee King–
Liza Jane), Agazizz (Juzan–Gizea) and Congo (Tarron–Black Dee).

The O'Neil family of Manteno, Illinois, have also been raising Morgans
for three generations beginning in 1916 when Charles J. O'Neil bought his
first mare, Byrrh (Handy Allen–Bay by Allen Morgan), to breed to the stallion Selim (Aureolus–Topsy), which he had acquired the previous year. Archie
Hudson (Archie L.–Turvey Hudson) was bought in 1927 and, crossed with
Byrrh, got the incomparable Archie O. Archie O lived to be thirty, traveled
widely, was leased to several state universities and to the United States Army.
His progeny are all over the United States. There are even a few in Europe.
He retained his fertility well into his twenties, siring Yancy Derringer "O"
out of Sue Travelmore when he was twenty-six.

Robert Lippitt Knight's 1,500-acre Green Mountain Stock Farm produced some of the finest old type Morgans bred in the twentieth century between 1916 and its dispersal in 1962. Among the first Morgans Mr. Knight acquired were the stallions Ashbrook (Croydon Prince–Nancy by Ethan Allen 3rd), and Moro (Welcome–Polly Rogers); the mares NeKomia (Ashbrook–Bridgett), Green Mountain Twilight (Rob Roy–Emily), Adeline Bundy (Rob Roy–Rose of Sutton) and Croydon Mary (Croydon Prince–Kate by the Radway Horse). Mr. Knight said, "I, perhaps, am elementary in my reasoning, but I like to think that I am adhering to the Morgan line as closely as possible." The wisdom of his program was borne out. Lippitt Morgans have traveled widely, have become the herd sires and foundation mares for other successful breeding operations and have, in general, given a good account of themselves wherever they went or whatever they were asked to do. At the herd's dispersal following Mr. Knight's death, 48 lots were auctioned, for a total of over $100,000. Lippitt Ethan Georgia brought the unprecedented price of $4,500 for a three-year-old filly, while the eighteen-year-old brood mare Lippitt Georgia brought $2,100.

Owen Moon, Jr., on the other hand, introduced a great deal of American saddle Horse blood into the *Register*, principally through 19 horses brought to Upwey Farm from Missouri and Illinois, including the five-year-old registered Saddlebred stallion King Peavine, purchased in 1937 from N. H. Hite of Auxvasse, Missouri. Renamed Upwey King Peavine, he is recorded in Volume V of the *Register* as X–8074, although he had neither Morgan sire nor dam; Morgan ancestors are several generations removed on his pedigree. Many of the mares on which he was used were also more Saddlebred than Morgan and some authorities criticized their produce as being neither good Morgans nor good Saddlebreds.

Captor (Mansfield–Narissa) bred by Department of Agriculture. (Courtesy Merle D. Evans, Massilon, Ohio)

The Orcutt family of Orcland Farm, West Newbury, Massachusetts, have been breeders of Morgans for many years. Frank Harrison Orcutt a charter member of the Morgan Horse Club, and for 65 years a breeder of fine horses, produced such good Morgans as Orcland Leader, Orcland Vigildon and the great Artemesia, which when crossed with Bennington founded a whole new empire.

Each year the United States Morgan Horse Farm sold a few surplus animals. In 1934 Merle D. Evans bought the full brother and sister, Captor and Dimity (Mansfield–Narissa by Troubadour of Willowmoor). In 1937 he bought five young mares, five-year-old Ceres (Bennington–Lady Sealect) in foal to Delmont (Ulysses–Ladelle), the yearling fillies Gleneida (Mansfield–Ulwina), Gorgeous (Delmont–Romance) and Gracious Lady (Abbot–Walla Walla), and a weanling filly, later named Roz (Delmont–Ceres). The following year, Ceres dropped a full sister to Roz which was named Tippy Tin. At the same time Mr. Evans leased the Remount stallion Hawk Jim (Linsley–Lady Spar). From this foundation developed what is now the world's largest herd of registered Morgans with a broodmare band that annually produces approximately fifty foals. The only "outside" blood added was Captain Fillmore (Fillmore–Gadabbot) also of Government Farm background, and recently, Payday (Mansfield–Glady) from Mansfield's last crop and believed to be one of his few remaining entire sons. The various combinations of the seven mares and two principal stallions resulted in hundreds of outstanding Morgans which became in turn herd sires and broodmares, both at Evans' Crabapple Valley Farm and for other breeders all over the United States. Others were excellent show and pleasure horses. Some outstanding Morgans bred at Devan Stud are: O C R (Captor–Roz), Great Hawk (Hawk Jim–Dimity), King Captor (Captor–Tippy Tin), Fleetwing (Captor–Gorgeous), Arrow-Hawk (Hawk Jim–Ceres), Tippy Dee (Hawk Jim–Tippy Tin), Holly Hawk (Hawk Jim–Gorgeous), Nugget (Captor–Gleneida), Wingfoot (Captor–Gleneida), Captor's Princess (Captor–Gleneida), Chief Hawk (Hawk Jim–Dimity), Caprice (Captor–Ceres), Starflake (Captor–Ceres), Lady Hawk (Hawk Jim–Ceres), Easterday (Hawk Jim–Roz), Glohawk (Hawk Jim–Gleneida), Hawk Eagle (Hawk Jim–Dimity), Lady Cap (Captor–Roz), Devan Comet (Captor–Ceres), Devan Diamond (Captor–Gorgeous), Devan Hawk (Hawk Jim–Starflake), Devan Chief (Captor–Lady Hawk), Devan Tip (Captor–Tippy Tin), Evening Star (Hawk Jim–Starflake), Foxy Prince (Captain Fillmore–Tippy Dee), Hawk Shaw (Hawk Jim–Lady Cap) and Devan Donna (Captor–Capricious). A certain amount of inbreeding was practiced, as seen by Devan Barb (Captor–Caprice by Captor) and Charm (Captor–Dimity), which has resulted in a high degree of uniformity of type.

The mighty O C R (Captor–Roz) at age seventeen. He has sired 103 outstanding Morgans. (Courtesy Tas Tee Farms, Hinkley, Ohio)

Devan Marsh Hawk (Devan Duke–Devan Dimglow), Debt (Devan Marsh Hawk–Tippy Dee), and Tippy Dee (Hawk Jim–Tippy Tin), horses of Government farm breeding at Blackacre, Peninsula, Ohio.

Government Farm breeding: Devan Marsh Hawk is the product of intensive inbreeding as practiced at Crabapple Valley Farm. Note persistence of Mansfield type. Owned by J. T. Urbank and Blackacre. (Photo by Denise Urbank; courtesy John T. Urbank)

O C R far right, winning the Get of Sire Class at the 1965 Gold Cup Show at the age of twenty-four. (Courtesy Dr. and Mrs. John R. Boswell, Strongsville, Ohio)

O C R was senior sire at Tas Tee farm in Hinkley Ohio and later at Willow-Moor Farm in Strongsville and left 103 outstanding descendants. Devan Hawk stood several seasons in Alabama and Florida and sired Little Hawk, now senior sire at Sunset Farm in Bethel, Maine. Fleetwing served a select band of broodmares at Reata Farm, and his sons and daughters have been shown with great success all over the East and Midwest. Mrs. John Junk of Mt. Sterling, has bred many outstanding Morgans from Nugget. A son, Big Bill B., is a champion parade horse. The list could be extended almost indefinitely.

PART V

Today

17

Horses in a Changing World

THE INTERNAL COMBUSTION ENGINE BROUGHT ABOUT PROFOUND CHANGES in the pattern and structure of American culture, changes which amounted to a revolution. Formerly it had been necessary to live close to one's business or place of employment. Automobiles and the ever-widening network of hard-surfaced roads that followed their proliferation did away with that necessity and made possible such modern phenomena as the decay of the central city, the cult of suburbia, indiscriminate urban sprawl and a degree of mobility undreamed of a generation ago. New land marks appeared: the drive-in theatre, the supermarket, the motel, the shopping center, the billboard, the automobile graveyard, the hamburger joint and tasteless, anonymous tracts of identical, shoddy own-your-own-homes, which began deteriorating almost before completion. Old landmarks were bulldozed into oblivion to make way for super roads which gobbled up millions of acres, yet often were obsolete before completion.

It seemed that the horse was soon to be another victim of mechanization. As tractors and trucks replaced horses as sources of farm power and transportation, their number declined steadily. By 1945 the total horse and mule population of the United States had dropped to 10,000,000. By 1955 it was less than 3,000,000. Morgan registrations slowed to a mere trickle. Other breeds became highly specialized. The Standardbred and Thoroughbred, by their superiority as harness and flat racers, excluded all others from the country's tracks. The American Saddle Horse, increasingly bred for show rather than utility, dominated both harness and saddle classes in the ring. Little more than a decade ago the non-specialized horse seemed headed for

HUNTER: Kennebeck Flaming Lady (Lippit Ethan Don–Aflame) owned and bred by Margaret Gardiner. In Northern New England the country is too trappy for a regular hunt, so bloodhounds are used. (Courtesy Margaret Gardiner; Warren Patriquin photo)

PLEASURE: Parade (Cornwallis–Mansphyllis) and his dam Mansphyllis (Mansfield–Paragraph) the only mare to win Produce of Dam four years in succession at the National Morgan Horse Show. (Mr. and Mrs. J. Cecil Ferguson up. Photo used by their courtesy)

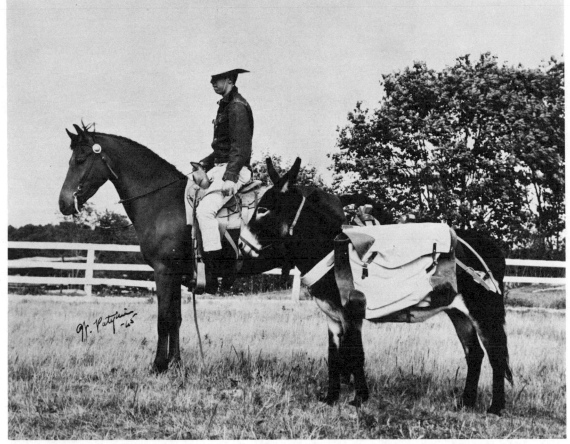

PLEASURE: Kennebec Alazan (Kennebec Ethan–Kennebec Alice May). (Courtesy Margaret Gardiner)

oblivion — as obsolete as the one-horse sleigh, butter mold, or spinning wheel.

The new prosperity and leisure of the fifties and sixties, however, caused a dramatic reversal of the trend. An unofficial estimate places the present horse population of the United States at double the 1959 farm census figure, or more than 6,000,000.

The reasons for the horse's return to favor are fairly complex. In our heritage there are deep-rooted feelings which ascribe nobility both to the horse and to his rider. Mythology is full of super horses and the demi-gods who tamed and rode them: Pegasus and Bellerophon, Siegfried and Greyfel, Frigga and Hofvarpnir. Fairy horses, demon horses, ghost horses, sea horses, wind

PLEASURE: The Fergusons on Broadwall Goldie and Broadwall Trumpeter (Parade–Debutanesque). (Courtesy Mr. J. Cecil Ferguson)

PLEASURE: Mrs. J. Cecil Ferguson and Meg on Broadwall King Midas (Silgal's Improver–Baroosa) and Broadwall Goldie, taken in Vermont on B Ride. (Courtesy Mr. J. Cecil Ferguson; Warren Patriquin photo)

PLEASURE: Mr. and Mrs. Harold Jenkins of Medina, Ohio, on their registered Morgan mares.

PLEASURE: Debbie Shepard on Tippy Dee. (Hawk Jim–Tippy Tin). (George Shepard photo)

PLEASURE: Little Hawk (Devan Hawk–Double H. Cindy) Phyllis Dock up. (Courtesy Norman and Phyllis Dock, Sunset Farm, Bethel, Maine)

PLEASURE: Kennebec Cory 08499 (Bayfield–Royalton Joan Darling) owned and bred by Margaret Gardiner. (Photo by Warren E. Patriquin)

horses, all have been part of tradition and legend. The words "chivalry" and "cavalier," with their implications of aristocracy and *noblesse oblige*, both derive from the French *cheval*, meaning horse. Knights and their ladies rode while peasants and common folk walked. Even the mounted highwayman had about him an aura of distinction which the common thief, burglar or pick-pocket lacked. The cavalryman was considered elite, a far more dashing fellow than the foot soldier, while infantry officers customarily reviewed their troops from the superior height of the saddle. In our highly mobile, status seeking, symbol-laden society, the new horse owner — subconsciously at least — pictures himself in a quasi-heroic role, and hopes that some of the lustrous residue of the past will rub off on him.

Horses have a very special meaning for adolescent and preadolescent girls, especially those with an absent or unsatisfactory father or father-figure. Psychoanalytic literature is rich in examples of horses appearing as phallic symbols in the fantasy life of female neurotics.

Perhaps the most potent factor in the horse's return to popularity in recent years is that Americans as a whole are experiencing a tremendous nostalgia for the past, their own recently vanished pioneer past. This nostalgia is evident in the popularity of gaslights in the newest subdivisions, or the hobbies of collecting artifacts from the past. Antique furniture, china, glassware, firearms, all have their avid collectors. Carriages, muzzle loading muskets, steam powered farm equipment are painstakingly restored. Civil War buffs reenact famous battles of the War Between the States. The Western, a highly stylized art form, glorifying the frontier has contributed tremendously to the upsurge in horse interest.

Lippitt Saul Moro (Lippitt Moro- Lippitt Sally Ash) foaled 1938. Picture taken when gelding was twenty-one. (Courtesy *Morgan Horse Magazine*)

PLEASURE DRIVING: Morgan stallion Parade and his son Broadwall Drum Major. (Courtesy Mr. J. Cecil Ferguson; painting by Harold Bruel)

PLEASURE DRIVING: Morgan four-in-hand at Morven Stud near Charlottesville during the 1964 Virginia Yearling Tour. (Courtesy *Morgan Horse Magazine*)

PLEASURE DRIVING: Morgan four-in-hand owned by Whitney Stone at Morgan Stud near Charlottesville, Virginia. (Courtesy J. Cecil Ferguson)

American tradition and morality are rural. Many people feel a nameless discontent that comes from being out of contact with the rhythms of nature. Life in our cities is often over-close and over-confining. Lemmings react to over crowding by rushing into the sea; certain other rodents become vicious, attacking and destroying each other when they become too numerous. The soaring rate of adult and juvenile crime in our large cities would tend to indicate that man reacts in a similar manner when population density becomes too great. As a retreat, Americans have become very involved in skiing, hiking, riding, camping, fishing and other semi-solitary pursuits.

Contact with horses is an excellent antidote to the tensions resulting from excessive competition, materialism and over-organization. Horse sports have such great therapeutic value that some psychiatric clinics have used riding as part of their treatment of patients.

In spite of increasing urbanization, there are many parts of the United States which are still seen best on horseback. The agile, tractable, easy-gaited, tireless Morgan is an ideal trail and pleasure horse. This fact is reflected in the breed's recent increase in numbers; registrations more than tripled in the ten years between 1954 and 1964. Due to his tremendous individual versatility, the Morgan did not die out as did other less adaptable utility animals such as the Narragansett Pacer, Norman Horse, Vermont Draft Horse or Conestoga Horse. The Morgan remains the ideal family horse, equally at home on the ranches of the West and the bridle paths of the East.

18

Morgans Today

THE GREAT MAJORITY OF PRESENT-DAY MORGANS ARE BEING USED AS family pleasure horses. Because of his ability to be the jack-of-all-trades the Morgan makes an ideal mount for the one-horse stable. Kind and small enough to be ridden and handled by children, yet large enough to carry a father no longer at his best varsity weight, the adaptable Morgan can take on just about any job imaginable. He will go swimming with the youngsters or carry them safely on venturesome cross-country rides. Gaily done up, he can take part in a costume class on Sunday, earn a 4-H ribbon as a saddle horse project at the county fair, or take the whole family for a ride behind him in a buggy or sleigh. He will prance at the Fourth of July parade or pull the manure cart with equal willingness, carry his owner to hounds or win a purse in a cutting contest. Driving for pleasure is again a popular pastime and one for which the Morgan is ideally suited.

Because of their intelligence and docility, a high percentage of males are kept entire. They even make quiet, dependable children's mounts. In 1952, as a three-year-old, Manito (Lippitt Mandate–Vixen) was trained and shown by ten-year old Ann Hopkins, of Green Village, New Jersey. The pair entered every type of competition from which Manito was not excluded by virtue of being a stallion. Similarly, in Cincinnati, the colt Devan Reggie (Star Hawk–Devan Regina) was trained, ridden for pleasure, schooled over the Indian Hills Hunt course and successfully shown by fourteen-year-old Wendy Artzt. He won ribbons in English Pleasure, Road Hack and In Hand both locally and at large regional shows such as the Ohio State Fair and the Morgan Gold Cup Show.

In addition to Western trails and suburban backyards, Morgans are found

PLEASURE DRIVING: Robin Selassie (Dyberry Robin–Lippitt Cecelia) and Manito (Lippitt Mandate–Vixen) hitched to a 1905 Brewster Surrey. (Courtesy of William Hopkins, Green Village, New Jersey)

PLEASURE DRIVING: Chadwick (Jubilee's Courage–Lippitt Dulcie). (Courtesy of Harold Jenkins)

PLEASURE DRIVING: Parade with Mrs. J. Cecil Ferguson and Mrs. Sanders Watney. (Courtesy J. Cecil Ferguson)

PLEASURE DRIVING: Parade. (Courtesy J. Cecil Ferguson)

PLEASURE DRIVING: Morgan mare Kane's Spring Hope (Kane's Jon–Bar-K-Torchee), in 1900-style heavy harness, to basket phaeton. Morgans are widely used for costume harness classes. (Courtesy Margaret Gardiner; Warren E. Patriquin photo)

at the better camps and riding schools. In the thirties, the backbone of the riding string at Camp Wabasso near Bradford, New Hampshire, was Morgan, headed by the lively but gentle red chestnut stallion Wildfire. Ralston Fox Smith, of Red Raider Camp and Riding School near Novelty, Ohio, has high praise for Morgans as the most durable and dependable mounts in his stable. The only complaint he has is that pupils fall in love with them, buy them, and take them home; as in the case of Foxy Prince (Captain Fillmore–Tippy Dee) purchased by the Berkobein family, of Chesterland. The gelding would ride double with Dad and six-year-old daughter and twelve-year-old Leslie entered him in many shows both on the flat and over fences, winning many ribbons.

Whippoorwill Tempo (Whippoorwill Duke–Merry Lyric), many times a blue-ribbon winner. McCulloch Farm, Old Lyme, Connecticut. (Courtesy *Morgan Horse Magazine*)

FUN: Morgans (Holly's Gay B) and children (Sammy Brackman, Jr.) are a natural combination. (Owned by Mr. and Mrs. Sam Brackman, Jackson, Ohio; photo courtesy *Morgan Horse Magazine*)

DISPOSITION PLUS: Elvis (Fleetfield–Felicity) and five grandchildren of Mr. and Mrs. W. W. Peterson, Joliet, Montana. (Courtesy Mrs. Peterson)

Morgan stallion Devan Reggie (Starhawk–Devan Regina), Wendy Artzt up. He was trained, ridden, and shown by his young owner. (Courtesy Ed Artzt, Cincinnati)

Gentle Morgan stallion Lippitt Moro Alert (Lippitt Rob Roy–Lippitt Gladys Moro) owned by John Mahoney, Jamesville, New York. (Courtesy Mr. Mahoney; Warren E. Patriquin photo)

Emerald's Cochise (Sky Chief–Arcie's Nekomia) black Morgan stallion, thirteen-year-old Timothy Morrell up. (Courtesy Mr. and Mrs. Leight Morrell, Tamarlei, Brattleboro, Vermont; photo by Mike Northrup)

Quite a few colleges, including the University of Connecticut, the University of New Hampshire and Earlham College use Morgans in their equitation program.

Morgans are not only used for recreation. In spite of urbanization and mechanization, there are still some jobs which are best performed by a man on horseback. Parts of the country are so mountainous, wild, and inaccessible that not even a jeep can get the mail through, so mounted postmen still make their rounds in a few remote areas; 39 star routes are served on horseback.

The Frontier Nursing Service in the Appalachian region uses horses to reach isolated settlements. Horses can swim a flooded ford, scramble up an icy mountain track or wade through axle-deep mud, which would stop a jeep or force it to turn back. Many babies have been delivered and first aid dispensed by nurses on horseback.

A mounted policeman can see over the tops of cars and make his way through stalled vehicles to unsnarl traffic, where a motorized policeman would be stymied. Nothing forestalls or quells a riot as efficiently as the presence of

Devan Marsh Hawk (Devan Duke–Devan Dimglow). Dana Baker up.

police mounted on calm, disciplined horses. Reese says of the New York Police: "The police horses of New York City have a national reputation for their uniformity of type, color (all being bays), good looks, intelligence, and altogether suitability for the job. They are probably nearer the type of good-sized Morgans than any other present day American breed." Jetmore (Red Oak–Puwanish Maid), a registered Morgan gelding bred by A. H. Barnett, of Derby, Vermont, served with the New York City Police. He won first prize at both the Brooklyn and New York shows as best police horse when shown with the pick of the force. Harvey (Mansfield–Carolyn), a Morgan stallion, served with the Buffalo Police for eight years until he was retired in 1956. The only occasion on which he defected from duty was when his rider, Officer Jabcuga, dismounted to write out a parking ticket. While his master's back was turned, Harvey decided to follow a vegetable wagon in which carrots were temptingly displayed. Justinson (Justin Jubilee–Dorset's Proud Lady) serves with the Boston Police.

In many of our National Parks, the Rangers are mounted on Morgans.

The pride of the Boston Police: Justinson (Justin Jubilee–Dorset's Proud Lady) a chestnut foaled May 27, 1954. (Courtesy Warren Patriquin)

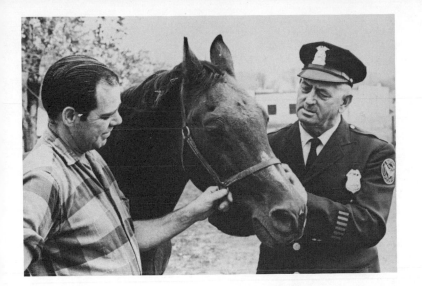

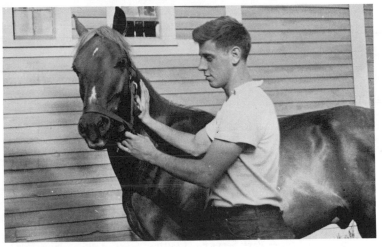

Morgan gelding at Camp Wabasso, Bradford, New Hampshire, 1937.

STOCK: Morgan gelding Red Cloud, age nineteen, owned by T. W. Daniels, Rock Spring, Wyoming. Used in park service. (Courtesy *Morgan Horse Magazine*)

Old Buffalo on top of 11,000-Foot Mount Kent. Morgan gelding used by T. W. Daniels in the United States Park Service. (Courtesy *Morgan Horse Magazine*)

STOCK: Packing a bull elk from Big Horn Mountain. All the horses are Morgans. Champion cutting horse Dee Dee Chocolate (Double Chocolate–Diamond Lil) in center. (Courtesy Charley Hamilton, Triangle A Ranch, Parkman, Wyoming)

Writing in the *Western Horseman*, U.S. Park Ranger, T. W. Daniels described the stamina and savvy of the Morgans he had ridden. A gelding, Red Cloud, covered an average of 800 miles during the busy summer and fall seasons; one year he logged over 1,200 miles. On some fire calls he traveled as much as 55 miles without a stop, over hazardous mountainous trails, often after dark had fallen. "The horse never missed putting his feet in the trail and at bad windfalls he knew the detour without a misstep, although it was pitch dark to me. . . . At the end of these trips he never showed any leg weariness or tiredness . . . Even in his old age, he loved to show a bunch of horses that did not want to be coralled where the corral gate was. All you had to do was stay on him and he loved every bit of it." In his years with the Rangers Mr. Daniels used many Morgans. Even at the advanced age of thirty they "could still do a good day's work. They had heart and legs of steel for the roughest of mountain trails."

Automation has failed to devise a better way of separating one critter from a bunch of cattle than the cowboy and his horse. Large ranches may use from 50 to 100 horses for their routine work. On Robert Anderson's Lincoln County Livestock Company, a spread of about 1,125,000 acres in New Mexico and Texas, 500 horses are needed for handling 557,000 cattle. Another job best done on horseback is inspecting and mending fences. A horse can scramble over boulders, slide down arroyos and snake through dense brush where no vehicle could go. Horses also pack salt to cattle in summer pasture high in the mountainous uplands. They round up the herd and bring them down to lower ranges before bad weather sets in, or drive them to the rail head to be loaded in boxcars and shipped to feeder stations or to market. In the fall they pack elk and deer carcasses down from the high country where wheels have never been. If the ranch has a few paying guests, they see the country on horseback.

Many people in a position to know, because the horse is still very much a necessary part of their way of life, consider the purebred Morgan to be tops as a working stock horse.

Because of their agility, intelligence and dogged willingness to go the last mile when the going is tough, Morgans are second to no other breed as ranch horses. Due to their compact build they develop relatively more energy than a larger, more strung-out animal. For the same reason, they can get by when the pickings are lean and are less subject to dehydration in desert country. The Morgan's springy pasterns and elastic way of moving make him a more comfortable ride, less tiring to the rider and far safer in rough country than the Quarter Horse, which tends to have short, stubby, upright pasterns. The Morgan's quick, energetic step, activated by powerful muscles upon short cannons, eats up the miles. An added bonus is that because of his natural beauty and animation he makes his rider proud to be seen on his back.

In *The Horse,* Kays quotes Roland G. Hill as saying, "I have been raising Morgans for thirty-five years. . . . We have large cattle ranches and use them for cowhorses. . . . I find the Morgan the best cow horse we have ever used and I like the registered ones better than the half-breeds. We use them for the hardest kind of riding and they stand up fine."[1]

CUTTING: Morgan gelding Chesty (Congo–Judith). (Courtesy Joseph E. Olsen, St. George, Utah, Harvey Caplin photo)

Cutting

As an outgrowth of routine ranch work — separating a calf from the herd so it can be branded, castrated, dehorned or medicated — cutting contests

[1] Kays, *The Horse,* A. S. Barnes and Company, New York, 1953, p. 249.

CUTTING: Chesty (Congo–Judith) a top performer at cutting and all Western performance classes. (Courtesy Joseph E. Olsen)

have grown into a major equine sport. Although Morgans excel as cow horses, very few compete in organized cutting. Those which have, however, have given a good account of themselves.

In open cutting meets, horses of all breeds, grade, cross-bred and those of unknown breeding may enter. The National Cutting Horse Association also authorizes single breed shows such as Arabian Cutting or Morgan Cutting. The Morgan Cutting Horse Association is an affiliate of the National Cutting Horse Association and the Morgan Horse Club, Inc. At the present time, open cutting is completely dominated by the Quarter Horse, of which approximately 5,000 are trained and actively campaigned, as compared to few more than a dozen Morgans.

In 1961 the Directors of the Morgan Horse Club, Inc., voted $1,000 to be added to at the rate of $1,000 annually, to a purse to be awarded to the owner of the first registered Morgan to reach the Top Ten Cutting Horse List

CUTTING: Echo's Pixie (Homestake–Majoret P.) Morgan mare, Charley Hamilton up. (Owned by Pendleton Farms, Belle Rive, Illinois; courtesy Charley Hamilton; Alexander photo)

CUTTING: Dee Dee Chocolate; Charley Hamilton up. (Courtesy *Morgan Horse Magazine*)

CUTTING: Dapper Dolly, owned by Tay Mattern with Billy Warne up, participating in open cutting. Dolly took a second in both classes entered. (Courtesy *Morgan Horse Magazine*)

CUTTING: Classy Boy (Condo–Sassy Sue) Morgan stallion. (Courtesy Mosher Brothers, Salt Lake City)

nationally. As of 1966, there is $6,025 in the pot, including an anonymous donation of $25. Since it did not seem likely that anyone was going to step forward and claim the big pot — which was annually getting bigger — the Directors at a board meeting held in Dayton, Ohio on October 22, 1966 voted to make an annual award, beginning in 1967, to the top three Morgan cutting horses based upon points won in open competition in National Cutting Horse Association approved shows. The awards are to be $250 for first, $200 for second, and $100 for third.

It takes years to perfect the skills necessary to a finished cutting horse. His balanced motions, unguided by the rider, and the quick lateral moves are reminiscent of *haute école* dressage. It is a beautiful sight to see a good cutting horse at work, moving with all the catlike grace of a ballet dancer. We in the East see so much bad Western riding with excessive spurring and jawing that it is a revelation to see a master of the art such as Charley Hamilton or Marlin Manning demonstrate his skill.

CONTESTING: Madison Lad (Major R. M.–Detta), owner Warren Ward, Eugene, Oregon, up. A barrel race winning combination. (Courtesy *Morgan Horse Magazine*)

CUTTING: Dee Dee Chocolate, age eleven, open Morgan Cutting champion in 1963. Charley Hamilton up; owned by Patsye Brown, L A Ranch, Oshoto, Wyoming. (Courtesy Charley Hamilton)

Rex Linsley 11550 stallion, owned by Windmere Farm, Albuquerque, New Mexico. Winner of Western Pleasure, Santa Fe Horse Show for third consecutive year. A challenge Cup will be offered in his name in this class at the 1964 show. Also winner of Reining, N. M. Pattern, and Stock Horse. Owner Mrs. W. C. Byers up.

CONTESTING: (Courtesy *Morgan Horse Magazine*)

The majority of Morgan cutting horses are also ridden for pleasure by their owners, and pitch in with the routine ranch work as needed. The motto of the Jackson Ranch in Harrison, Montana, is "We use our show horses and show our using horses." Cutting competition sharpens the horse's skills rather than making him unfit for other use as, unfortunately, do some other types of showing. Chesty Boy (Congo–Judith), a Morgan cutting horse owned by Joseph Olsen of St. George, Utah, is ridden both English and Western, has placed well in dressage trials, drives in double or single harness and jumps well up to 3′6″. Dee Dee Chocolate (Double Chocolate–Diamond Lil), open Morgan cutting champion in 1963, trained by Charley Hamilton of Triangle A Ranch, Parkman, Wyoming, does her share of the work around the ranch and takes hunters into the mountains after big game.

DRESSAGE: High Pastures Sampson (Ethan Eldon–Lippitt Ramona), Phillipa Crow, Woodstock, Vermont, up. First place open dressage competition, Woodstock Horse Show, August, 1963. Owned by High Pastures Morgan Horse Farm, Brownsville, Vermont. (Courtesy Mary Turgeon)

Dressage

Because of their natural balance and agility, Morgans are excellent candidates for dressage. Many people confuse the word, which literally means training, with *haute école,* which is dressage carried to the highest level.

By use of the natural aids — hands, legs, seat and voice — the horse is trained and learns to become responsive to the rider. His balance under saddle, suppleness and muscular strength are developed, while he becomes light in hand and obedient to the rider's will.

According to the 1965 A. H. S. A. rule book, "The object of dressage is the harmonious and progressive development of the physique and ability of the horse. As a result it makes the horse calm, supple and keen, resulting in a perfect understanding with its rider. The horse gives the impression of doing of his own accord that which is required of him by the rider."

Although dressage is a long, painstaking process, the effects are far more lasting than those achieved by short-cut methods — gimmicks, overbitting and the use and misuse of artificial aids such as whips, spurs, martingales —

DRESSAGE: High Pastures Sampson, Dr. Hans Van Schaik, Cavendish, Vermont, up. Shows half pass. (Courtesy Mary Turgeon)

DRESSAGE: High Pastures Sampson. (Courtesy Mary Turgeon)

DRESSAGE: Prince of Pride (Dickie's Pride–Utah Queen) winning the Dressage Class at the 1964 Western National Morgan Horse Show. (Alexander photo; courtesy Mary Wolverton, Littleton, Colorado)

which are, too often the detriment of the horse's mouth, manners and soundness.

Dressage is the classic European method of training the horse; it had its origin in the need for the officer's charger to maneuver at close quarters in mounted combat. It was employed by the United States Cavalry in schooling remounts as early as 1862. It is one of the three major phases of international equestrian competition, both as a separate event and as the first part of combined training events.

Until recently dressage was one phase of horsemanship that enjoyed little civilian participation in the United States. Morgan owners especially seemed to ignore it. The United States Pony Clubs have introduced many youngsters to dressage, but as a field of competition it has been Thoroughbred-dominated. Prince of Pride, Manito, Chesty, Kennebec Archbrook and George Dulaney's grade mare Vixen have all done well in open dressage competition.

No small measure of Suncrest Cavalier's tremendous show ring success is due to his thorough foundation in dressage.

One of the most distinguished Morgan dressage horses is High Pastures Sampson (Ethan Eldon–Lippit Ramona). As a five-year-old, after only a few months of training under Hans Van Shaik, Sammy entered a B 2 Test at the United States Equestrian Team headquarters at Gladstone, New Jersey. He placed third among a large field of experienced performers. The following year he was first in the Open Dressage Competition at the Woodstock Horse Show. In 1966, Margaret Gardiner's six year old Morgan stallion Kennebec Archbrook (Kennebec Ethan–Sunday News), also trained by Dr. Van Shaik, won the second level Dressage Class at the International Equestrian Organization Show held at York, Pennsylvania.

During the Vienna Spanish School's triumphant tour of the United States, two Morgans joined the Lipizzaner stallions. Sixteen-year-old stallion Parade

DRESSAGE: Kennebec Archbrook 12750 (Kennebec Ethan–Sunday News) six-year-old owned and bred by Margaret Gardiner. Dr. Van Shaik up. The 14:2-hand stallion won the second level Dressage Class at the International Equestrian Organization Show, York, Pennsylvania, 1966. (Warren Patriquin photo; courtesy Margaret Gardiner)

DRESSAGE: Parade, Johann Isbinger up. This horse toured the United States with the Lipizanners of the Spanish Riding School of Vienna. (Courtesy J. Cecil Ferguson; Freudy photo)

DRESSAGE: Royalton Billy Roberts (Ethan Eldon–Justine Morgan), first-place winner in Dressage Class at National Morgan Horse Show. Owned and ridden by Mary Turgeon. (Photo courtesy Mrs. Turgeon; Freudy photo)

(Cornwallis–Mansphyllis) and his son, Broadwall Drum Major, were loaned by Mr. and Mrs. J. Cecil Ferguson of Broadwall Farm, Greene, Rhode Island. Colonel Alois Podhajsky, director of the School, had the highest praise of the Morgans' ability.

Undoubtedly dressage will be a continuing and increasingly important factor in Morgan activities. An exhibition by High Pastures Sampson at the 1963 National Morgan Horse Show was so well received that a dressage class was offered the following year. In 1965 the class had so many entries that it was necessary to divide it into junior (rider under eighteen) and senior (over eighteen).

Even at the elementary level, dressage trials are an excellent measure of a horse's skill and physical capabilities.

Competitive Long Distance Rides

The oldest and most famous of all competitive 100 mile rides is the one sponsored by the Green Mountain Horse Association, of South Woodstock, Vermont. Its purpose is to stimulate increased interest in the breeding and development of using horses with stamina and endurance. It also demonstrates the type of animal most suited to a long ride, the proper methods of conditioning for such a ride and the best methods of caring for a horse during a long ride. The use of medication, stimulants and linaments is strictly forbidden.

The Vermont 100 Mile Ride grew out of the endurance rides of 300 miles in five days, which were sponsored by the United States Cavalry in conjunction with the Morgan Horse Club. The 300 mile rides were gruelling affairs held, for the greater part, over hard surfaced roads. In 1921, 27 horses started but only six finished. In 1924 none of the 17 starters was able to finish. Lady Wentworth, the Arab's most outspoken champion, felt that because of their relatively small size, "A great weight handicap was placed on the Arabs and Morgans, but they were able to carry it with less leg trouble, but at a sacrifice to speed."

C. C. Stillman, one of the founders of the Morgan Horse Club and keeper of the stud book from 1919 to 1926, contributed to the Morgans' success in the endurance rides of the early twenties. He personally selected and purchased Morgans, both registered and grade, and then hired riders to condition them and ride them in the competition.

Between 1919 and 1924 the sons and daughters of General Gates were outstanding in these events, bearing out Joseph Battell's confidence in the horse as a sire. Although hundreds of horses of all breeds and types were put into training with the 300-Mile Ride as a goal, only 118 ever started of

Morgan gelding Gladstone (General Gates–Minnehaha) placed second in the 1922 300-mile endurance ride sponsored by the United States Cavalry. (Photo courtesy Department of Agriculture)

Castor (General Gates-Babe by Bob Morgan) a stallion used in the Remount Service, placed well on three 300-mile competitive rides sponsored by the Cavalry. (Courtesy Department of Agriculture)

which 48 actually finished the course. Of the 48 to finish, 5 were Morgans, which accounted for nine finishes and six of the placings in the money. Castor (General Gates–Babe by Bob Morgan) and two Arabians were the only horses able to complete three rides. Castor completed the ride in the second-best time in 1919. In 1921 he carried the required 245 pounds — almost one-third of his slight 800 pounds — without developing any leg trouble. He lost only 12½ pounds during the contest. The gelding Gladstone (General Gates–Minnehaha), and the mares Dolly (Dewey–Nelly) and Jessie (Scotland–Ellen), granddaughters of General Gates; Eudora, a full sister to Castor; and Major S. (St.S.Superb–Jewel M.), a grandson, all finished or placed on the ride. In 1925, Gurney C. Gue pronounced General Gates to be the "outstanding sire in cavalry tests."

Over a period of four years, the Morgans had the highest percentage of finishers to starters of any other breed entered — 54.55 per cent as compared to 45.15 per cent for the Arabs and 31.25 per cent for the Thoroughbreds.

The year 1965 marked the 30th anniversary of the Vermont 100 Mile Trail Ride. There were 60 horses from eleven states entered, of which 47 finished.

Before the ride begins, each horse receives a detailed veterinary inspection to determine the animal's probable soundness. All horses are weighed and the amount of weight lost by a horse during the ride is used as a measure of the animal's condition. Scars and blemishes must be declared before the start of the ride. Unsound and unfit animals are not permitted to start and each year a few are eliminated at the preliminary inspection.

On the first two days, entries cover 40 miles, which must be completed between six and one-half and seven hours. Time penalties are imposed for early as well as late finishes, so the contest is in no way a race. On the third day, the remaining 20 miles are to be covered between two and three-quarters and three hours. Each horse is carefully inspected at the end of each day's ride, as well as at several checkpoints along the way. The entry that covers ground at a steady, moderate gait — usually a brisk trot — has an advantage. Horses of medium size seem to be the most efficient, with balanced action being more important than height or length of stride. Entries are judged 80 per cent on condition, based upon soundness, weight loss, and general appearance; 10 per cent on manners and way of going; and 10 per cent on time.

Because of the number of entries, the ride is now held in three divisions: Junior (twelve to eighteen years), Lightweight (155 pounds to 180 pounds), and Heavyweight (Over 180 pounds). If rider, tack and equipment do not add up to the minimum, dead weight is added. Juniors must complete a 50-mile ride prior to being eligible to enter the Junior Division of the 100-Mile Ride.

Although formerly the Vermont 100 Mile Ride was Morgan-dominated — not only in number of horses entering, but in percentage finishing and in placings — unfortunately, in recent years not enough good Morgans have been properly trained and conditioned to make the showing of which the breed is capable. In 1939, 14 registered Morgans entered as compared with 4 Arabs and 3 Thoroughbreds. But, of late, Arabian enthusiasts have taken over, dominate this particular field of competition and win the top honors — at least in part due to default by Morgan owners.

During the first three years of the ride, a Morgan was among the top three horses, taking third place in 1936, both first and third in 1937 and third in 1938. Lady Luck (Saltram–Kate by the Wright Horse), ridden by R. S. Hall, won the 1937 ride. In 1938, Ruth Worthington hacked her half-Morgan mare Valerie (Kalitan–Sufragette) 200 miles from Lake Saranac to Woodstock, won the 100 Mile Ride, and hacked home again! The mare was out of a registered Morgan and was sired by a Thoroughbred, winner of the 1917 Preakness Stakes. She carried 225 pounds during her long journey. The same year, Mrs. Ruth Dickson, of Townshend Farm, Weston, Massachusetts, had four entries, including Sadwin (John A. Darling–Gladwin) ridden by Mary Turgeon, which placed third. Sadwin also won the Maine 80 Mile Trail Ride on three occasions. In 1939 a half-Morgan, Upwey Princess, was winner.

One of the most outstanding Morgan trail horses was Friendly (Mansfield–Ulwina by Bennington) owned and ridden by Miss Lucie Brown, of Milton, Massachusetts, who won the Lightweight Division in 1942 and 1943, the only horse ever to win a division in two successive years. The first stallion to win either a division or a sweepstakes was a son of Mansfield, Lippit Morman. Placed second in 1945, he came back to win both Heavyweight and Sweepstakes in 1946. Another son of Mansfield, Buddy — out of the Brunk bred mare Jana — placed second in the Heavyweight in 1942, second in the Lightweight in 1944, fifth in the Heavyweight in 1945 and seventh in 1946.

In 1961, Morgans made a poor showing with only eight entered, of which five were able to finish. Of the five completing the ride, however, four placed in the Junior Division. At least the youngsters were in there trying, even if the adults were not.

The following year, the Morgans made a strong comeback. Although fewer horses were entered, they were better conditioned and all six to enter finished, the first time in the history of the ride that 100 per cent of one breed

Lippitt Morman (Mansfield–Lippitt Kate Moro) a full brother to Lippitt Mandate, and Sadwin (John A. Darling–Gladwin) on the 1946 Vermont 100-mile ride. Lippitt Morman was the first stallion ever to take first place in a division of the ride. Sadwin was third in the 1938 ride. (Courtesy *Morgan Horse Magazine*)

On the 1962 Vermont 100-mile ride. (Courtesy *Morgan Horse Magazine*)

Broadwall Bugler (Parade–Lyndrita), full brother to Broadwall Rhythm, winning the Junior Division of the 1964 Vermont 100-mile ride. Owned and ridden by Pamela Brassard, Seekonk, Massachusetts. (Courtesy *Morgan Horse Magazine*)

had done so, although one entry was disqualified for time. Townshend Lady-O-Peace was the highest placed Morgan, earning second in the Sweepstakes. UVM Deborah won the best trail horse award and was fourth in the Heavyweight Division, an impressive record for her first attempt at competitive long distance riding.

In 1964, six of the seven Morgans entered started. Timber Trails (Easter Twilight–Penn State Co-ed) was third in the Heavyweight Division. Earlier in the year he had placed second in the New Jersey 100 Mile Ride. Pamela Brassard won the Junior Division with her Broadwall Bugler (Parade–Lyndrita). Top honors of the competition went to an eleven-year-old mare of Moyle breeding owned and ridden by Mrs. W. E. Mackay-Smith. As we have seen, the Moyle breed developed in Utah is of probable Morgan origin. Mrs. Mackay-Smith's mare won both the Sweepstakes and Heavyweight Division.

In 1965 for the first time in recent years Morgans outnumbered Arabs both in number of entries — 14 to 11 — and in number finishing — 9 to 7 — although the percentages finishing were virtually identical: 64 percent of the Morgans completed the ride as compared with 63½ per cent of the Arabs. The honors, too, were almost equally divided. A Thoroughbred, Nike, took the Heavyweight, an Arab the Lightweight and Sweepstakes, while a Morgan, Equinox Welcome (Dyberry Buddy–Royalton Samantha), owned by **Orin Beattie**, of Manchester Center, Vermont, and ridden by Lynda Beattie won the Junior Division. Captain Paleface (Easter Twilight–Lavender Lassie) won the coveted Best Trail Horse in the Senior Division while placing second in the Heavyweight Division.

Broadwall Rhythm placed second in the Lightweight Division of the 1965 Vermont 100-Mile Ride. (Courtesy *Morgan Horse Magazine*)

Competitive Trail Riding: Ten-year-old gelding Captain Paleface (Easter Twilight–Lavender Lassie) owned and ridden by Mrs. Gabrielle Le Paige, Woodstock, New York. Horse placed second in Heavyweight Division and won best trail horse award in 1965 Vermont 100-Mile Ride. (Courtesy Mrs. Le Paige)

Susie Belle (Lippitt Morman–Anita Belle) owned by Dr. Elvin Stanton, Glendora, California, at the start of the Los Compadres Invitational Trail Ride. Her sire, Lippitt Morman was the first stallion to win the Vermont 100-Mile Ride. (Courtesy *Morgan Horse Magazine*)

In 1961, Lucille Kenyon of Altoona, Florida, a veteran of 24 hundred-mile rides placed second in the Heavyweight Division of a North Carolina 100 mile ride with her five-year-old Morgan mare Priscilla Alden (Parade–Baroosa), an extremely rare animal, a horse absolutely without scar, blemish or unsoundness to be declared.

In 1964, Little Joe Morgan won the Lightweight and Keystone's Rome Beauty took second in the Heavyweight Division in a one-day ride sponsored by the Southern California Morgan Club, but open to horses of all breeds.

Morgans have placed well in other competitive trail rides wherever and whenever their owners have taken the time and effort necessary to condition them for such demanding activity.

Showing

Because of their natural style, action, animation, and beauty Morgans make excellent show horses. Their short, slick coats take on a lovely bloom with a little extra grooming. Their flowing manes and tails accent each motion. There is a little ham in all Morgans. They willingly strut their stuff at the sight of a crowd or a group of other horses. It was because of this lightness and jaunty manner that the original Morgan Horse and his sons were in such demand to lead parades or to drill with the local militia at their musters.

Wherever there were state fairs, there were Morgans to take first premium

Tas Tee's Indian Summer. She is the first mare ever to win the Morgan Versatility Show Championship. Mike Goebig, Philadelphia, up. (Courtesy *Morgan Horse Magazine*)

Chico's Flame (L. U. Colonel–Tippy Dee), a distinguished Morgan show horse. He is shown both English and Western and was high-point Morgan in Ohio, 1963. Owner Dorothy Chapman, Spencer, Ohio, up. (Courtesy the *Morgan Horse Magazine*)

ROADSTER: Anna-Marie Mar-Lo (Mickey Finn–Ruthven's Barbara Ann) at the Mid-Atlantic Horse Show, Frederick, Maryland. Owned by Cascade Farm. (Courtesy Ethel Gardner, Philadelphia)

as all-purpose horses and as roadsters. In 1849, Grey Hawk (Harlow Horse) received the first premium at the Windsor County Fair in Vermont and at the New York State Fair. At the first Vermont State Fair, held at Middlebury, 75 sons and daughters of Old Black Hawk were on hand to follow him around the track.

During the twenties and thirties Morgans were often shown under saddle in open three-gaited classes with roached manes and tails; judging from the old photographs, some of them had had their tails nicked and set.

As the general interest in horses increased, Morgan numbers also grew. Shows began offering classes restricted to registered Morgans and rules were set up for showing them. Artificial appliances such as braids and quarter boots (except in roadster classes) were specifically excluded; the horses were to be shown with full mane and tail, the latter unset and ungingered.

Many outstanding show horses were also used for work or pleasure during the week, given an extra-special grooming on Sunday and taken into the ring to perform under saddle or in harness. In 1939, after completing the Vermont 100 Mile Ride, Mountain Sheik (Mendon Boy–Rachel) showed in the first Morgan Horse Show at South Woodstock. "He was fresh as a daisy, in

Kennebec Ethel (011038) (Kennebec Ethan–Helen May) with owner-breeder Margaret Gardiner up. Placed 2nd on Maine 100-mile ride. (Photo courtesy Margaret Gardiner)

Lippitt Mandate (Mansfield– Lippitt Kate Moro) successful show stallion, sire, and sire of sires. (Courtesy Mrs. Harold Childs, Tunbridge, Vermont)

Lippitt Mandate in saddle class. Note natural action and tail, beautiful balance, and animation. (Courtesy Mrs. Harold Childs)

fact a little too fresh for horse show etiquette," wrote a correspondent in the *Vermont Horse*. One of the most notable stallions to combine pleasure with show ring success is Parade. On one occasion his owner, J. Cecil Ferguson, rode him on a 20 mile trail ride in the Berkshires on a Saturday and on Sunday placed second with him in a performance class at Weston. It was not at all unusual for a horse to hack to the show, collect several ribbons of the preferred colors and hack home again.

The outstanding Morgan Lippitt Mandate (Mansfield–Lippitt Kate Moro) was equally successful in the ring and out. He has won ribbons in saddle, fine harness, stock, roadster and jumping classes. He was New England Morgan Champion as a five-year-old and continued to win championships consistently until he last showed in 1955 at the age of fifteen. In his best years he met and defeated every other champion of the breed. He was shown in Ohio, Michigan, Iowa and Illinois in addition to the New England and Mid-Atlantic circuits. For several years he was regularly hunted with the Beaufort Hunt near Harrisburg, Pennsylvania. He never wore anything but a keg shoe in the ring and out, and during his entire show career was used regularly by his owner for pleasure. He participated in three Green Mountain Trail Association Fifty Mile Rides. He further distinguished himself by siring

Vixen (Virgil–Althea) extremely successful show mare, bred by Stone Family Association, Charlottesville, Virginia. (Courtesy Mrs. Harold Childs)

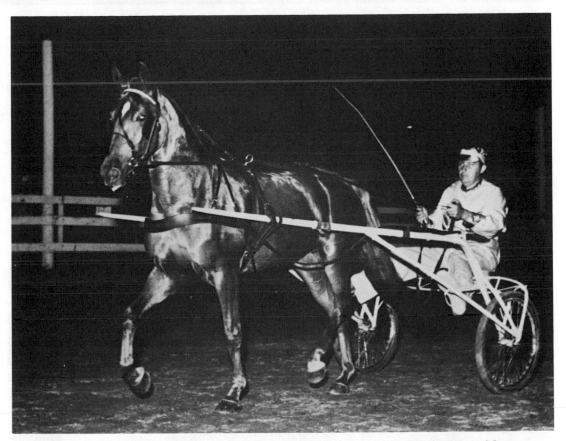

ROADSTER: Anna-Marie Mar-Lo at the National Morgan Horse Show, Northampton, Massachusetts. One of the fastest trotting Morgans of modern times. Owned by Cascade Farm. (Courtesy Ethel Gardner)

Lippitt Mandate; winning roadster in harness, National Morgan Horse Show, 1953: Harold Childs, whip. (Courtesy Mrs. Harold Childs; Freudy photo)

Lippitt Mandate jumping. (Courtesy Mrs. Harold Childs; E. Morgan Savage photo)

numerous champions, including versatile Manito, The Third Man, Mr. Showman, Lippman Hawk, Man O'Day, Carolina, Talisman, Romance, Minute Man, Man O'Destiny, The Marksman and Mandate's Peggy Lou.

The National Morgan Horse Show has become one of the most outstanding one-breed shows in the United States. It grew out of the Eastern Morgan Horse Show organized by Owen Moon, Jr., in 1939 to celebrate the 150th anniversary of the birth of Justin Morgan. The first show was held at Mr. Moon's summer home, a farm near South Woodstock. It followed the Green Mountain Trail Association's 100 Mile Trail Ride with many horses participating in both events; 110 Morgans showed in eighteen classes. The show

Harness Pairs: Town-Ayr Echo (Lippitt Rob Roy–Lantz' Beauty) and Towne-Ayr Baythorne (same parents): Morgan geldings owned by Mrs. Seth Holcombe; E. A. Wolcott, Jr., whip. (Courtesy Seth Holcombe; Freudy photo)

Pairs: Broadwall Drum Major and his sire, Parade: Morgan stallions ridden by Mrs. Bruce Ferguson and Meg Ferguson. (Courtesy J. Cecil Ferguson; Warren Patriquin photo)

soon outgrew its original site and since 1952 has been held at the Tri-County Fair Grounds near Northampton, Massachusetts. In 1957 there were 250 entries and by 1962 there were 396; 464 in 1963 and in 1964, 528. Increasing interest in Morgans for pleasure has been reflected in the number of entries and the number of classes. In 1958 there was one Western Pleasure Class with 14 entered; the event was divided in 1963 with 24 showing. Two English Pleasure Classes in 1958 have expanded to four with 80 Morgans entered. In Pleasure Driving, one class in 1958 has become five classes with 78 entries in 1963. Road Hack also doubled during the same period from two classes and 42 entries to four classes with 62 entries.

The caliber of the horses competing is the highest and the competition is extremely keen. Horses come not only from New England but also from the entire Eastern United States, Florida, the Mid-West and even a few from the Far West.

One of the most interesting shows from the spectator standpoint is Ethel

U. C. Hermes (Meade–Hermina), ten-year-old stallion in the Trail Class at the 1963 Morgan Versatility Show. (Owner: Eugene Holden)

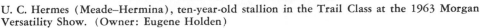

Gardner's unique Morgan Versatility Show held each fall near Philadelphia. It is an exacting test of a horse's all round ability and endurance. For a single entry fee a horse may enter as many as 10 of 13 classes, earning points toward a championship. Each horse in a class is rated from 0 to 10 on each of ten criteria and can earn up to 100 points a class or 1,000 for the entire show. Because each horse's performance can be evaluated in each phase against every other horse, the show is a highly educational experience for the rider. He can see in exactly what areas his and his horse's shortcomings lie. Although the horse that enters the greatest number of classes has the best chance of earning a placing in the Championship, no points are awarded for a horse that is obviously not working. The contest is an A. H. S. A. Honor Show and confers quadruple points.

Held on a single day, the show demands a well-conditioned horse, which is thoroughly capable of doing an honest day's work. The classes held under A. H. S. A. rules are Stock, English Pleasure, Trail, Fine Harness, Flat Race of One-Half Mile, In Hand, Saddle, Western Pleasure, Half-Mile Harness

U. S. Panez 10446 (Panfield–Inez) owned by Mr. Richard Nelson, Amherst, Massachusetts.

Kane's Spring Delight (John Geddes–Barbette) owned by Camelot Farms, Fort Lauderdale.

Bar-T Superman (Orcland Leader–Orcland Victoria), Molly Pickett, whip, in Fine Harness Class at 1963 Morgan Versatility Show. The pair won the Championship in 1964, and Reserve in 1965.

Race, Pleasure Driving, Jumping, Walking Race and Work Harness. The Pleasure Driving is a beautiful class with antique vehicles, carefully restored, furnished by the show committee.

The Morgans exhibited at the Versatility Show have breed character to a marked degree, combined with quality and finish. All of the show champions have been outstanding individuals: the stallions Manito in 1961 and 1963, Prince of Pride in 1962, the geldings Bar-T Superman in 1964 and Suncrest Cavalier in 1965, and the mare Tas-Tee's Indian Summer in 1966.

In addition to showing in classes limited to Morgans, many horses have been shown successfully in open classes such as Road Hack, Trail, English Pleasure, Western Pleasure, Hunter, Jumper, Stock, Equitation, 4-H Fairs and contests such as barrel racing, pole bending, and cutting. Many Morgans are under 14:2 hands, and therefore are technically ponies and may be shown as such, but not at the same show at which they enter breed classes. The A. H. S. A. Rule III, Section 3 (c) states that, "No animal shall compete as a horse in one class and as a pony in another during the same show."

One of the most distinguished horses to compete in 4-H was Devan Hawk (Hawk Jim–Starflake). Bred by Merle D. Evans and foaled in 1949, he was sold as a yearling to Martha Moore, of Hampshire Hill Farm in Prattville, Alabama. He placed well on the 1956 Florida 100 Mile Trail Ride,

Bar-T Superman, owned by Mr. and Mrs. R. D. Pickett, Amherst, Massachusetts, at Versatility Show.

VERSATILITY CHAMPION: Suncrest Cavalier winning the Western Pleasure class at the 1965 Mid-Atlantic Morgan Show. Jane Blue up. (Tarrance photo; courtesy Dr. Ann Pressman)

Versatile Suncrest Cavalier at the 1965 Mid-Atlantic Morgan Show. (Tarrance photo; courtesy Dr. Ann Pressman)

Suncrest Cavalier, another view. (Bobbie photo; courtesy Dr. Ann Pressman)

Bar-T Superman and his thirteen-year-old rider, Molly Pickett, Amherst, Massachusetts. (Courtesy *Morgan Horse Magazine*)

Registered with both the Morgan and Palomino Horse Breeder's Association, Prince of Pride (Dickie's Pride–Utah Queen) is shown winning the Palomino Stake at the 1963 National Western Stock Show in Denver. Owner Mary Wolverton up. (Courtesy Miss Wolverton)

The Third Man (Lippitt Mandate–Dottie Irene) in the Trail Class at the 1963 Morgan Versatility Show. The bay gelding excels as a hunter and jumper.

Captain Paleface (Easter Twilight–Lavender Lassie) after the ½ mile Running Race at the 1963 Morgan Versatility Show. (Owned by Gabrielle Le Paige)

Manito (Lippitt Mandate–Vixen) twice Champion of the Morgan Versatility Show. Ann Hopkins up.

Stock Horse Kilgoran Bonni, at 1965 Versatility Show.

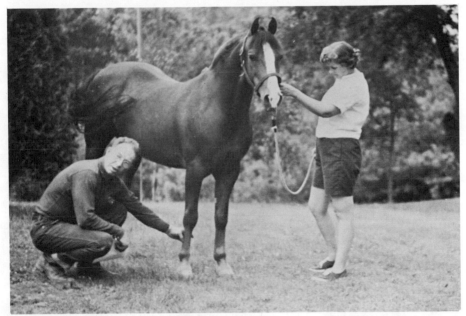

Devan Pambroke (O C R–Devan Pam). Russell Scott points out short cannons and clean tendons, while Mrs. Don Shook holds halter and shank.

Sea Mist (Sea Breeze–Red Jewell) at the Summit County, Ohio, 4-H Judging Clinic. Owned by Bob Rutledge.

Devan Dale (O C R–Glenhawk) with Don Shook and Sea Mist with Bob Rutledge at the Summit County clinic.

is skilled at basic dressage, is a delightful pleasure horse, drives, pulls in work harness, hunts with local packs and has won quite a bit of money barrel racing and cutting. Really an all-round Morgan! He was Reserve Champion of the All-American Morgan Horse Show in Chicago and Junior Champion Stallion. He also had a highly successful career at stud, siring the very typey Little Hawk, now standing at Norman and Phyllis Dock's Sunset Farm in Bethel, Maine. At the age of fourteen he was gelded and sold to Bob Juve of Copley, Ohio, for his young daughter, Tina, to use in 4-H. Tina showed him in local shows and at several Summit County Junior Fairs. Among their many winnings were first in a huge halter class, and firsts in English Pleasure and English Equitation. One year Hawk was high point English Horse, and in 1962 he was third high point horse of the Fair in a county that is not only dominated, but swamped with Quarter Horses. Hawk is back in Alabama with his former owner, now Mrs. M. H. von Redlich, teaching her youngsters, age three and five, to ride.

Devan Hawk (Hawk Jim–Starflake) Tina Juve up. (Courtesy Bob Juve, Copley, Ohio)

Little Hawk (Devan Hawk–Cindy) in Justin Morgan Performance Class at Maine Morgan Horse Show. Norm Dock is on the lines. Hawk pulls rake and cultivator at Sunset Farm, where he is senior sire. (Courtesy Norman and Phyllis Dock)

In 1958, George W. Dulaney, a riding instructor and trainer of hunters in Baltimore, attended a horse auction looking for durable, school-horse types. He bought a couple of Morgans, which their Mid-West breeder had culled and shipped to the sale, an unbroken mare and a green-broke gelding. The horses came to hand more readily than anything Mr. Dulaney had seen in 20 years as a professional. The Morgans were schooled in jumping and elementary dressage and were used in advanced equitation classes. At the end of three months the trainer allowed a pupil who had been riding for less

HUNTER: Champion hunter-jumper General (breeding unknown. Said to be Morgan). George W. Dulaney up. (Courtesy Mr. Dulaney)

than a year to take the mare, which he called Vixen, to a junior combined training event to participate only in the dressage phase, thinking the competition would be extremely valuable experience for both green horse and rider. Not much was expected in the way of placing. Through some mix-up in communications, the youngster entered all three phases, winning the dressage and stadium jumping, and placing third in the stiff cross-country course in a field of 40 horses, principally Thoroughbred or Thoroughbred type! Both horses that finished ahead of Vixen had had a great deal of experience, having hunted several seasons, shown and run in local hunt races. One was an imported Irish horse standing 17 hands. The remarkable thing about the whole performance was that the mare stood a scant 15 hands, had never galloped cross country, had never jumped at speed and had never been asked

The Third Man (Lippitt Mandate–Dottie Irene). (Courtesy *Morgan Horse Magazine*)

JUMPING: Broadwall King Midas (Silgal's Improver–Baroosa), Morgan gelding owned by Mrs. Lawrence Earl. (Courtesy J. Cecil Ferguson; Earnest L. Mauger photo)

to take such obstacles as faced her on the 22-fence course. Truly an amazing performance. After that, Vixen was shown widely in hunter and jumper classes and was never out of the ribbons. In hunt country for a 15 hand horse to be looked at he has to be a real performer. The gelding General did every bit as well as the mare. Both became too valuable to retain as school horses and were sold. They were shown throughout the East and on the tough New York circuit. General once changed hands for a reported $5,000, a bargain considering that his steadiness and competence in fencing amounted to life insurance in the hunting field.

JUMPING: April Surprise; Ann Hopkins up. (Courtesy William R. Hopkins)

Another outstanding Morgan performer is Manito, a son of the great Lippitt Mandate and the Virginia bred registered Morgan mare Vixen (Virgil–Althea). The gallant little chestnut stallion, twice winner of the Morgan Versatility Show, was bred by Marilyn C. Childs and is owned by William Hopkins, of Green Village, New Jersey. He has entered almost every type of competition — trail rides, combined training, pairs, harness, saddle, stock — and as a sire he passes on his versatility to his get. His son A. B. Dillon has been shown by a ten-year-old in hunter seat equitation and hunter classes. Also bred and trained by Bill Hopkins and his daughter Ann is April Surprise (Nekomia's Archie–Lantz's Flicka), a hunter champion. Robin Selassie

ROADSTER: Manito (Lippitt Mandate–Vixen). (Courtesy William R. Hopkins)

(Dyberry Robin–Lippitt Cecelia) another outstanding performer is following in the Hopkins tradition of demonstrating that whether hitched to a cart, running a race, or jumping a fence, a Morgan can do the job efficiently and with his own unique style.

Another outstanding performer shown principally in open rather than breed classes is Cap's Stormy (Devan Cap–Tippy Dee by Hawk Jim). He was bred by Milford Fox, of Chesterland, Ohio, from Evans stock. As a two-year-old started in reining, he was acquired by the Jess Baker family, of Solon, Ohio. He was a family project, first ridden by Carolyn, and later taken over by her thirteen-year-old sister, Dana. Sonny, as the gelding is always called, hunted with the Chagrin Valley Hounds, pulled his mistress behind him on skis, took a dressage course at Lake Erie College and was shown all over northern Ohio in local and regional shows. Between 1959 and 1961 he was out of the ribbons in only three classes. Because artificial methods of showing Morgans were, unfortunately, quite prevalent in Ohio at that time, and because the Bakers preferred to keep him natural so that he could be enjoyed between shows, Sonny was entered in breed classes on only two occasions, in which he was pinned third and fourth against the

Cap's Stormy (Devan Cap–Tippy Dee) at the Chagrin Valley Show in 1961. Dana Baker up. (*Plain Dealer* photo)

WESTERN PAIRS: Morgan Cap's Stormy (Devan Cap–Tippy Dee), left. Dana Baker up. (Courtesy Alice Baker)

Cap's Stormy (Devan Cap–Tippy Dee) schooling over a four-foot coop, Cameron York (age twelve) up. (Courtesy Martha York, Memphis)

area's top saddle performance horses. He was shown in Paris, Costume, Road Hack, Hunter Seat Equitation and Pleasure. Shown only once in hand, as a yearling at the Geauga County Fair, he won the blue in a colt class over many entries of all breeds. In 1961 he was Central Ohio Champion Road Hack, Champion Hunter Seat Equitation Horse (14–17) and Reserve Champion English Pleasure Horse. He was many times a junior show champion.

In 1962 Cap's Stormy was sold to the Cordra York family, of Memphis, Tennessee, for their ten-year-old daughter, Cameron. Sonny continued his winning ways on the Mid-South Circuit, and his outstanding performance as a jumper have won him mention in the *Chronicle* on many occasions. One of his most glorious moments came when he won a jumper class at Germantown, Tennessee in a class of 50. Many of the other horses could

Cap's Stormy and Cameron York. (Courtesy Martha York)

have jumped over him flatfooted, for Sonny stands only 14:3. When he came into the ring the crowd laughed to see all those big fences and such a little horse, but when he jumped they applauded, for he soared over the obstacles as if he had wings, scoring the only clean round in the class. He is one of the very few registered Morgans in Tennessee, but is making an excellent name for his breed by his high standing in the Hunter-Jumper Division, of which he was Reserve Champion in 1965.

Prince of Pride (Dickie's Pride–Utah Queen) is another who shows the world that the Morgan takes a back seat to none. He is owned by Mary Woolverton, a Denver social worker. The stallion is registered both with the Morgan Horse Club, Inc. and the Palomino Horse Breeder's Association. He is shown both English and Western, as a hunter, jumper, dressage horse, cutting horse and harness horse. His versatility earned him the championship of Morgan Versatility Show in 1962, although at that time he had had only two weeks' previous training in harness. Similarly, he had been schooled over fences on only one occasion before the Mid-Atlantic show at which he placed first in the hunter class and third in jumping! Back in Denver after the triumphant Eastern tour, Miss Woolverton entered Prince in a dressage trial. He was second in a class of 30 preliminary division horses, edged out of first by a single point.

Suncrest Cavalier (Redberry–Brooklyn Scarlet) was bought as a two-year-old at an Estes Park auction by Dr. Ann Pressman, of Lexington, Kentucky. The colt was so unpromising that nobody bid on him at the sale, and Dr. Pressman bought him in a private transaction after the auction. He was ridden for pleasure for several years before his remarkable potential was realized. He was first shown in a few small shows in English and Western pleasure classes and was so successful that his owner, and his trainer Jane Blue, decided to try for the big time. After making an excellent showing at the Morgan Gold Cup Show in Lebanon, Ohio, the trio went to the National Morgan Horse Show, where the gelding accounted for four firsts, including Senior Dressage. At the Morgan Versatility Show he completely overwhelmed the opposition, distancing his nearest rival, 1964 champion Bar-T Superman, by more than 100 points and taking the blue in five of ten classes: Stock, English Pleasure, Western Pleasure, Pleasure Driving and Jumping. He was second in the Running Race and third in Trail and Geldings in Hand.

Prince of Pride taking a fence in the stadium jumping phase of the annual Equitation Center of Colorado Three-Day Trials,, an event in which he placed second. (Dick King photo; courtesy Mary Wolverton)

Bibliography

A., R. C., "Hailing the Hackneys," *Wallace's Monthly* (New York, 1892).

ALEXANDER, DAVID, *The History and Romance of the Horse.* Cooper Square Publishers, Inc., New York, 1963.

ANDREAS, ALFRED T., Charles W. Davis and William Eliot Furness, eds., *Military Essays and Recollections.* A. C., McClurg and Company, Chicago, 1891.

ARNETT, A. M., PH.D., "Philip Henry Sheridan," *Encyclopaedia Britannica.* Encyclopaedia Britannica, Inc., 1929 (Vol. XX).

BAILEY, L. H., ed., *Cyclopedia of American Agriculture.* The MacMillan Company, New York, 1908.

BALCH, DONALD J., "Breeding Morgans Today at the University of Vermont." *The Morgan Horse Magazine,* Leominster, Mass., 1965.

BARWOOD, JUDEEN C., "Morgan Places in Dressage Event." *The Morgan Horse Magazine,* Leominster, Mass., 1963.

BATTELL, JOSEPH, *The Morgan Horse and Register.* Register Printing Company, Middlebury, Vermont, 1894, Vol. I.

BELLOWS, JOHN, letter, The Boston Cultivator, Boston, Sept. 1855.

BENEDICT, G. G., "The First Cavalry Regiment," *Vermont in the Civil War,* Vol. II.

BLISS, D. W., "The Centennial of Justin Morgan." *Vermont Agricultural Report,* Montpelier, 1890.

BRUNNER, JOHN, *Horses at Home.* Spring Books, London, n.d.

BUECHNER, ALAN C., "The New England Harmony." Folkway Records, New York, 1964.

CARTER, MAJOR GENERAL WILLIAM HARDING, U. S. A., *The Horses of the World.* The National Geographic Society, Washington, 1923.

CARTER, W. T., "California Morgans of Yesterday: 20th Century." *Morgan Horse Directory,* Northern California Morgan Horse Club, Inc., Modesto, California, 1966.

CATTON, BRUCE, *This Hallowed Ground.* Doubleday & Company, Inc., Garden City, New York, 1956.

CLEMENT, JOHN P., "100 Years Ago This Week," Rutland, Vermont *Herald,* Oct. 6, 1962.

CROWELL, PERS, *Cavalcade of American Horses.* McGraw-Hill Book Company, Inc., New York, 1951.

COLE, BARBARA, "Abraham Lincoln Owned Morgans." *The Morgan Horse Magazine,* 1964.

———— "Morgans as Cavalry Horses." *The Morgan Horse Magazine,* Leominster, Massachusette, 1964.

———— "Morgans in California 100 Years Ago." *The Morgan Horse Magazine,* Leominster, Massachusetts, 1964.

———— "The Early Years of the *Morgan Horse Magazine." The Morgan Horse Magazine,* Leominster, Massachusetts, 1964.

COOK, O. W., "True Briton and Justin Morgan." *The Maine Horse Breeder's Monthly,* Canton, Maine, 1882.

DAKIN, JANET W., "I Stand to be Counted." *The Morgan Horse Magazine,* Leominster, Massachusetts, 1964.

———— "Vermont 100 Mile Ride." *The Morgan Horse Magazine,* Leominster, Massachusetts, 1965.

DANIELS, T. W., "The Morgan as a Cowpony and Mountain Horse." *The Western Horseman,* reprinted, *The Morgan Horse Magazine,* 1962.

DIMON, JOHN, "Horse Papers." *The Cultivator and Country Gentleman,* Albany, New York, 1873.

DISSTON, HARRY, *Know About Horses.* The Devin-Adair Company, New York, 1961.

DRENNAN, *Report of the Operations in the War of the Rebellion by the Troops under the Command of General P. H. Sheridan.* Chicago, 1871.

DULANEY, GEORGE W., "Morgans as Jumpers." *The Morgan Horse Magazine,* Leominster, Massachusetts, 1961.

EARLE, DR. I. P., Biochemist, United States Department of Agriculture, Animal Husbandry Division, Beltsville, Maryland. (Letter January 22, 1966).

ELA, ANNA, "Green Mountain Horse Association 100 Mile Trail Ride." *The Morgan Horse Magazine,* Leominster, Massachusetts, 1961.

————"Green Mountain 100 Mile Ride." *The Morgan Horse Magazine,* Leominster, Massachusetts, 1962.

———— "Vermont 100 Mile Trail Ride." *The Morgan Horse Magazine,* Leominster, Massachusetts, 1964.

ENGLISH, MAURICE, ed., "The Neighs Have it." *Chicago,* Chicago, 1955.

FREEMAN, DOUGLAS S., "Little Sorrel." *Richmond News Leader,* Richmond, Virginia, 1939.

FULLER, ERASMUS D., "The Morgans of Seventy-Five Years Ago." *The Vermont Horse,* Rutland, Vermont, 1937.

FULLER, COLONEL JOHN FREDERICK CHARLES, "Cavalry." *The Encyclopaedia Britannica.* The Encyclopaedia Britannica Company, Ltd., London, 1929 (Vol. V).

GARDINER, MARGARET, "Justin Morgan, the Man." *The Chronicle of the Horse,* Middleburg, Virginia, 1966.

GARRARD, KENNER, *Nolan's System for Training Cavalry Horses.* D. Van

Nostrand, New York, 1862.

GOCHER, W. H., "Morgan Migration." *The Vermont Horse,* Rutland, Vermont, 1937.

HALL, EDWARD T., "Territorial Needs and Limits." *Natural History,* New York, 1965.

HAMILTON, CHARLEY, "As the Morgan Goes." *The Western Horseman,* 1965.

HAMMOND, CHARLES L., "Morgan Horses in the Civil War." *The Vermont Horse,* Rutland, Vermont ,1938.

HAYWOOD, MAJOR EUGENE B., "Morgan Horses in the Civil War." *The Vermont Horse,* Rutland, Vermont, 1938.

HERRICK, JEANNE MELLIN, "Rough Riding." *Horse Illustrated,* Springville, New York, 1961.

HERVEY, JOHN, *The American Trotter.* Coward-McCann, Inc., New York, 1947.

HOLLOWAY, MRS. C. C., "Morgan Portrait from England." *The Morgan Horse Magazine,* Leominster, Massachusetts, 1965.

HORTON, BOB, "Army Down to 40 Horses, And Only 27 Of Them Work." *Akron Beacon Journal,* Beacon Journal Publishing Co., Akron, March 30, 1966.

HOULTON, LA VONNE, "California Morgans of Yesterday: 19th Century." *Morgan Horse Directory,* Northern California Morgan Horse Club, Inc., Modesta, California, 1966.

HOWEY, M. OLDFIELD, *The Horse in Myth and Magic.* Castle Books, New York, 1848.

HUNT, FRAZIER and ROBERT HUNT, *Horses and Heroes.* Charles Scribner's Sons, New York, 1949.

H., S. T., "Ethan Allen." *Wallace Monthly* in *The Vermont Horse,* Rutland, Vermont, 1939.

JOHNSON, JAMES RALPH and ALFRED HOYT BILL, *Horsemen, Blue and Gray.* Oxford University Press, New York, 1960.

LANE, ROSE WILDER, *Free Land.* Longmans, Green and Company, New York, 1938.

KAYS, D. J., *The Horse.* A. S. Barnes and Company, Inc., New York, 1953.

KOIER, LOUISE, "Justin Morgan, Horseman and Composer." *The Christian Science Monitor,* Boston, 1964.

KRANTZ, EARL B., "Breeding Morgans at the United States Morgan Horse Farm." *The Morgan Horse Magazine,* 1947.

M. "Tired Out." *Spirit of the Times* in *The Maine Horse Breeder's Monthly,* Canton, Maine, 1887.

MACKAY-SMITH, ALEXANDER, "The Great Justin Morgan Pedigree Controversy." *The Chronicle of the Horse,* Middleburg, Virginia, 1966.

MACKAY-SMITH, M. P., D.V.M., "Is There Morgan Blood in Moyle Horses?"

The Morgan Horse Magazine, Leominster, Massachusetts, 1964.

MILLER, IDA, "The Most Hoss." *Farm Tempo U. S. A.,* Clarinda, Iowa, 1964.

NORCROSS, E. L., "Maine Horses in England." *The Maine Horse Breeder's Monthly,* Canton, Maine, 1886.

Ohio Farmer, The (Cleveland, Ohio, 1852 *et seq.*).

ORCUTT, ROBERT, "Morgan Performance Horses." *The Morgan Horse Magazine,* Leominster, Massachusetts, 1961.

OWEN, MABEL, "Principal Sire Lines and Families of the Morgan Breed." *The Morgan Horse Magazine,* Leominster, Massachusetts, March 1965 *et seq.*

———— "Sherman Morgan AMHR 5." *The Morgan Horse Magazine,* Leominster, Massachusetts, 1963.

PARKS, C. D., V.M.D., "Judging Morgan Breed Classes." *The Morgan Horse Magazine,* Leominster, Massachusetts, 1961.

PATRIQUIN, WARREN E., "Professional Horse Photography." *The Morgan Horse Magazine,* Leominster, Massachusetts, 1963.

PATTEN, JOHN W., *The Light Horse Breeds.* A. S. Barnes and Company, Inc., New York, 1960.

PEDLER, ERN, "The Morgan as a Stock Horse." *The Morgan Horse Magazine,* Leominster, Massachusetts, 1961.

PETERS, HARRY, *Currier & Ives: Printmakers to the American People.* Doubleday, Doran & Company, Inc., Garden City, New York, 1942.

PHILLIPS, LANCE, *The American Saddle Horse.* A. S. Barnes and Company, Inc., New York, 1964.

PHILLIPS, RALPH W., "The United States Morgan Horse Farm: its Work and its Objectives." *The Morgan Horse Magazine,* February, 1946.

Program 15th Annual National Morgan Horse Show. (The Morgan Horse Magazine, Leominster, Massachusetts, July, 1957).

RAY, PHIL, "The Half-Breed." *The Western Horseman,* (1965).

REDWAY, GEORGE WILLIAM, "Shenandoah Valley Campaigns." *Encyclopaedia Britannica,* Encyclopaedia Britannica Company, Ltd., London, 1929 (Vol. XX).

REESE, H. H., "Breeding Horses for the United States Army." *Department of Agriculture Year Book,* Government Printing Office, Washington, D. C., 1917.

———— *Breeding Morgan Horses at the U. S. Morgan Horse Farm.* Government Printing Office, Washington, D. C., 1921.

———— *Breeding Morgan Horses at the U. S. Morgan Horse Farm.* Government Printing Office, Washington, Revised 1923.

———— *The Road Horse, with Special Application to his Selection and Management in the Rural Delivery Service.* Government Printing Office, Washington, D. C., 1912.

REID, DR. HOWARD, "The First Endurance Ride." *The Vermont Horse,* Rutland, Vermont, 1937.

RHINE, JERRY, "Red Flash, 26 Years Old." *The Morgan Horse Magazine,* Leominster, Massachusetts, 1966.

1967 *Rule Book,* The American Horse Shows Association, Inc., New York, 1967.

SELF, MARGARET CABELL, *The American Horse Show,* A. S. Barnes and Company, Inc., New York, 1958.

SHERIDAN, PHILIP, *Sheridan's Reports* (n.d.).

———— *Personal Memoirs.* Charles L. Webster & Company, New York, 1888.

STEPHENS, JOYCE, "Nurse Arrives on Horseback." *The Pony Club Book No. 10,* The British Horse Society, Kingswood, Surrey, 1957.

STONG, PHIL, *Horses and Americans.* Frederick A. Stokes, New York, 1939.

TAYLOR, JAMES E., *With Sheridan Up the Shenandoah Valley, 1864: Leaves from a Special Artist's Sketch Book and Diary* (manuscript, 1900).

TAYLOR, LEWIS, *The Horse America Made.* Harper and Brothers, New York, 1961.

THWAITES, REUBEN GOLD, Ll.D., ed., *Early Western Travels 1784–1846.* The Arthur H. Clark Co., Cleveland, 1906.

TURGEON, MARY, "Why Dressage?" *The Morgan Horse Magazine,* Leominster, Massachusetts, 1965.

———— "Why Dressage Competitions?" *The Morgan Horse Magazine,* Leominster, Massachusetts, 1964.

VESEY-FITZGERALD, ed., *The Book of the Horse.* Nicholson & Watson, London, 1946.

WALLACE, JOHN H., ed., "A Great Pedigree Expert?" *Wallace's Monthly,* New York, 1886.

———— "Joe Battell's Law Suit." *Wallace's Monthly,* New York, 1887.

———— "The End of Battell vs. Wallace." *Wallace's Monthly,* New York, 1888.

WALKER, COLONEL S. P., Assistant Commandant, *Horsemanship and Horsemastership.* The Cavalry School, Fort Riley, Kansas, 1944.

WEIR, F. A., "Origin of the Morgan Horse." *The Maine Horse Breeder's Monthly,* Canton, Maine, 1883.

WENTWORTH, LADY, *Thoroughbred Racing Stock.* George Allen and Unwin, Ltd., London, 1938, Rev. 1960.

WILLIAMS, DUVAL, "Morgan Blood in Western Stock Horses." *The Vermont Horse,* Rutland, Vermont, 1939.

WORTHINGTON, RUTH D., "From Aderondacks to Green Mountains." *The Vermont Horse,* Rutland, Vermont, 1939.

———— "Breeding Horses at the U. S. Morgan Horse Farm." *The Vermont Horse,* Rutland, Vermont, 1939.

Index

Note: names of horses and numbers of pages with illustrations are italicized.